THE STORY OF MODERN EUROPE

THE STORY OF MODERN EUROPE

FROM 1870 TO THE PRESENT DAY

by

H. A. CLEMENT M.A.

Adult Education Tutor Cambridge University
Former Senior History Master Audenshaw Grammar School
Late Senior Scholar in History Trinity College Cambridge
Former Examiner in History for the Northern Universities
Examiner in History for London University

Author of
"The Story of the Ancient World,"
"The Story of Britain," etc.

With eight plates in half-tone
and twelve maps in the text

GEORGE G. HARRAP & CO. LTD
LONDON   TORONTO   WELLINGTON   SYDNEY

First published in Great Britain 1956
by GEORGE G. HARRAP & CO. LTD
182 High Holborn, London, W.C.1

Composed in Plantin type and printed by
The Pitman Press, Bath

Made in Great Britain

PREFACE

THIS book is intended to present the main outlines of the history of Europe from 1870 to the present day. It is written primarily for pupils taking the European History period after 1870 at the Ordinary level in the General Certificate of Education, though it might also be found useful for the general reader and as a background book for Current Affairs in sixth forms. The standard of treatment from 1870 to 1939 is maintained at a uniform level; but after 1939 the story is more condensed, and may be regarded as in the nature of a postscript. Otherwise the book would grow out of proportion for the purpose it is intended to serve.

Divisions in history, whether of time or space, are necessarily somewhat arbitrary. Although the year 1870 is a well-marked turning-point in European history, it has been found desirable in many cases to sketch briefly the preceding events in order to make the story intelligible to those with little or no previous knowledge. Similarly, no history of Europe in modern times can be isolated from the history of other continents. There is in consequence frequent reference to events in the U.S.A., Africa, and Asia where they affect the course of events in Europe.

Suitable examination text-books upon this worth-while period of European history are still scarce. It is hoped that this book will help to fill the gap.

H. A. C.

CONTENTS

ILLUSTRATIONS

MAPS

INTRODUCTION

To intrude upon the drama of history at any given point is bound to create its own difficulties. Past scenes cannot be recalled, and actors who have held the stage for some time are surprised in the middle of their performances. None the less, history books must begin somewhere, and the year 1870 is a convenient starting-point for a history of modern Europe, especially if this starting-point is loosely interpreted according to the requirements of each topic introduced in the opening chapters.

The decade 1870–80 saw the emergence of new European states and the virtual completion of the process by which the Europe of the Vienna settlement of 1815 was transformed into the Europe of our own age. The Franco-German War of 1870–71 was the occasion summing up many of these changes. It completed Bismarck's task of unifying Germany, and in 1871 the new German Empire was born. It gave the new Kingdom of Italy, which Cavour had patiently constructed only a few years earlier, the opportunity of taking Rome, and thus acquiring its natural capital and completing its unification. It dethroned Napoleon III and ended the Second French Empire; by 1875 the constitution of the Third Republic had been adopted, and France had chosen the form of government which was to last down to the Second World War. At the same time the Balkans were undergoing a transformation. The Treaty of Berlin (1878) created new Balkan states and marked, in fact, the biggest single break-up of the Ottoman Empire in Europe during the nineteenth century. It also demonstrated the increased interest that Austria-Hungary was taking in South-eastern Europe since the expulsion of Austria from Germany in 1866. Austro-Russian rivalry in this area increased, and the seeds of Sarajevo (immediate cause of the First World War in 1914) were sown in 1878.

Not only in its political state-system, but also in social and economic matters, was Europe witnessing far-reaching changes at this time. In 1867 Disraeli's Reform Act gave the town-workers in England the vote for the first time; it symbolized the beginning of that process whereby the countries of Western Europe developed into the democracies of the twentieth century. But in the very same year Karl Marx published the first volume of his *Das Kapital*, the Bible of modern communism. Herein the emphasis was upon 'bread-and-butter' rather than the Parliamentary vote, upon economic questions such as the ownership of the means of production and the alleged exploitation of the workers under the capitalist system. The first short-lived attempt to put those ideas into practice took place with the Paris Commune of 1871. In other words, the seeds of communism were already sown, to produce their harvest in the twentieth century. Further significant changes of an economic nature were also apparent at this time. In 1861 Russia emancipated her millions of serfs—the last European country to emerge from the Middle Ages. Modern industrialization, which had begun in Britain, was fast spreading to other countries, to Bismarck's new German Empire, to the U.S.A., and even to the recently opened-up Japan. Most countries, Britain excepted, abandoned free trade about this time and embarked on policies of protection and economic nationalism. Industrialization brought with it new needs for raw materials and markets, and a fresh wave of imperialism swept over the world. Africa was almost completely carved up by the European powers in the 1880's.

The years around 1870 do, then, in many ways mark the beginning of a new era. Europe, both at home and beyond the seas, was acquiring a 'new look' of distinctively modern design.

Chapter 1

FRANCE: INTERNAL AFFAIRS (1870–1914)

France in Defeat (1870–71)

SINCE the revolution of 1848 France had been under the rule of Louis Napoleon, nephew of the great Napoleon I. For four years he had ruled as President of the Second French Republic, and then in 1852 he had transformed the Republic into an Empire and assumed the title of Napoleon III. (Napoleon I's son, who had died in 1832, was regarded by Bonapartists as Napoleon II.) With his uncle's example to inspire him, Napoleon III had pursued an active foreign policy. For the first ten years he achieved success: in 1849 he restored Pope Pius IX to his throne in Rome; in 1854 he embarked, together with England, on the Crimean War against Russia; in 1859 he aided Cavour in his work of expelling the Austrians from Italy, and received in return Savoy and Nice. After 1860 he was less successful: he interfered disastrously in Mexican affairs at a time when he should have been giving more attention to the growing power of Prussia under Bismarck; he miscalculated the outcome of the Austro-Prussian War of 1866, and received none of the rewards he had asked for in return for his neutrality. His power and popularity were fast declining. For the first ten years he had ruled as a dictator; during the last ten he tried by concessions to win the support, or at any rate to lessen the criticism, of republicans and others who attacked his government. But it was in the sphere of foreign policy that the final test eventually came.

In July 1870 France declared war on Germany. The war was as necessary for Bismarck's final moves in his unification of Germany as it was to give Napoleon III his last chance of restoring his fortunes, and both statesmen must share the blame for its outbreak. What concerns us more is its outcome. Napoleon III had long been in ill-health, and his country was unprepared. The French generals and their armies proved no match for the Germans, and France was over-whelmingly defeated. On September 2, 1870, Napoleon III sur-rendered with a large French army at Sedan. This was the end of his rule, though not yet the end of French resistance to the invader.

The Germans marched upon Paris, but before they reached there the Parisians under the leadership of Léon Gambetta once more declared France a republic, with the intention of resisting the national enemy to the last. The Germans besieged Paris, and Gam-betta escaped in a balloon to organize French resistance from the out-side. But it was to no avail. One after another French armies and fortresses capitulated, and on January 28, 1871, Paris itself sur-rendered. On the same day an armistice ended the fighting. This was followed two weeks later by the election by universal male suffrage of a French National Assembly sitting at Bordeaux. One of France's most respected statesmen, Thiers, who had already given forty years' service to his country, was chosen "Head of the Executive Power of the French Republic."

It was Thiers and Bismarck who negotiated the terms of peace which were embodied in the Treaty of Frankfort (May 1871). France ceded to Germany Alsace (except for the fortress of Belfort) and Eastern Lorraine: she agreed to pay an indemnity of five thousand million francs—*i.e.*, £200,000,000—within the next three years, and undertook to support a German army of occupation till it was paid.

The Paris Commune (1871)

With the Second Empire of Napoleon III gone, the problem of what to put in its place soon occupied the attention of France. The first crisis in this connexion arose during March to May 1871—*i.e.*, in the interval between the armistice and the signing of the Treaty of Frankfort. Paris was traditionally more advanced than the rest of France, which, composed mainly of peasants, was fonder of the old ways. The newly elected National Assembly contained a majority of royalists (although, as we shall shortly see, the royalists themselves were by no means united), and the prospect of a restored monarchy provoked strong opposition from republican Paris. Matters were brought to a head when Thiers' government and the Assembly moved from Bordeaux to Versailles—just outside Paris, and full of royalist associations—and proceeded to take unpopular measures against Paris. All back payments of rents and debts, suspended during the war, were to be made up, and the Paris National Guard was to have its pay stopped, and to be disarmed. When troops from Versailles tried to enforce disarmament a clash occurred and Paris revolted. The Parisians elected a Council, or Commune, and defied the National Assembly. The Paris Commune was inspired by vague socialist or communist ideas, and was hailed by Karl Marx from his exile in London as the beginning of the workers' revolution. It demanded as a first step the right of other French cities to organize themselves into communes, and to be independent of the conservative countryside.

Thiers' government could obviously not allow its authority to be thus flouted. Paris was once more besieged—this time by Frenchmen —with German occupation forces outside the city as contemptuous spectators. As often, civil war produced the greater horrors. After a seven weeks' bombardment Paris was entered by the troops of the National Assembly. Fierce street-fighting ensued, resulting in the wilful destruction of much property, and the loss of thousands of lives. Victory was followed by the imprisonment or exile of many thousands more. For a long time to come the memories associated with the Commune and its suppression embittered French politics. It has since occupied an honourable place in the history of communist revolution; Karl Marx sought to draw lessons from its failure— lessons later used by the Russian revolutionaries in 1917.

The Establishment of the Third Republic

After the suppression of the Paris Commune the National Assembly gave Thiers the title of President. In 1872 a system of compulsory military service of up to five years was established. Early in 1873 the new President, by means of loans, paid off the last of the war indemnity, and the German occupying forces left France six months earlier than the Treaty had specified. Germany was not pleased at this speedy revival of her ancient foe. Thiers was hailed as the "Liberator of the Fatherland," and the Assembly declared he had "deserved well of his country."

The problem of a Constitution proved more difficult. The majority of the National Assembly were monarchist in principle and opposed to a republic. But the tangled history of France since 1789 divided the monarchists themselves into three main parties. First there were those who supported Henry, Count of Chambord, the descendant of the Bourbons who had been dethroned in 1789 and again in 1830. Secondly, the Count of Paris was supported by those who favoured the less absolute monarchy represented by the Orleanists, who had been dethroned in 1848. Thirdly, there were still some Bonapartists who favoured the exiled Napoleon III or his son, the Prince Imperial. Thiers himself favoured a constitutional monarchy, but, remarking that three people cannot sit on one throne, became converted to the idea of a republic. "It is the Republic which divides us least," he said. The Assembly forced Thiers to resign the Presidency in 1873, and replaced him by the monarchical Marshal MacMahon.

The death of Napoleon III in 1873 lessened the prospects of the Bonapartists, which in the circumstances had never been very bright. A compromise between the Bourbons and the Orleanists seemed possible when the Count of Paris agreed that the Count of Chambord should rule first, but that on the latter's death (Chambord being childless) Paris should succeed. But this plan broke down over the question of a flag. Chambord refused to renounce the Bourbon traditions of his forefathers, as symbolized by the white flag with its *fleur-de-lis*. "Henry V cannot desert the flag of Henry IV." In consequence he rejected the tricolour of the Revolution and of Napoleon I's victories—the only flag France would accept, as even the Orleanists admitted. The issue thus became clear: a return to the Bourbonism of the *ancien régime* or a Republic. The former being unacceptable to the majority of Frenchmen, the National Assembly in 1875 established the Third French Republic by a majority of one vote. Gambetta had played a great part in securing the Republic, helping to win many by-elections for republican candidates in the fateful months preceding the Assembly's decision.

Even so, the new Constitution reflected certain monarchical tendencies. The head of the Republic was to be a President, elected, not by the people, but by the two Houses of the French Parliament sitting together. He was to hold office for seven years. His powers were strictly limited, like those of a constitutional monarch, and in effect he was little more than the ceremonial head of the State. Parliament was to consist of two Houses: (1) a Chamber of Deputies elected by universal male suffrage every four years; (2) a Senate elected by representatives of municipal councils and other local interests and holding office for nine years. The government was to be in the hands of a Prime Minister, assisted by other ministers, and responsible to Parliament, much as in Britain.

The Third Republic was faced at the outset with many enemies in Church and State. As it developed other difficulties appeared. The number of political parties grew too large. Governments were often uneasy coalitions between different groups, and were frequently dismissed by a Parliament which (unlike its British counterpart) could not be dissolved by the outgoing Prime Minister. The average life of a French government under the Third Republic has been estimated at about ten months. Yet, strangely, the new Constitution lasted much longer than any French form of government since 1789, and was not altered till 1946, when, after the upheaval of the Second World War, the so-called Fourth Republic was established.

The Early Years of the Third Republic

In 1877 President MacMahon, who was a monarchist at heart, dismissed a republican ministry and made the Duke of Broglie, a monarchist, Prime Minister. With the consent of the Senate, he then dissolved the Chamber of Deputies and appealed to the country. Gambetta, the outstanding republican leader, took up the challenge implied in these actions. Was France to be republican or monarchist? Was the popularly elected Chamber of Deputies to be at the mercy of a President, with all the dangers this involved of a return to dictatorship? The royalists, strongly supported by the Church, hit back hard, but the result was a victory for the republicans, and in 1879 MacMahon was obliged to resign. His successor, Grévy, was politically 'sound.' Republicanism was further strengthened at this time by declaring July 14 (the anniversary of the fall of the Bastille) a national holiday, and by a revision of the Constitution which made the republican form of government unalterable, and which excluded members of former royal families from ever becoming President.

B

Soon after 1880 laws were passed establishing freedom of the Press, of public meeting, and of association; the latter permitted the growth of trade unions. A national system of education, free and compulsory between the ages of six and thirteen, was set up, and in the new publicly provided schools priests and monks were forbidden to teach, and religious education was barred. The Catholic Church still controlled many schools of its own, however, and, with its traditions of Divine Right and association with the monarchy, was regarded with hostility by many republicans. "Clericalism is the enemy," Gambetta had remarked during the election of 1877.

During Grévy's presidency French colonial power was extended to Tunis, Madagascar, parts of West Africa, and in Indo-China, as more fully described in Chapter 6. This active colonial policy recalled to many the Mexican adventure of Napoleon III, and was by no means popular.

General Boulanger

For several years after 1886 the Republic was threatened by the Boulangist movement. Financial scandals, weak governments, and an unpopular colonial policy were now added to the usual discontents, and in the person of General Boulanger, who cut a handsome figure seated on his favourite black horse, the enemies of the Republic found a champion. In 1886 Boulanger was ex-military governor of Tunis, Minister of War, and popular with the Army. He denounced the weakness of the French Parliamentary system, and called for a revision of the Constitution to give the President greater powers. For three years Boulanger's popularity made him a possible dictator, had he possessed the courage to seize his opportunity. He came to control many newspapers, and, finding it was possible to be elected for more than one constituency, he stood for different places as vacancies occurred, and was elected in many by large majorities. At length, in 1889, the government in alarm demanded his trial for plotting against the safety of the State. Boulanger's nerve failed him; he fled to Belgium, and committed suicide two years later.

Boulanger's death almost coincided with the Panama scandal. In 1880 an international company had been formed, under French leadership, to construct a canal through the Isthmus of Panama.

Ferdinand de Lesseps, builder of the Suez Canal, was its president. For ten years the work proceeded, but the company made little progress, and was declared bankrupt in 1889. A few years later the scandals attaching to its operations were revealed. Disease and miscalculations had hampered the work. Worse still, while thousands of French investors had lost their money, others, including de Lesseps, Parliamentary deputies, and senators, had by fraud and corruption waxed rich. Many were sentenced to imprisonment, among them being de Lesseps himself and his son. The confidence of France in the integrity of its rulers was sadly shaken. The present canal was begun in 1904 by the U.S.A., and completed in 1914 (see page 82).

L'Affaire Dreyfus

First Boulanger; then Panama; and now Dreyfus. Alfred Dreyfus was of Jewish birth, and a captain in the French Army. In 1894 he was charged with selling military secrets to a foreign power, which presumably meant Germany. The evidence rested chiefly on a document known as the *bordereau*, which some experts, but not all, said was in Dreyfus' handwriting. The accused protested his innocence and his loyalty to France, but was found guilty by court-martial, degraded from his rank, and sent to Devil's Island for life.

In 1896 Colonel Picquart, a man of high principles in charge of the French Intelligence Department, declared that the *bordereau* had been forged by an unscrupulous Army officer, Major Esterhazy, and that Dreyfus was consequently innocent. But it took another ten years before the matter was finally settled, as passions were soon aroused which obscured the merits of the case itself. Dreyfus, in fact, became a symbol splitting France into two camps. Those who demanded justice (which they believed would mean acquittal) included the convinced republicans and anti-clericals and all who thought that the vested interests of the Army should be subordinated to the civil government and law courts. In the other camp, resisting any reopening of the case, were monarchists and clericals, the Army, and those who condemned a man merely on account of his Jewish blood.

The anti-Dreyfusards won the opening rounds. Colonel Picquart was removed from his position, and although Esterhazy was tried, the trial was a farce, and he was acquitted. This provoked Zola's famous letter in 1898 beginning *J'accuse*, in which the author charged the judges in both the Dreyfus and Esterhazy cases with a deliberate miscarriage of justice. Zola was condemned, but fled to Britain. In vain the authorities produced new documents to implicate Dreyfus; they were shown to be forgeries, and matters were once more brought to a head when Esterhazy, having fled to Britain, confessed that he had forged the original *bordereau*. Thereupon a retrial of Dreyfus was held at Rennes in 1899. By five votes to two the judges again declared Dreyfus guilty, but with extenuating circumstances, and reduced his term of imprisonment to ten years. They had obviously acted under pressure from the Army officers. The French President hoped to terminate the scandal by pardoning Dreyfus, but the Dreyfusards rightly demanded, not pardon, but a declaration of innocence. It was not till 1906 that the law courts declared Dreyfus innocent, and found Esterhazy guilty of having forged the *bordereau*. Dreyfus was reinstated in the Army, with the promotion to the rank of major, and was awarded the Cross of the Legion of Honour. The affair thus ended in a victory for the republicans over the vested interests of the Army and the unreasoning passions of anti-republicans and anti-Semites.

The Conflict between State and Church

In 1899 a new French Premier, Waldeck-Rousseau, formed a government supported by extreme republicans and the growing body of socialists. He soon began an attack upon the Roman Catholic Church which within a few years completely altered the relations between Church and State. In every crisis since 1870, and particularly during the Dreyfus affair, the Church had ranged itself alongside the enemies of the Republic. Its religious orders and their membership had increased considerably; so too had its property over the last half-century. Through its schools it controlled a great deal of education, and did not hesitate to teach doctrines hostile to republican ideas and forms of government.

The first blow was delivered in 1901 by the Law of Associations, which obliged all religious orders to submit their rules for the State's approval, and forbade their existence unless they received definite

Parliamentary authority. Unauthorized orders were excluded from any educational work. A new Premier, Combes, enforced the law with vigour, and many orders were dissolved. In 1904 it was further enacted that even authorized religious orders must discontinue their teaching work within the next ten years. This was stoutly resisted by a newly elected Pope, Pius X, and very soon disputes between Church and State over the appointment of bishops brought matters to a head.

The Law of Separation (1905) repealed Napoleon's Concordat of 1801, which still regulated the relations between the two powers. Under the new law the State ceased to recognize any religion at all, so that in effect the Roman Catholic Church was disestablished. The State renounced its responsibility for the salaries of Church officials, though providing certain pensions to existing clergy to mitigate hardship. The State in return gave up its control over Church appointments. As far as churches, cathedrals, and other property were concerned, the State asserted its ultimate rights to control these, but was willing to allow their use by specially formed Associations of Public Worship.

All religious bodies were affected by the law, but, naturally, it hit the Catholic Church hardest of all. The Pope condemned it, and Catholics refused to form Associations of Public Worship. A compromise in 1907 allowed churches to be opened by a contract between priests and local authorities.

Later Parliamentary elections confirmed this policy of separating Church and State. The majority of Frenchmen had come to distrust a religion which had so often ranged itself alongside the enemies of the Republic. While many continued to remain Catholic, many others left the Church, to become freethinkers or atheists.

Social and Industrial Unrest

Under the Third Republic important economic and social developments took place. French industries and communications were developed, but with the loss of the valuable iron ores of Lorraine, and with her small supplies of coal, France has never become an industrial giant on the scale of Britain, Germany, or the U.S.A. She has remained primarily agricultural.

Nevertheless, sufficient developments occurred to produce a strong working-class movement centred mainly in the industrial towns and the seaports. Trade unions had been legalized in 1884, and by the beginning of the twentieth century there was a strong socialist movement which was henceforth to exercise an important influence on political affairs. The socialists co-operated with the radical republicans in the legislation against the Church, and they secured a reduction in the terms of compulsory military service—a decision reversed on the eve of the 1914 war.

An extreme section, known as syndicalists (French *syndicat*=trade union), refused to co-operate any longer with radical Premiers like Clemenceau, or even moderate socialists like Briand. The French Parliament was slow to pass social service legislation, such as Bismarck had done twenty years before in Germany, and Lloyd George was then doing in Britain. The syndicalists turned to direct industrial action, seeking to paralyse the nation's life by means of strikes. Their ultimate aim was to take over the nation's industries and run them through the trade unions. A wave of unrest culminated in the railway strike of 1910, when the moderate socialist Premier, Briand, outwitted the strikers by calling them back as soldiers under the terms of their military reserve commitments. Thereafter matters quietened down somewhat, but unrest had by no means disappeared when the First World War broke out in 1914.

Chapter 2

GERMANY: INTERNAL AFFAIRS (1870–1914)

The German Empire (1871–1918)

As described in Chapter 1, Bismarck's unification of Germany reached its completion with the defeat of France in 1870–71. On January 18, 1871, the new German Empire was proclaimed in the Hall of Mirrors at the Palace of Versailles; the first Emperor was William I, the King of Prussia whom Bismarck had served for the previous nine years.

The German Empire consisted of twenty-five states, plus the newly acquired territory of Alsace-Lorraine. The different state-rulers (kings, dukes, etc.) were allowed to continue with quite important powers over the internal affairs of their territories. For the most part these states were under the absolute control of their rulers, thinly disguised in places by a sham Parliamentary system. This was particularly the case in the largest state of all, Prussia, where the Parliamentary franchise was so arranged as to give the greatest power to the wealthy classes, such as the Junkers, or large landowners of East Prussia.

The Empire as a whole was to be governed by an Emperor, assisted by ministers and advised by an Imperial Legislature. In many respects the new Constitution was based upon that of the North German Confederation which had been established after the Austro-Prussian War of 1866. The King of Prussia was *ipso facto* German Emperor, or Kaiser, with the power to make treaties, declare war, and control the armed forces of the Empire, without any real check from the other rulers, or from the Imperial Legislature. Again, the Emperor appointed his own ministers, who were responsible to him, and not to the elected representatives of the people. The foremost minister was the Imperial Chancellor, who supervised the other ministers individually, rather than as a collective body like the British or French Cabinets. In this way the Chancellor's authority was considerably enhanced. The Imperial Legislature consisted of two Houses. The lower House, or Reichstag, was elected by male suffrage for a period of five years. Although its consent was necessary for new taxes, it could not interfere with existing taxes, and had no power in appointing the Chancellor and his ministers or in controlling their policy. The more important House was the Bundesrath, or Federal Council, consisting of delegates appointed by the different state-rulers; it was thus very conservative in outlook. Out of 58 members, Prussia appointed 17, the next highest contribution being from Bavaria, with 6. As Prussian influence was strong over many North German states, she could usually control the Bundesrath. She also had the power of vetoing any proposal affecting the Army or Navy or any amendment to the Constitution.

The most striking features of this new German Empire were the power of the Kaiser (or his nominee, the Chancellor) over the other organs of government, and the power of Prussia over the other states. The strongest pressure-groups soon became evident: the Prussian landowners, or Junkers, the industrial magnates of the Ruhr, the General Staff of the Army, and the Civil Service. Although the people could elect the Reichstag they really had few powers, and little opportunity of learning democratic ways of government.

The German Empire lasted from its creation in 1871 to the end of the First World War in 1918. It had three Emperors: (1) William I, who lived till 1888; (2) his son, Frederick III, who reigned for only three months; and (3) Frederick's son, William II (1888–1918). In effect it was governed by Bismarck till 1890, and thereafter by the Kaiser William II.

Bismarck's Problems (1870–90)

Bismarck's work after 1870 consisted in maintaining and strengthening the structure he had built up in the previous years. At home this meant preventing some of the South German states from breaking away from the newly created Empire—a problem fairly easily solved, as Prussia's domination was strongly rooted, and Bismarck could turn to advantage the jealousies between some of the German

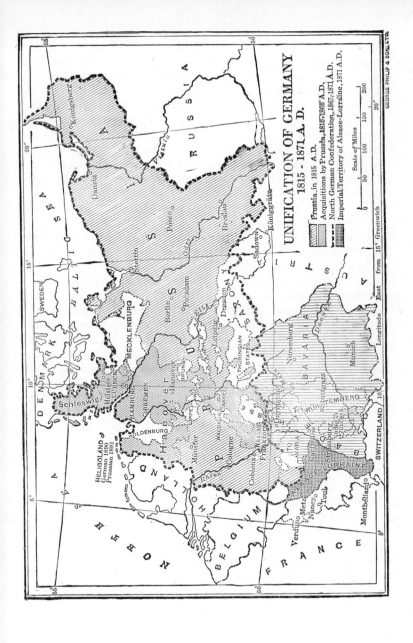

UNIFICATION OF GERMANY
1815 - 1871 A. D.

Prussia, in 1815 A.D.
Acquisitions by Prussia, 1815-1866 A.D.
North German Confederation, 1867-1871 A.D.
Imperial Territory of Alsace-Lorraine, 1871 A.D.

Scale of Miles
0   50   100   150   200

Longitude East from 15° Greenwich

GEORGE PHILIP & SON, LTD.

princes themselves. For the first ten years he was also engaged in a struggle with the Roman Catholic Church. Economic development proceeded apace, creating social and economic problems. Finally, Bismarck had to deal with the growth of socialism, as represented by the Social Democratic Party. Overseas he became involved, somewhat against his wishes, in the scramble for colonies in the 1880's. In the sphere of foreign policy his chief concern was to prevent the recovery of France, and to set at nought her desire to avenge 1870. Colonial and foreign policy can be understood only in their wider setting, and will be considered in detail in later chapters.

The *Kulturkampf*

Bismarck's contest with the Roman Catholic Church is usually referred to as the *Kulturkampf*, or struggle (*Kampf*) over civilization (*Kultur*). It arose out of several causes, and was conducted over a variety of issues; but fundamentally it was a clash between the claims of an almighty State and those of an almighty Church. As such it was in direct line with the struggle between Popes and Emperors in the Middle Ages, or even, going further back, between the rival claims of God and Cæsar mentioned in the New Testament. The distinction between the things that are God's and the things that are Cæsar's is not easy to draw in practice, and the greater the claims of the rival parties (as in the case now being considered) the more difficult it is to reach any agreement. The problem was aggravated by obvious political factors. Prussia was predominantly Protestant, and had antagonized many Catholics by her recent defeats of Austria and France. The new German Empire was about two-thirds Protestant and one-third Catholic, and it was Catholic states like Bavaria and Württemberg which resented the dominance of Prussia. The Catholics, in fact, soon organized a political party of their own, called the Centre. It returned many members at elections, and, under the skilful leadership of Windthorst, was able to exert considerable influence in the Reichstag. This was not at all to Bismarck's liking.

The struggle was precipitated by a split between the Catholics themselves over a question which symbolized the fundamental issues at stake. At the Vatican Council in 1870 the Pope had been declared infallible in matters of faith and morals. Bismarck was not interested in the finer theological arguments which lay behind this decree, but it did appear to him as a challenge to his authority over his own Catholic subjects. He was strengthened by the fact that a number of German Catholics themselves, led by the historian Döllinger, disagreed with the decree, and, declaring it to be an innovation, formed themselves into an Old Catholic party. The Roman Catholic authorities proceeded to expel Old Catholics from their posts, to excommunicate them, to forbid students to attend their lectures or the faithful to attend their services, whereupon the Old Catholics appealed to the German government for protection. Bismarck took up their cause, and was soon involved in a struggle covering the whole field of relations between Church and State.

His first acts were to forbid members of religious orders to engage in teaching, and to expel the Jesuits from the country. The German envoy was withdrawn from the Vatican in 1872. Bismarck expressed his determination never to surrender in the words: "To Canossa we will not go, either in the flesh or in the spirit"—Canossa being the place in North Italy where, eight centuries earlier, the Emperor Henry IV had waited barefoot in the snow for three days to crave forgiveness from the victorious Pope Gregory VII. Soon all schools were placed under lay inspection, and all marriages were to take place before civil authorities, being then valid whether followed by a religious ceremony or not. In the years 1873, 1874, and 1875 the Prussian Parliament passed the most stringent laws of all, applicable to its own state. These were the celebrated May Laws (passed in May in each of the three years) or Falk Laws, after the minister who introduced them. Under these candidates for the priesthood had to study at a State university for three years; priests were forbidden to utter public excommunications; the State's sanction was declared necessary for appointments of Roman Catholic clergy; Catholic colleges were to be open to State inspection; and Catholic orders were to be dissolved or expelled.

Pope Pius IX declared the May Laws null and void, and a bitter conflict ensued. Roman Catholic clergy defied the laws, in face of expulsion, fines, and imprisonment. As a result over a thousand parishes were without priests, and opinion began to turn more strongly against Bismarck. In 1877 the Centre Party was returned as the largest single party in the Reichstag elections. Bismarck offered to resign the Chancellorship, but the Emperor William refused. Soon several factors eased the tension and brought the *Kulturkampf* to an end. Socialism was growing in strength, and appeared to Bismarck a greater danger than Catholicism; if he could placate the Catholics he would win the support of the Centre Party in the coming political struggle. In 1878 Pius IX was succeeded by the more conciliatory Leo XIII, and the prospects of a settlement increased. A German representative was once again sent to the Vatican, and in 1879 the May Laws were suspended, to be repealed finally in 1886. Apart from the Jesuits, religious orders were allowed to return. The State kept a few of its gains, notably the laws relating to civil marriage and the State inspection of schools; otherwise victory lay with the Church. In effect Bismarck *had* gone to Canossa—in the spirit, if not in the flesh.

Bismarck and Socialism

At the 1871 Reichstag elections a party known as the Social Democrats polled about 125,000 votes, and secured the election of two members, one of them being August Bebel, its leader. German socialist doctrines were derived from the teachings of Karl Marx and Ferdinand Lassalle. Marx was an extreme revolutionary who in 1848 had published the *Communist Manifesto* and in 1867 the first part of *Das Kapital*. Lassalle was more moderate in his views, though still very critical of the capitalist system. For some time the German socialists were weakened by the existence of an extreme and a moderate section, but in 1875 at a conference at Gotha the two composed their differences and issued an agreed programme for the Social Democratic Party. First, it demanded more democracy: male *and female* suffrage, the power of the Reichstag to control the Government, freedom of speech, of the Press, of meeting and association, universal education, and such-like. Secondly, the capitalist system based upon private ownership of the means of production and the profit-motive was to be replaced by State ownership of the major industries, run for the benefit of the nation as a whole. To Bismarck as a conservative, a Junker, and an imperialist who distrusted peoples and Parliaments, this programme spelt ruin to the edifice he had so laboriously built up. When the Reichstag elections of 1877 gave the socialists twelve members, with about half a million popular votes behind them, he determined to take action. Attempts on the Emperor's life in 1878, although not made by Socialists, gave him his opportunity. He patched up his quarrel with the Church, and secured the support of the Centre Party, to which socialism was as distasteful as to himself.

In 1878 Bismarck secured a law which launched a frontal attack upon socialism. Socialist societies, meetings, and publications were forbidden, and the police were given wide powers of enforcement. Although passed in the first instance for four years, the law was renewed till 1890, the year of Bismarck's fall. The German police, as might be expected, enforced the law energetically, and many hundreds of people were imprisoned or exiled. But socialism was only driven underground, where its roots continued to spread. Many harmless-sounding societies were secretly socialist, and literature was printed in Switzerland and smuggled into Germany.

Bismarck's second line of action was to steal some of the socialists' thunder, and by a policy of State-help to undermine the causes of socialism. In Germany as elsewhere industrialization brought with it insecurity, and it was this insecurity which Bismarck tackled in his State Insurance schemes. In 1883 a scheme for insurance against sickness was launched, followed by another against accidents in 1884, and an old-age pension scheme in 1889. The cost was shared between employer and employee, with the government making a small contribution. The benefits deriving from such measures are obvious, and most countries nowadays have similar schemes on even wider lines. Bismarck was a pioneer in State Insurance—it was not till over twenty years later that Great Britain followed suit. But the German Social Democrats merely redoubled their propaganda. Such sops as Bismarck had thrown to the workers, they argued, could not obscure the essential autocracy of the German Empire, or the injustices of the prevailing social and economic system. Socialism continued to grow. In 1890, after twelve years of persecution and six years of 'killing by kindness,' the Social Democrats polled 1,500,000 votes, and obtained 35 seats in the Reichstag. Bismarck's fall in 1890 was occasioned partly by disagreement with the new Kaiser over the socialist issue.

The Kaiser disapproved of Bismarck's repressive legislation. But new policies proved no more effective than the old; by 1914 the Social Democrats commanded well over 4,000,000 votes and over 100 seats, and formed the largest single party in the State.

Economic Development

Germany's economic life underwent rapid changes in the years following 1870. It was now possible, and indeed essential, to weld the different German states more closely together. For the past half-century the Prussian customs union (*Zollverein*) had done much to break down internal trade-barriers and to give Germany a single customs policy. This was now completed. Further steps now taken included the establishment of a single currency and banking system, the extension of communications by rail, road, and water, and the expansion of technical education.

Germany in 1870 was still mainly agricultural; before the end of the century the balance had tilted in favour of industry and commerce. By far the most significant development took place in the heavy industries of iron and steel. The newly acquired province of Lorraine possessed rich deposits of iron ore, but these were unsuitable for steel-production on a large scale owing to their high phosphoric content. But in the 1870's an English chemist, Sidney Gilchrist Thomas, invented a process whereby phosphoric ores could be utilized in the manufacture of steel. The iron ores of Lorraine could now be wedded to the coal of the Ruhr, and before the century was ended German steel-production exceeded Great Britain's, and was second only to that of the U.S.A. Bismarck had founded the German Empire by 'blood and iron,' but it was coal and iron that now gave it its strength. Important developments also took place in other industries, notably textiles and chemicals. German inventive genius, coupled with German thoroughness and industry, soon made the country a powerful competitor in the world's markets, which became increasingly flooded with goods 'made in Germany.' At the same time her population was increasing. Whereas France remained steady at about 40,000,000, Germany advanced between 1870 and 1914 from 41,000,000 to 65,000,000. The needs for raw materials, markets, and outlets for the energies of the expanding population were factors behind Germany's desire for colonies in the years before 1914.

In 1879 Bismarck decided to impose tariffs to protect German industry and agriculture from foreign competition. He had noted the general drift away from free trade on the part of most countries except Britain. In particular the U.S.A. was fast developing her industries under a system of protection, while the prairie provinces were now beginning to pour their agricultural products into the Old World. As a landowning Junker himself Bismarck lent a ready ear to the agricultural interests, and his system of protection was designed not only to foster Germany's growing industries, but also to safe-guard her ancient agriculture. Financial considerations also played a part. Social reforms and the maintenance of a large army, in view of French revival, cost money. To ask the individual German states might raise difficulties; but revenue from customs duties ranked as imperial taxation, and as such was under the Chancellor's control once the Reichstag had passed the necessary laws.

'Dropping the Pilot' (1890)

In 1888 the Emperor William I died at the ripe age of ninety. He was succeeded by his son, Frederick III, whose short reign (March to June 1888) was a pitiful fight against the disease which soon ended his life. Frederick's son, William II, a young man of twenty-nine, succeeded his father. The new Kaiser possessed much ability, but was vain and headstrong, and his reign culminated in the First World War, which cost him his throne in 1918.

A young and inexperienced ruler of a different character might have been glad of the continued services of his grandfather's Chan-cellor. Not so William II, who had ideas of his own, and was deter-mined to have his own way. He disagreed with Bismarck's policy of repressing the socialists. He also wanted a bolder foreign policy. Bismarck had remained friends with both Austria and Russia, who were rivals in the Balkans, and had avoided colonial and naval policies which might antagonize Britain (see Chapter 7). The new Emperor was resolved to side openly with Austria even if it antagon-ized Russia, and to make Germany a leading naval power even if it antagonized Britain. In 1890 the old Chancellor, somewhat to his amazement, was forced to resign. In a famous cartoon *Punch* depicted the young captain dropping the old pilot. Bismarck lived in retirement for another eight years.

Internal Affairs under William II

William II believed firmly in the doctrine of Divine Right. The Chancellors succeeding Bismarck were the following: Caprivi (1890–94), Hohenlohe (1894–1900), Bülow (1900–9), and Bethmann-Hollweg (1909–17); but none of these exercised a shadow of Bismarck's power. In effect Germany was now ruled by her ambitious and often unstable Kaiser. With his dreams of world conquest, the chief interest of his reign lies in the realm of foreign affairs—in the 'armed camps' and the international crises preceding 1914, in Germany's colonial ambitions, and in the development of her naval power, which more than anything else antagonized Britain.

Internally German industry and commerce made great strides. German scientists and technicians led the world in many spheres, and pre-1914 Germany excelled in many branches of metallurgy, in the production of dyestuffs, optical instruments, and in artificial fertilizers. Her future seemed assured, had she not risked it in the gamble of war.

Constitutional questions assumed increasing importance. After Bismarck's dismissal the Emperor allowed the repressive anti-socialist laws to lapse, hoping that a conciliatory policy and the benefits of social legislation would combine to lessen the effectiveness of socialist propaganda. He was sadly disillusioned. The Social Democratic Party grew from strength to strength, till it became the largest single party in the Empire. William tried in vain to reverse his policy of conciliation; the Reichstag refused to pass fresh repressive laws. But although the socialists came to command the largest number of votes in the country, the German Constitution denied them any real power. The constituencies continued the same as when Bismarck had mapped them out; growing towns like Berlin (where the socialists were strong) were grossly under-represented compared with the conservative countryside. The Reichstag still had no control over the ministers, and the ministers had little control over the Emperor. At times the Army chiefs exercised more political power than the ministers. Matters came to a head in 1908, when William II's personal views on Anglo-German relations were published in the *Daily Telegraph*. When published they were such as nearly to provoke war. All parties protested against the Emperor thus acting without consulting his ministers, and the Chancellor Bülow was only dissuaded from resigning by William promising to be more discreet in future. The absence of any real democratic tradition was badly felt after the First World War, when efforts were made to bring Germany more in line with western democracy.

Chapter 3

RUSSIA: INTERNAL AFFAIRS (1870–1914)

The Reforms of Alexander II (1855–81)

THE Tsar Alexander II ascended the Russian throne in the middle of the Crimean War. The new ruler was by nature more liberal-minded than his predecessor, Nicholas I. Moreover (as is often the case, and particularly so in the history of Russia), defeat in war aggravated existing discontents and stimulated the demand for reform. The first part of Alexander's reign was an honest attempt to meet this demand, at any rate up to a point.

Most notable of all Alexander's reforms was his emancipation of the serfs—an act which earned for him the title of "the Liberator Tsar." Serfdom was still the common lot of the Russian peasant, although elsewhere in Europe it had disappeared. The liberation of the serfs on the Crown lands was a relatively easy matter for the Tsar. Elsewhere serfs were freed by a series of laws, known collectively as the Edict of Emancipation, issued in 1861. Henceforth the serf was a free man, no longer subject to the authority, and often the knout or chain, of his overlord. Altogether more than 20,000,000 serfs were emancipated. But freedom without the means of livelihood is a mockery, and the Russian government had to attempt the difficult task of settling the land-question on terms satisfactory to both lords and peasants. Hitherto the serfs in each *mir*, or village community, had worked several days a week for their lord, and in return had been allowed large holdings for their own use. What was to be done now that the serf was exempt from labour-services and other obligations? The lords claimed that *all* the land was theirs; but if the peasantry were given their freedom without land they would obviously be in a worse position than before. A compromise was eventually adopted. The lord retained about half the land of the village; the remainder went to the *mir* for the use of the peasantry. A very rough average gives each peasant about 20 acres under the new arrangement. But the peasantry through the *mir* had to purchase their share, by reason of the lord's claim that all the land was originally his. In practice the government paid over the purchase price to the lords, and the peasantry had to repay the government by instalments over the next forty-nine years. This caused widespread discontent, and it is recorded that in some villages the peasantry had to be forced into freedom when they realized what freedom implied!

Alexander also introduced a certain amount of self-government into local affairs. He divided Russia into 34 provinces with 360 districts. Each district elected its council, or *zemstvo*, and the district *zemstvos* sent representatives to provincial councils. Important powers were assigned to these *zemstvos* over primary education, sanitation and public health, roads and bridges, the relief of the poor, and the management of hospitals and asylums. A few years later similar elected councils were established in the towns. For the next half-century the *zemstvos* did extremely useful work.

Other reforms of Alexander included greater equality before the law by making judges more independent of the government and by introducing trial by jury; more freedom for the Press and for universities; the pardon of many exiles and increased facilities for travel abroad; and, to repair the deficiencies exposed by the Crimean War, the introduction of a system of military conscription with exemptions for university students and breadwinners.

Continuing Discontent

These reforms failed to satisfy Russia. The Tsar's non-Russian subjects longed for greater independence. Prominent among these were the Poles, who revolted in 1863. They were crushed with severity, and incorporated more closely into the Russian Empire.

Military conscription was irksome to many. The new judicial reforms did not apply to political offences, and critics of the government could still be condemned without fair trial. Between 1863 and 1874 over 150,000 political offenders were deported to Siberia. The success of the *zemstvos* only increased the desire of the people for some control over their central government, which was still an autocracy unchecked by any elected Parliament.

In the countryside emancipation had substituted new hardships for the old. The peasant had less land than before—and now had to find money for redemption payments over the next forty-nine years! Moreover, the land was still not entirely his own, but belonged to the village, or *mir*, which was jointly responsible for the payment of the village taxes and loan repayments. Because of this the *mir* could refuse to allow peasants to leave the village unless they had made satisfactory arrangements regarding their payments. Every so often the land of the village was redistributed, and as the population increased the amount allotted to each peasant diminished. To find the money needed for taxes and redemption payments the *mir* had often to export corn, despite the fact that with the primitive methods of agriculture then practised it could hardly produce enough for its own needs. The Russian peasant lived in conditions of indescribable poverty, borne only because he had never known anything different. But if the peasants' problem was one of land, the lords' was one of labour. After emancipation the lord could no longer enforce labour-services, and was often obliged to sell part of his land for lack of labour.

Revolutionary Movements and the Assassination of Alexander II (1881)

Prevailing discontent, together with the Tsar's growing reaction in the latter part of his reign, inevitably bred ideas of revolution. 'Intellectuals,' who had imbibed liberal and scientific doctrines from Western Europe, were prominent in this connexion. The Russian is sometimes said to be a natural anarchist, the vast distances of the surrounding plains producing a nomadic outlook which chafes under governmental restraints. Whether this be so or not, early Russian revolutionary thought certainly aimed at the overthrow and destruction of existing governments. The leading anarchist at this time was the Russian Count Bakunin, now in exile. Inside Russia the fashionable revolutionary doctrine was nihilism (Latin *nihil*=nothing). The nihilists were convinced that Russian society—its government, religion, class system, and social structure—was rotten to the core, and should be completely swept away. Then, starting afresh from nothing, a new order would be built up based upon reason and science.

The fate of the Paris Commune of 1871 impressed upon the nihilists the importance of winning over the conservative-minded peasantry. During the 1870's a movement called 'going to the people' developed. Several thousand nihilist intellectuals, mostly young men and women, went among the peasantry performing useful educational and social work, but above all trying to win them over to revolution. Countrymen everywhere take slowly to new ideas, and are suspicious of townsfolk and their book-learning, and although the Russian peasant had many grounds for discontent, he was unmoved by the doctrines of the nihilists. The latter now turned increasingly to methods of terrorism, substituting the knife, pistol, or bomb for the spoken word. Leading officials were done to death—and, in return, many revolutionaries executed or exiled to Siberia. Attempts were made to murder the Tsar himself. At length, after several miraculous escapes, Alexander II was killed by bombs thrown at his coach (March 1881).

Alexander III (1881–94): Reaction Triumphant

The bombs which killed Alexander II killed also any further chance of reform, and the end of the century has aptly been called the 'twilight' of Russian history. The new Tsar, Alexander III, was the embodiment of reaction. His chief adviser, Pobiedonostsev, preached autocracy as a philosophy and pursued it ruthlessly as a policy. Wherever possible Alexander II's reforms were undone or whittled down. Contact with western civilization was discouraged, Russia, it was held, being sufficient unto herself, with no need for new-fangled notions from outside. The so-called 'Iron Curtain' of the twentieth century has its counterpart throughout the long centuries of Russian history, and at few times has been more in evidence than in the twenty years following the murder of Alexander II.

Liberal and reformist ideas suffered the same fate as those of the extreme revolutionaries. The universities were controlled, the Press muzzled, the franchise for the *zemstvos* limited, and their powers diminished, the jury system curtailed, and even the emancipation of the serfs to some extent undone by the establishment of Land Captains (sometimes the old nobility in a new guise) to control the peasantry. The secret police—symbol of Russian autocracy through the ages—was increased in numbers, and its powers enlarged.

Russification was as much the government's policy as repression. The many non-Russian races of the Empire were denied wherever possible their separate rights of language, religion, culture, and custom, until Russia became, in Lenin's later vivid phrase, "a prison-house of the nations." None suffered so much as the 5,000,000 Jews, who were confined to the ghettoes in certain towns, excluded from engaging in agriculture, deprived of many civil rights, and from time to time subjected to murderous outbursts of popular fury known as pogroms. Such pogroms served the government's purpose in another way, the Jews becoming a scapegoat for the shortcomings of the government itself. Between 1880 and 1890 about 1,500,000 Jews left Russia, the majority going to the United States, where expanding 'Big Business' readily absorbed their labour.

Russian literature reflects the age in many ways. One of the greatest of all Russian writers, Count Leo Tolstoy, author of *War and Peace* and *Anna Karenina*, revolted against the materialism and physical barbarities around him. Retiring to his country estate, he lived the life of a simple peasant, renouncing bodily pleasures and the use of force. The short stories and plays of Anton Chekhov reflect the sharp awareness of human pain and suffering that weighed heavily upon the more sensitive minds during this 'twilight' period of Russian history.

Economic Development

The reigns of Alexander III and of his successor, Nicholas II (1894–1917), saw the beginnings of an Industrial Revolution in Russia. Till the latter part of the nineteenth century Russia was almost entirely agricultural, what few factories there were being often run by serf-labour. The emancipation of the serfs and the growing pressure of population upon the land produced a migration of labour from country to town. Factories grew up in the large towns, and the iron and coal of the Ukraine were exploited. The usual evils of factory-life soon appeared, and from 1880 the government tried by factory laws to remedy them.

Rapid strides were made under Witte, Minister of Finance from 1892 to 1903. Witte aimed at so developing Russia's natural resources

as to make her largely independent of other countries. He passed laws
for the protection of growing industries. He reformed the currency,
and placed Russia upon the gold standard. By so doing he gave confidence to the foreign investor, and much capital was attracted from
abroad, especially from France after she became Russia's ally in the
1890's. Witte realized the importance of communications in such a
vast country as Russia. He promoted railway construction, and
brought many railways under State ownership. His ministry coin-
cides almost exactly with the building of the Trans-Siberian Railway,
4500 miles long, which was commenced in 1891 and completed in the
early years of the twentieth century.

Industrial and commercial progress increased the country's wealth,
but it was too small and unequally shared to allay the growing discontent. The peasant was falling behind in his redemption payments,
and famine often swept the land. But the peasant lived in small com-
munities separated by wide distances, and concerted action was
difficult in his case. Not so with the town-worker. The law forbade
him to strike; but it could not prevent him from forming secret trade
unions and other associations, or from listening to the growing murmurs of revolution.

Nicholas II (1894–1917): Early Years

Any hopes that the new Tsar, Nicholas II, would prove more
liberal than his predecessor were quickly dispelled. A request for
representative government was dismissed as "a senseless dream."
Intellectuals in particular were the object of attack. The censorship
was tightened up, and university teachers and students were watched
for 'dangerous' opinions. Thousands of political prisoners were
arbitrarily arrested and dispatched to Siberia. In 1903 Witte was
dismissed as being too lenient, and his place taken by Plehve, a
thoroughgoing reactionary. The attack on the subject races, particularly Finns and Jews, reached new heights. Since its transference
from Sweden to Russia in Napoleonic times, Finland had been
allowed considerable independence under the Tsar, who ruled in the
capacity of Grand Duke. It had prospered, and was many years in
advance of its mother-country. As such it presented a dangerous
example to the Tsar's Russian subjects, and in 1899 it was shorn of

its national rights and absorbed into Russia. Pogroms against the Jews continued on a large scale, at times with the definite encouragement of Plehve.

Reformist and Revolutionary Movements to 1905

Movements to end this state of affairs abounded. Two kinds can be broadly distinguished: those which sought improvements inside the existing framework, and those which thought the framework so rotten that only by scrapping it could any improvements be made.

Among the first was the Zemstvo Movement. Despite frequent obstruction by the central government, the *zemstvos*, or local councils, established by Alexander II continued to do good work. Professional and social workers, such as doctors, teachers, nurses, and engineers, had performed miracles, but realized acutely how much more needed to be done, and how helpless they were without reform at the centre. The Moscow *zemstvo* took the lead in summoning conferences of *zemstvo* chairmen to co-ordinate activities and press for further powers. Witte encouraged their efforts, but his successor, Plehve, tried to limit their activities. Closely connected with the Zemstvo Movement was the Russian Liberal Party, under the leadership of Struve and others; their newspaper, *Liberation*, was printed in Germany and smuggled across the frontier.

Just before the end of the century several revolutionary parties were formed, the two most important being the Social Revolutionaries and the Social Democrats. The Social Revolutionary Party had grown out of the earlier movement of 'going to the people,' and as such it carried out propaganda mainly among the peasantry. It had no well-defined political philosophy, but attacked the many specific abuses it found in the countryside, and it had no hesitation in preaching and practising methods of terrorism. The Social Democrats, on the other hand, were in essence the Russian version of the international Marxist movement, which had already formed similar parties in other countries. As such they preached the complete overthrow of the existing system, and, in accordance with Marxist doctrines, concentrated mainly upon the workers in the large towns. Somewhat strangely, many of them opposed the violent methods of the Social Revolutionaries. The leaders of both societies were forced to live in exile, and in 1903 the Social Democrats held a conference in London, where an important decision was taken. The party had for some time contained two wings, the more extreme being led by Lenin. At the London Conference the extremists obtained a majority, and formed the Bolshevik party—so called from the Russian *bolshe*, meaning 'more.' Not only had they *more* votes, but they were *more* extreme in their methods and objects—what we should call 'whole-hoggers.' Their more moderate rivals formed the Menshevik, or minority, party. From now on the Bolsheviks and the Social Revolutionaries drew closer together.

Matters came to a head during the Russo-Japanese War of 1904–5 (see Chapter 6). Had the Russian government been victorious it might have quelled the clamour for reform; but defeat exposed its corruption and incompetence, and soon led to disturbances. In July 1904 Plehve was assassinated. In November a meeting of the *zemstvo* chairmen, led by the Moscow council, drew up an extensive programme of reform, which won widespread approval from the professional classes and the Liberals generally. It demanded a Parliament, the abolition of arbitrary arrest, and an extension of personal liberty to include freedom of speech, of association, of conscience, and of the Press. Throughout the year 1905 Russia was in a state bordering at times upon anarchy. In January a priest, Father Gapon, led a large body of demonstrators to the Winter Palace at St Petersburg to lay their grievances before the Tsar in person. They were mown down in cold blood by the military, and many hundreds were killed or wounded. The barbarities of "Bloody Sunday," as it came to be called, sank deep into the popular consciousness. Strikes of city-workers and mutinies among the armed forces broke out, and in February the Grand Duke Sergius (the Tsar's uncle, and a noted reactionary) was murdered. In August Nicholas II promised concessions, but they were inadequate, and in October a General Strike threatened to paralyse the nation's life. Some of the large cities now for the first time established soviets, or workers' councils, as rivals to the established authorities; Lenin and Trotsky, revisiting Russia from exile, noted and encouraged this experiment. At length the Tsar restored order by recalling Witte as chief minister, and promising a Parliament elected on a wide franchise. One of Witte's first acts was to abolish all further land-redemption payments, which in many cases had fallen hopelessly in arrears. The unrest of 1905 was over, but it was to serve as a rehearsal for the full-length drama of 1917.

The Dumas: A Constitutional Experiment

The word *duma* means 'a thinking-place' (just as our 'parliament' means a 'talking-place'), and was the name given to the Parliaments elected from 1906 onward in accordance with the Tsar's promise. The maximum length of a Duma was to be five years, and its consent was declared necessary for all new laws, except emergency decrees. Before the first election, however, the Tsar safeguarded his position in two ways. He created a Second Chamber composed of government nominees, and he issued certain fundamental laws, outside the Duma's control, which reserved all final power to the Tsar and his ministers.

The first Duma met in May 1906, and contained a majority of the progressive party known as Constitutional Democrats, or Cadets. Witte soon resigned; he was too liberal to work amicably with the Tsar, yet not liberal enough to throw in his lot with the Duma. Thereafter the Tsar's ministers were mostly thoroughgoing reactionaries. Very soon the government and the Duma were involved in bitter argument. The Duma wanted the Second Chamber remodelled, they wanted land reforms, and an extension of personal liberty, including the abolition of arbitrary arrest; above all, they wanted control over the appointment and policy of the Tsar's ministers. This would have made the Tsar a constitutional monarch, as in Britain, and was too much to expect. In July, after two months, the Tsar dissolved the Duma.

In March 1907 a second Duma met. The anti-government parties were again in a majority, this time containing a large number of extreme Socialists, as distinct from the more moderate Cadets. Disputes again broke out, and the Tsar arrested a number of delegates. In June—this time after three months—the Tsar again dissolved his Duma.

Before the next election the Tsar altered the franchise to deprive many of the peasantry of the vote, and to give the wealthy landowners greater powers. The result was that the third Duma, which lasted from November 1907 to 1912, was a more docile body than its predecessors. This at any rate had the advantage of allowing something to be done. A few reforms in education and State insurance were passed. Most important, the Tsar's chief minister, Stolypin, continued certain rural reforms which he had begun in 1906. By a law of 1909 the Russian village, or *mir*, could, if it so desired, end its arrangement of common land ownership and communal farming, and the peasant could consolidate his lands into one holding without the prospect of periodical reallotment. It is reckoned that about one-tenth of the peasantry took advantage of this law before the Bolshevik revolution of 1917. It encouraged individual initiative and pride of ownership, and produced an era of comparative prosperity. But the mass of the peasantry was still poverty-stricken and land-hungry, and Stolypin's law allowed the growth of the *kulaks* (literally 'fists'), the more prosperous and enterprising peasants who could now buy up the lands of their needy neighbours. The *kulaks* increased production, but soon earned the envy of their less fortunate or less thrifty brethren.

The fourth Duma (1912–17) was, like the third, composed largely of reactionaries. Russia presented a pitiable spectacle on the eve of the First World War. Stolypin had been assassinated, and the weak-willed Tsar allowed the Tsarina undue influence over affairs of government. Her chief concern was to preserve all authority intact for the heir to the throne, and she earned public disgrace by her association with the disreputable peasant-monk Rasputin. Repression of all reformers, and of the subject-races—Poles, Finns, Jews, Ukrainians—was intensified; the prison-camps of Siberia were busy. The constitutional experiment of the Dumas had failed, and the discontented were resorting once more to violence. In the big cities strikes and disorders were increasing. But August 1914 witnessed an outburst of patriotism, and the nation united in defence of its country. Tsarism had been given one more chance. Could it use it?

Chapter 4

OTHER COUNTRIES (1870–1914)

Italy

ITALIAN unification was largely the work of Cavour, who in 1859 had obtained French assistance in driving the Austrians out of Lombardy. During the following year other states joined Piedmont— namely, the northern duchies (Parma, Modena, and Tuscany), and, after Garibaldi's expedition, Naples and the major part of the Papal States. In 1861 the Kingdom of Italy was proclaimed. Cavour died soon afterwards, leaving Venetia and Rome still unattached to the new kingdom. In 1866 Italy acquired Venetia as a result of her alliance with Prussia in the war against Austria. In 1870 she obtained Rome when the French troops which had been guarding the Holy City for the past twenty years were withdrawn during the Franco-German War. Italy now had her natural and historic capital, Rome, and her unity was complete—unless we except so-called Unredeemed Italy (*Italia Irredenta*), still in Austrian hands. This consisted of the Trentino district in the Tyrol and the Istrian peninsula in the Adriatic.

The Constitution of modern Italy was in effect that of the former Kingdom of Piedmont. The royal House was the Piedmontese House of Savoy, represented by Victor Emmanuel II, who reigned till 1878. The Parliamentary system consisted of two Houses: a Senate nominated by the king, and a Chamber of Deputies elected by males of twenty-five years or over paying a certain amount of direct taxes. The king's ministers, as in Britain, were responsible to the Lower House.

The history of Italy since 1870 can be understood only if the problems facing the new kingdom are first considered. In matters of government she had to weld together what had hitherto been about

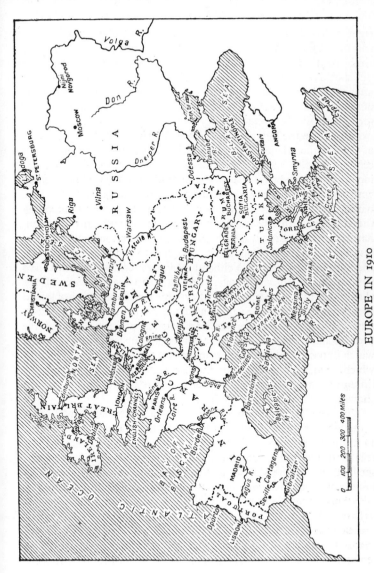

EUROPE IN 1910.   See the map on page 67.

The only changes between 1910 and 1914 were in the Balkan Peninsula.

eight different states; most of these had been autocratically ruled, and the people had no experience in Parliamentary self-government. In the relations between Church and State she was faced with unique difficulties as a result of her seizure of Rome in 1870, just a few months after the Vatican Council had declared the Pope infallible in matters of faith and morals. Nor were her social and economic problems less formidable. Poverty and illiteracy were the lot of most of her people, particularly in the South; it is estimated that in 1861 over 75 per cent. of the total population was illiterate, with the figure reaching 90 per cent. in Naples and Sicily. The new kingdom took over the not inconsiderable debts of the former states, and was faced in addition with the need for heavy expenditure on public works such as roads, harbours, and railways. All this necessitated heavy taxation, which the country, with few natural resources and (except in the North) hardly any industries, was ill-fitted to bear. Her population, too, was fast increasing, rising from 25,000,000 in 1870 to 35,000,000 in 1914. Many millions sought a livelihood in emigration to the U.S.A. and various South American states, and although many returned after some years to their native land, they were for the time being lost to their mother-country. Such considerations contributed to Italy's final problem, that of foreign and colonial policy. The need for prestige and for greater economic self-sufficiency led her into policies which imposed still further demands upon her limited resources, and which, in view of her late start and her inadequate strength, brought little in the way of returns. A brief review of events since 1870 will show how Italy attempted to tackle these problems.

When the Italians occupied Rome in 1870 the Pope, Pius IX, protested against their action, and retired to his palace of the Vatican. Refusing to recognize Victor Emmanuel as King of Italy, or the legality of the Italian seizure of the Papal lands, Pius IX never again set foot outside the Vatican and its grounds. His example was followed by his successors, and the Pope henceforth became the "Prisoner of the Vatican." Italy genuinely desired a settlement, not only out of respect and affection for the Pope himself, but also because of the offence given to Catholics in all lands, and the likelihood that some time or other a Catholic power, maybe France, would be tempted to espouse openly the Pope's cause. As the Pope himself refused to treat with the so-called usurpers, the Italian Parliament attempted a settlement alone. In 1871 it passed the Law of Papal Guarantees. The Pope's spiritual powers were guaranteed, his person given royal immunity, the Vatican City granted sovereign status, and an income promised as compensation for the loss of his temporal estates. The Pope refused the income, and forbade Catholics to vote or accept office in the new kingdom. Although in practice many Italian Catholics compromised upon the rival claims of Church and State in accordance with their own conscience, the differences between the two powers remained a constant source of embarrassment to the Italian government. Not till Mussolini's Lateran Treaty of 1929 (see p. 171) was the breach healed.

In 1878 Victor Emmanuel II was succeeded by his son, Humbert I. The next twenty years saw many attempts made, with varying success, to solve Italy's other problems. Early in the new reign the national budget balanced for the first time; but taxes continued high, and mismanagement and even corruption characterized some of her governments. A law of 1877 providing for compulsory education was only partially enforced. In 1882 the franchise was trebled by reducing the age-limit to twenty-one, and lowering the qualifications. In the same year Italy enhanced, as she thought, her national prestige by forming the Triple Alliance with Germany and Austria (see Chapter 7). This heralded a more active colonial policy. Excluded by France from Tunisia, she sought consolation along the Red Sea. In 1885 she seized the port of Massawa, and laid the foundations for her colony in Eritrea. Francesco Crispi, Prime Minister for the greater part of the period 1887–96, soon embarked on wider schemes. Italian forces advanced inland to threaten the independence of Abyssinia, but they were cut to pieces and forced back to the coast. By 1889 Italy had consolidated her power in the two coastal strips of Eritrea and Italian Somaliland, but she still cast envious eyes upon Abyssinia. In 1896, in an attempt to occupy a small state which was tributary to Abyssinia, the Italians suffered a severe defeat at Adowa, and for the time being all hopes of inland penetration had to be abandoned. Forty years later they were revived by Mussolini.

Adowa ended the ministry of Crispi; but there were other reasons. The wars had proved costly, taxation was heavy, and budget deficits were once more accumulating. Moreover, the wars had produced only two colonies, whose usefulness in solving Italy's difficulties was highly questionable. Crispi had ruled as a dictator, suppressing the growing socialist and republican parties. After his fall the discontent took uglier shape. In the South hunger and poverty produced 'bread riots'; in the North disturbances occurred which threatened the very form of government itself. In 1900 King Humbert was assassinated.

Humbert's son, Victor Emmanuel III (1900–47), entered upon his difficult task with many personal advantages: youth, energy, intelligence, and above all a genuine desire to promote the welfare of his people. Conditions improved somewhat, especially with the extension of the silk and cotton industries in the North. But even this was not all gain. Working conditions were bad, and socialist and anarchist movements flourished. In 1904 a general strike paralysed the nation's life in the big cities of the North. From the poverty-stricken South emigrants continued to seek a better life in the New World and elsewhere. Again Italy sought relief, or at any rate diversion, in overseas adventures. In 1911 she engaged in war with Turkey for the possession of Tripoli, and when the war ended in 1912 she had gained her prize, and was also left in actual, if not entirely legal, possession of Rhodes and the Dodecanese. Her actions had not met with the support of her German ally. What with her differences with Austria over *Italia Irredenta*, her traditional affection for Britain, and the easing of Franco-Italian tension over the North African coast, her loyalty to the Triple Alliance had for long been weakening, and when war broke out in 1914 she declared her neutrality.

Austria-Hungary

The old Austrian Empire, built up laboriously over the centuries, was a patchwork of many different races. The nucleus of this ramshackle empire was the Austrians themselves, of Germanic stock. To their east were the Magyars of Hungary, descendants of Hun settlers of the Dark Ages, characterized by an extreme form of feudal society in which the oppressed serfs were ruled by a proud, landowning nobility. East of the Magyars lay the Roumanians of Transylvania, blood-brothers of the Turkish subjects of Moldavia and Wallachia. To the north and the south of this central line of Austrians, Maygars, and Roumanians lay races mainly of Slavonic blood. North were the Czechs of Bohemia, the Slovaks, and some Poles and Ruthenians; south were Croats and Serbs. In addition, there were Italians in the Tyrol and, since 1815, in the Austrian-ruled provinces of Lombardy and Venetia. Furthermore, Austria proper and Bohemia were included in the boundaries of the 1815 German Confederation, of which Austria was the president; the rest of the Austrian Empire was outside.

In 1848–49 widespread but unsuccessful revolutions occurred in the Austrian Empire. In the midst of these revolutions a new Austrian Hapsburg emperor, Francis Joseph, succeeded to the throne. A youth of eighteen at his accession, he was destined to reign from 1848 till his death in 1916, in the middle of the First World War. The first twenty years of his reign saw important changes. In 1859 Lombardy was lost to Piedmont. In 1866 Austria was defeated by Bismarck's Prussia. Austria was obliged to withdraw from the German Confederation, which now passed under Prussian control, to become in 1871 the German Empire. Austria also lost Venetia to Italy. Thus Austrian leadership of the German states, going back over six centuries, was dramatically ended.

The Magyars of Hungary had not ceased since 1848–49 to agitate for self-government, and the defeat of Austria in 1866 brought them their reward. In 1867, by an arrangement known as the *Ausgleich*, or "Compromise," the internal government of the Austrian Empire was recast. The Empire was split in two, and Hungary became a separate kingdom, and assumed rule over some of the subject-races; Francis Joseph took the title of King of Hungary as well as Emperor of Austria. Both Austria and Hungary had their separate Parliaments and ministries, at Vienna and Budapest respectively. Only for foreign affairs, the Army, and finances was there joint government, controlled by delegations of sixty members each from the two Parliaments. Thus was established the Dual Monarchy; henceforth the Austrian Empire is more correctly described as Austria-Hungary.

The Dual Monarchy lasted intact to the First World War, but it was subject to many strains. There was the usual demand for a widening of the franchise, which was granted by Austria in 1907, but refused by Hungary to her subjects. The severest strain, however,

D

was the continued demand of the subject-races for equality of treatment with Austrians and Magyars. Racial discontent continued till the First World War gave it the opportunity to express itself in action.

Internal tension linked up closely with matters of foreign policy. Serbs and Roumanians outside Austria-Hungary supported the claims of their oppressed kinsfolk inside. Russia supported the Balkan peoples, partly on strategic and partly on racial grounds; she fostered Pan-Slav movements in an attempt to unite all Slavs in one common aim. Excluded from German affairs, and desirous of quelling Balkan discontent, Austria after 1866 turned increasingly towards the Balkans, and began her *Drang nach Osten*, or drive to the east. Germany supported her, and the two powers became firm allies. This naturally increased the tension between Austria on the one hand, and the Balkan races and Russia on the other.

The Low Countries

Belgium (the former Austrian Netherlands) had been joined to Holland in 1815 under William I, of the House of Orange, which for the first time assumed the title of a royal House. In 1830 the Belgians revolted, and after a struggle asserted their independence. Leopold of Saxe-Coburg became their king, and the chief powers of Europe guaranteed their neutrality in the Treaty of London (1839)—the famous 'scrap of paper' of 1914.

The history of Holland and Belgium since 1830 presents few features of outstanding importance. In Holland the House of Orange has been successively represented by William I (1815–40), William II (1840–49), William III (1849–90), and Wilhelmina, who while still a minor became queen in 1890. In 1898 Queen Wilhelmina assumed royal powers in her own person, and after reigning fifty years abdicated in 1948 in favour of her daughter Juliana. Holland has progressed from a somewhat autocratic state to a democratic one, and at the present day the royal House stands high in popular esteem.

In Belgium Leopold I had a long and successful reign from 1831 to 1865. From the outset the Belgian Constitution was liberal, and often served as a model for reformers elsewhere. Leopold accepted the limitations of constitutional monarchy, and, free from political strife, his country enjoyed a period of peaceful development. His successor, Leopold II (1865–1909), was less fortunate, and was faced with dissensions between Flemings and Walloons, and between Catholics and Liberals. Leopold II's reign also saw the 'scramble for Africa' (see Chapter 6). In his personal capacity the king encouraged H. M. Stanley's exploration of the Congo, which in 1878 became the Congo Free State run by a company under Leopold's direction. Thirty years later it passed as a national colony to Belgium. In 1909 Albert I succeeded to the throne. It was he who defied the German invader in 1914, and his reign ended in 1934. His successor, Leopold III, faced a second German invasion in 1940, but with different results from his predecessor. He was accused of having compromised with the enemy, and in 1950 he was obliged to hand his powers over to his son, Prince Baudouin, who assumed the royal title in the following year.

Scandinavia

Important changes have occurred in Scandinavia over the last 150 years. Before the Napoleonic period Denmark and Norway were united, and Sweden (once mistress of the Baltic) still possessed Finland. In the course of the Napoleonic wars Russia obtained Finland, which she kept till the First World War. Denmark's support of Napoleon lost her Norway; this was given to Sweden, which under Count Bernadotte (formerly one of Napoleon's marshals) had helped in the final overthrow of France. Bernadotte founded the royal House which still rules in Sweden.

Denmark was thus much reduced in size, and it took her long to recover from the blow. In 1864 she suffered further losses when Austria and Prussia seized the duchies of Schleswig and Holstein. Since then she has pursued a policy of peaceful internal development. Denmark, under her present king, Frederick IX, still possesses Greenland and the Faroe Islands. Iceland, which had for long enjoyed home rule under the King of Denmark, became an independent republic in 1944.

The union of Norway and Sweden in 1814–15 had to be forced upon an unwilling Norway. Even then there was no complete fusion. The king of Sweden ruled in another capacity as king of Norway, and the two countries had a common Minister of Foreign Affairs. Otherwise they retained their own governments and institutions. Continuing disagreements came to a head when Norway, having developed a strong mercantile marine, demanded a consular service separate from that of Sweden. The latter resisted on the grounds that it would lead to separate foreign policies. At length in 1905 the Norwegian Storthing (Parliament) declared that "the union with Sweden under one king has ceased." Although some in Sweden were prepared to use force, the Swedish government acquiesced on condition that the decision was approved by the Norwegian people. A popular vote showed over 368,000 in favour of separation and 184 against. Norway then chose a member of the Danish royal House as king. He assumed the title of Haakon VII, and at the time of writing still rules. Relations between the two countries have been friendly since the break, and both have advanced towards greater democracy.

Spain and Portugal

Spanish history in the nineteenth and twentieth centuries is complicated in detail, but in its main outlines presents a simple pattern. Since the War of the Spanish Succession and the Treaty of Utrecht (1713) its royal line had been the Bourbons, close relatives of the French former ruling House. The mass of the people were poor and illiterate, and were denied power and advancement by those in authority. The latter included the Bourbon monarchy, reactionary, absolute, and itself torn by dynastic disputes; the proud and effete nobility; the Army, which, as the possessor of the only effective force in the country, made and unmade revolutions; and the Roman Catholic Church, wealthy in land and other possessions, and determined to retain its privileged position in the State. The Bourbons were restored on the downfall of Napoleon, but were soon in difficulties. Internal revolutions were suppressed with the aid of France. In 1823 Spain was obliged to recognize the loss of her once mighty American empire. A period of dynastic strife was ended by the accession of Isabella II (1833–68), whose reign was marked by such reaction, corruption, and intolerance that in 1868 the queen fled the country. The vacancy thus created led to the candidature of Leopold of Hohenzollern for the Spanish throne—the immediate cause of the

Franco-German War of 1870. Leopold withdrew his candidature, and for the next few years Spain experimented with a king from the Italian house of Savoy, and with a republic. In 1874 the Army overthrew the latter and restored the Bourbons, in the person of Alfonso XII, son of Isabella. Two years later a new Constitution granted increased powers to the Spanish Parliament, or Cortes. Alfonso XII died in 1885, to be succeeded by his son Alfonso XIII, for whom a regency existed till 1902, when the king assumed royal powers. During the regency of Maria, Spain lost the Philippines, Cuba, and Porto Rico to the U.S.A. as a result of the Spanish-American War of 1898 (see Chapter 6). Her once widespread empire was now reduced to a few shreds: Spanish Morocco, Rio de Oro, Spanish Guinea, the Canaries, and a few other islands. In a later chapter we shall see how in 1931 Alfonso XIII was forced to leave Spain, which once more became a republic.

Portugal experienced much the same kind of royalist absolutism, dynastic quarrels, and revolutionary movements as Spain. Her royal House of Braganza fled to Brazil during the Napoleonic wars, and was reluctant to return afterwards. In 1822 Brazil declared its independence. From 1889 Portugal was ruled by Carlos I, who, faced with growing discontent, became more reactionary than before, and began to tamper with the Constitution. In 1908 Carlos and the Crown Prince were assassinated. The king's second son, Manuel, had a brief reign till 1910, when revolution broke out, and Portugal became a republic. A new Constitution granted the people greater powers, and, although the Portuguese Republic contains certain arbitrary features judged by British standards, it has won the support of the people, and subsequent royalist attempts to overthrow it have been easily defeated.

Switzerland

Switzerland is composed of twenty-two cantons, which were still only loosely associated in 1815, when the great powers guaranteed their neutrality. German and French are the important languages, while a small minority speak Italian. The Protestant and Roman Catholic religions are both strong. In 1845 the Catholic cantons formed a separate league called the Sonderbund, and attempted to defy the others. They were defeated after a short war, and in 1848 a new Constitution was adopted. This strengthened the Federation and made Switzerland in some ways the most democratic country in the world.

Under its new Constitution, and with its neutrality preserved through two world wars, Switzerland has enjoyed a century of peaceful development. More than any other country it has stood forth as an island of internationalism in the turbulent seas of national strife. Its citizens played a leading part in establishing the International Red Cross (see Chapter 8), whose symbol is simply the Swiss flag with the colours reversed. Geneva in particular has become the home of many international organizations, and the scene of international conferences and courts of arbitration. After the First World War it was chosen to be the headquarters of the League of Nations.

Chapter 5

THE EASTERN QUESTION (1870–1914)

The Eastern Question: Its Essentials

THE Eastern Question consisted of the problems raised by the threatened break-up of the Turkish, or Ottoman, Empire in Europe. The Turkish Empire stretched from the borders of Austria and Russia in the north through Asia Minor and Syria to Egypt and other parts of North Africa. In the Balkan peninsula—the part now under consideration—it contained numerous subject-races: Roumanians, Serbs, Bulgarians, Albanians, Greeks, and others. These peoples were mostly Christian in religion, and had suffered the Mohammedan yoke of the Turks for five centuries; but in the nineteenth century the movement began for their liberation. Already in the 1820's the Greeks had won their independence by force of arms.

The impending disintegration of the Turkish Empire raised serious issues for the great powers, especially those with interests in the eastern Mediterranean. Russia possessed racial and religious affinities with most of the Balkan peoples, who like her were Orthodox Christians in faith and largely Slavonic in blood. Hence she championed their cause and posed as their protector. Her motives were not entirely altruistic, for if she created new Balkan states under her protection her influence would reach the shores of the Mediterranean, and she might even command the Straits (Dardanelles and Bosphorus) controlling the sea-routes to the Black Sea.

These considerations led other powers to view Russian policy with suspicion. British colonial and commercial interests in India and the Far East were linked with the control of the Eastern Mediterranean and the Suez route (the Canal was not opened till 1869, but even before then an important overland route existed). But many Britons were faced with a dilemma. To oppose Russian designs seemed equivalent to propping up the effete and barbarous Turkish Empire and denying the Balkan Christians their independence. At times, therefore, we find men like Byron (who lost his life fighting for the Greeks) and Gladstone acting counter to the usual British official policy by supporting the independence of the Balkan peoples in the belief that other ways and means could be found of halting the Russian advance. On land the chief opponent of Russian advance into the Balkans was Austria. Not only had Austria her own ambitions in that area, but also her ramshackle empire itself contained Balkan races like Serbs and Roumanians. If these latter races now under Turkish rule became free, they would wish to unite with their fellow-nationals under Austrian rule, and the Austro-Hungarian Empire itself would break up. As time went on the Pan-Slav movement took shape—a movement for the independence of all Slavonic races, and their union under Russian leadership. This threatened still more the integrity of the Austro-Hungarian Empire, and it is not surprising, therefore, that Austria and Russia were bitter rivals in South-eastern Europe. One further country requires mention— France. The French had commercial interests and political ambitions of long standing in certain parts of the Ottoman Empire, notably in Syria and Egypt. These threatened to weaken the Sultan's power, and French designs were opposed by Britain. But France had equally no desire to see Russia in control of the Balkans, and this consideration usually lined her up with Britain and Austria where Balkan questions were concerned. As time went on the growing might of Germany counterbalanced certain aspects of the Eastern Question, and in 1914 we find Britain and France in the same camp as their Near Eastern rival, Russia.

The Situation by 1870

The first people to win their freedom from the Turks were the Greeks, whose independence was recognized in 1832; but their frontiers as then fixed still left many compatriots inside the Ottoman Empire.

Continued suspicion of Russian designs led in 1854 to the Crimean War, in which Britain and France assisted Turkey in opposing Russian aims. The war was ended by the Treaty of Paris (1856).

Russia and Turkey restored all conquests; but, although there were no boundary changes, there were other important provisions. The Black Sea was declared open to merchant ships of all nations, but closed to warships of all nations; Russia also had to dismantle her naval fortress of Sebastopol. The two provinces of Moldavia and Wallachia, as well as a rather small Serbia, were given self-government, but were still to owe allegiance to the Sultan. Russia was obliged to renounce her claims of protection over the Christian subjects of the Sultan, while the other European powers promised not to interfere in Turkey's internal affairs. In return the Sultan issued a solemn promise to govern his Christian subjects better. The general result was to check Russia's advance, for the time being, but to leave the fate of the Balkan peoples still unsolved.

In the 1860's Serbia strengthened her military forces, and obliged the Sultan to withdraw the Turkish garrison; the only symbol of Turkish suzerainty left was the Turkish flag flying side by side with the Serbian at Belgrade. Moldavia and Wallachia went even further. By the Treaty of Paris they were forbidden to unite, but were allowed to elect their own rulers. In 1859 they both elected the same ruler, and two years later the powers ratified the arrangement. The two provinces, now united, were henceforth known as Roumania, after their Roman origin. In 1866 they deposed their first ruler and chose a German prince, Charles of Hohenzollern-Sigmaringen, a capable sovereign who retained his throne till his death in 1914. Finally the defeat of France by Germany in 1871 gave Russia (who rightly reckoned that Britain would not interfere alone) the opportunity of denouncing the neutrality clauses of the Black Sea. Once more Russia began building a fleet and fortifying Sebastopol, but it took her many years to accomplish the task.

The Bulgarian Atrocities and the Treaty of Berlin (1878)

In 1875 the provinces of Bosnia and Herzegovina, inhabited by people closely akin to the Serbs, rose against their Turkish tax-gatherers. The Austrian Chancellor, Count Andrassy, with the support of Russia and Germany, presented the Sultan with a note demanding reform in the disaffected provinces. The Sultan as usual promised reforms, but—again as usual—with no guarantees that they would be carried out. The unrest spread, and in 1876 the Bulgarians revolted and killed over a hundred Turkish officials. The Turks proceeded to stamp out the Bulgarian rising with the utmost cruelty. In addition to their regular troops, they employed wild irregulars known as Bashi-Bazouks, who massacred many thousands (the exact figure being unascertainable) of men, women, and children in cold blood. The Bulgarian atrocities roused Europe to righteous anger. The British Liberal leader, Gladstone, then in opposition, called upon the government to join other countries in expelling the Turks "bag and baggage . . . from the province they have desolated and profaned." Gladstone was referring to Bulgaria, together with Bosnia and Herzegovina; but once started, the expulsion would almost certainly have spread to other European provinces of the Turkish Empire. The British Prime Minister, Disraeli, rejected Gladstone's appeal. The Turk was to him a symbol of Oriental glamour and romance; talk of atrocities he declared mere "coffee-house babble." Instead he preferred the old Palmerstonian policy of opposing Russia even at the expense of Christian life and liberty in the Balkans. Subsequent events were undoubtedly influenced by the Sultan's belief that, in any war with Russia, Britain would send assistance, as at the time of the Crimean War.

Meanwhile in 1876 two successive Sultans were deposed by Turkish rebels, and the throne was eventually occupied by Abdul Hamid II, a capable and unscrupulous ruler whose reign lasted till 1909. Serbia and Montenegro were now officially at war with Turkey, but, although assisted by numerous Russian volunteers, they were heavily defeated, and only a Russian ultimatum prevented the Turks from marching on Belgrade. The Pan-Slav movement (collaboration between the Slavonic races under Russian leadership) was growing in importance, and when it became obvious that the Sultan's promises of reform would never be implemented, the Tsar Alexander II declared war on Turkey (April 1877). The Russians advanced through Roumania and reached the fortress of Plevna before they were halted. For five months Osman Pasha with 40,000 men defied Russian forces three times as large. Eventually the Russians called upon Todleben, their veteran soldier of the Crimean War, to assist them, and by the end of the year Plevna had fallen. By January 1878 the Russian armies had reached Adrianople, and were soon within striking distance of Constantinople, in whose waters they could see the tops of a British fleet which Disraeli had moved up to guard the Straits. Hostilities were ended when the Russians forced upon the Sultan the Treaty of San Stefano (March 1878).

By this treaty Serbia, Montenegro, and Roumania were to become fully sovereign states, the last shreds of Turkish suzerainty disappearing. Roumania, however, was to cede to Russia the fertile district of Bessarabia in return for the barren Dobrudja, which was hardly generous treatment by Russia of her gallant ally in the recent war. The most important clauses related to the creation of a large state of Bulgaria, stretching from the Danube in the north to the Ægean coastline in the south, and containing all Macedonia, a region of very mixed racial groups, coveted by Greeks and Serbians as well as by Bulgarians. This new "Big Bulgaria" was still to be nominally under Turkish suzerainty. Objections were immediately raised by Austria, and more particularly by Britain. The new Bulgaria would almost certainly be under Russian domination, while its large extent would split the remains of the Turkish Empire into several scattered portions and give Russia (assuming she controlled Bulgaria) access to the Ægean and a base for future hostilities against Constantinople and the port of Salonika. Disraeli demanded a revision of the treaty, obtained a vote of money for military supplies, and moved Indian troops to Malta. Russia decided to adopt a conciliatory attitude, and consented to a congress at Berlin to work out a new agreement.

The Congress of Berlin (1878) met under the chairmanship of Bismarck, who, claiming to be a disinterested party, described his position as that of an "honest broker." But it was Disraeli who dominated the meeting. As Bismarck said: "*Der alte Jude, dass ist der Mann*" ("The old Jew, he's the fellow"). At length, after protracted negotiations over last-minute details, the following arrangements were agreed upon. Serbia, Montenegro, and Roumania achieved their independence, the first two being slightly enlarged. As at San Stefano, Russia obtained part of Bessarabia from Roumania; the latter was compensated by receiving the Dobrudja. The "Big Bulgaria" was split in three. One part, about a third the size of the original, continued as Bulgaria, enjoying self-government under a prince of its own, but still under nominal Turkish suzerainty. To its south was a state known as Eastern Roumelia, which was to remain inside the Turkish Empire as a useful bastion guarding the approaches to Adrianople and Constantinople; it was, however, to be ruled by a Christian governor appointed by the Sultan. The third part (Macedonia and the Ægean coastline) was to return to Turkey completely. As for Bosnia and Herzegovina, they were placed under the protection of Austria (whose frontiers they adjoined), but were not to be formally annexed into the Austro-Hungarian Empire. In Asiatic Turkey Russia obtained Kars and Batum; to counteract this threat to Turkey from the east Britain obtained the island of Cyprus.

The Treaty of Berlin established the political framework in the Balkans for the next thirty years, although, as we shall see, there were certain alterations in the years immediately following it. At the time it was regarded as a great act of statesmanship, especially in Britain, where it appeared to have checked Russian expansion. Disraeli claimed to have brought back "peace with honour." He was fêted by the London crowds, and the Queen bestowed the Order of the Garter upon both him and his Foreign Secretary, Lord Salisbury. Later generations have been less enthusiastic, at times, perhaps, erring in the other direction. They have pointed out that Russia, checked in the Balkans, promptly turned her attention farther east, to Persia, Afghanistan, and Manchuria; but this would have happened in any case, and is in itself no argument against checking Russian designs in Europe. Cyprus has been condemned as a useless acquisition, especially as Disraeli could have obtained Egypt instead; but its usefulness has increased in the twentieth century with the development of air power and the need for safeguarding the Middle Eastern oilfields.

Probably the most serious criticism that can be made is that the treaty fell between two stools; it neither re-established a strong and reformed Turkish Empire in Europe nor did it expel the Turk "bag and baggage" and create strong, independent Christian states. Instead it gave bits and pieces to every one, and insufficient to anyone. Thus Macedonia remained under unreformed Turkish rule, despite its mixed Greek, Serbian, and Bulgarian population. The Serbs of Bosnia-Herzegovina were left under the suzerainty of

THE BALKAN PENINSULA AFTER THE TREATY OF
BERLIN, 1878

Turkey, given the protection of Austria, while they increasingly
desired union with their fellow-countrymen in Serbia. Small wonder
that friction continued among all parties, eventually precipitating the
First World War. Gladstone had once urged the creation of strong

Balkan states as a "living barrier between Russia and Turkey."
"There is no barrier like the breasts of freemen." If this course had
been resolutely followed at Berlin it might have saved much future
trouble, though nothing short of a miracle could have brought complete peace to the Balkans.

One further point deserves notice. Bismarck, claiming to preside
over the conference as an "honest broker," found himself faced with
the rival claims of Austria and Russia to the Turkish heritage. Try as
he could to please both, he had to choose at times between one or the
other—and he chose Austria, as when he backed her claims over
Bosnia-Herzegovina. Austria and Germany drew closer together, and
in 1879 (one year after the Congress) concluded a secret alliance—the
first step in the creation of the European armed camps preceding the
war of 1914 (see Chapter 7). As for Russia, she realized where Bismarck's preference had lain, and she gradually cooled towards Germany and drew closer to France.

The Next Thirty Years (1878–1908)

The boundaries of Greece, drawn in 1832, still left many Greeks
under Turkish rule. In 1862 the first king of Greece, Otto of Bavaria,
was deposed, and in the following year Prince George of Denmark
accepted the vacant throne. As a coronation present Britain, under
Gladstone's influence, presented the new king with the Ionian
Islands, which had come under British protection in 1815. In 1881,
again largely as a result of Gladstone's influence, the Sultan ceded a
large part of Thessaly to Greece. Fifteen years later (1896) the people
of Crete, led by a 'coming' politician, Venizelos, revolted against
Turkish rule, and demanded union with Greece. The Greeks inter-
vened with arms, but were unsuccessful, and Crete continued under
Turkish rule till the twentieth century.

In 1885 the Bulgars of Eastern Roumelia revolted, expelled their
Turkish governors, and proclaimed their union with Bulgaria. This
was a direct defiance of the arrangements made at Berlin, when the
"Big Bulgaria" of Russia's creation had been split up. The powers
protested, but did not act, and the union was carried through. Somewhat ironically, the loudest protests came from Russia, who, having
discovered that the Bulgars were by no means the willing tools she

had hoped for, now desired to limit Bulgaria's frontiers. Such are the whirligigs of international politics!

Between 1894 and 1896 the news of Turkish atrocities again shocked the ears of Europe. This time it was the massacre of thousands of Armenian Christians, perpetrated on the pretext of suppressing rebellion. Britain, under Lord Salisbury, refused to act alone, lest a precedent be created for future interference by Russia, and so, political considerations outweighing humanitarian, nothing was done, unless one more promise of reform, extracted from the Sultan, can be counted an achievement.

Meanwhile Germany under her new Kaiser, William II, was taking an increasing interest in the affairs of Turkey. Germany saw in the Turkish Empire a land-route to the Middle East, by-passing the usual sea-routes controlled by Britain. The Kaiser visited the Sultan, toured parts of the Ottoman Empire, and made speeches proclaiming German friendship towards Turkey. German officers were sent to train the Turkish Army, and German bankers and businessmen acquired valuable economic interests inside the country. Concessions were granted and plans made for a German-controlled railway running from Berlin through the Balkans to Constantinople, and thence through Asia Minor to the Persian Gulf. This Berlin-to-Bagdad Railway was begun, but not completed before the First World War; it symbolized to Britain and Russia (both interested in Turkish affairs from their own different angles) the appearance of a third competitor.

In 1908 the most serious crisis since the Treaty of Berlin occurred. It was precipitated by the growing strength of a new party in Turkey. This was the party known as the Young Turks, formed largely of young Army officers under the leadership of Enver Bey. Their object was to modernize Turkey by giving her a Parliament, freedom of thought, of religion, and of the Press, and in addition to treat the subject-races more generously. In 1908 they staged a revolt, and forced the aged Sultan Abdul Hamid to grant a Constitution. Despite their liberal professions, the Young Turks proved as ruthless as ever towards the subject-races, their efficiency making them even more oppressive than previous Turkish governments. It is of interest to note that among their members was Mustapha Kemal, the creator of the reformed Turkish State after the First World War. The appearance of this party alarmed those powers whose interests lay in a weak and backward Turkey, and two events soon followed in 1908.

First, Prince Ferdinand of Bulgaria, who owed nominal allegiance to the Sultan under the Treaty of Berlin, proclaimed himself king, and renounced the last shreds of Turkish overlordship. The Sultan protested, but could do nothing effective.

Two days later (October 7, 1908) Austria-Hungary announced the outright annexation of Bosnia-Herzegovina, which she had been 'protecting' for the Sultan since 1878. This produced a first-class crisis, both inside the Balkans and among the great powers. The little state of Serbia, with about three million inhabitants, was aroused to a high pitch of anger. Already Austria-Hungary ruled over five million Serbo-Croats; she was now adding another million to her Empire. The tension between the two countries continued till it produced the Sarajevo crisis in 1914, the immediate cause of the First World War. Turkey was powerless to do anything herself, and the issue became one between the Berlin powers of 1878. Russia championed the cause of her fellow-Slavs, the Serbs, while Lord Grey, the British Foreign Minister, demanded a conference. But behind Austria stood the military might of Germany, and the Kaiser risked war in backing up the action of his ally. France did not feel strongly enough over the issue, and Russia and Britain withdrew before what the Kaiser later boasted of as the "shining armour" of Germany. The storm-clouds passed, but they left behind an embittered Serbia and a resentful and watchful Russia, determined on stronger measures next time to counter Austro-German designs.

The Balkan Wars (1912–13)

In 1909 a counter-revolution against the Young Turks failed. The leaders of the party regarded the Sultan Abdul Hamid II responsible for the plot, and deposed him. His brother, Mohammed V, was placed on the throne. The growing strength of the Young Turks, with their policy of excluding European interference from Turkish affairs and consolidating their hold on what remained of the Turkish Empire, was an important factor in precipitating the events of the next few years.

In 1911 Italy, which had for long coveted parts of the Turkish Empire in North Africa, and had seen Tunisia pass to France and Egypt to Britain in the 1880's, seized certain coastal towns in Tripoli and declared war on Turkey. By 1912 Turkey sued for peace, ceding Tripoli and the island of Rhodes to Italy, and leaving the other islands of the Dodecanese in Italian hands for the time being. Turkey's action was prompted by danger from another quarter—the Balkan states, which had temporarily settled their differences and formed a league.

The Balkan League (1912) was largely the work of the Greek Prime Minister, Venizelos. It consisted of Greece, Serbia, Montenegro, and Bulgaria, and its immediate object was to settle the question of Macedonia, which, it will be remembered, had been left in Turkish possession at the Congress of Berlin. The region was one of the most mixed in Europe, with Serbs, Greeks, and Bulgarians scattered among its wild mountains and remote villages. The League demanded certain much-needed reforms of government, and, on failing to obtain satisfaction, declared war on Turkey. In the First Balkan War (1912–13) the Turks were overwhelmingly defeated, the Greeks and Serbians overrunning Macedonia, and the Bulgarians capturing Adrianople and advancing within sight of Constantinople.

The great powers, though for different reasons, were alarmed at this sudden upset of the balance of power. A conference was arranged in London, and the contesting parties forced to accept the Treaty of London (May 1913). Turkey was to be deprived of all its European possessions except Constantinople and its immediate surroundings. Greece was to be allowed to annex the island of Crete, while Austria insisted on the creation of an independent Albania to prevent Serbian expansion to the Adriatic. But the division of Macedonia was left to the members of the League themselves—and the inevitable happened. Greece and Serbia were in military occupation of most of Macedonia, and the Serbs, thwarted of their Adriatic outlet by the creation of Albania, demanded the lion's share of Macedonia. The Bulgarians justifiably maintained that not only was much of Macedonia Bulgarian in race, but that they had played a vital part in the recent victories of the League by driving the Turks back to Constantinople.

E

A month after the Treaty of London the Bulgarians attacked their late allies, and the Second Balkan War (1913) resulted. Bulgaria was opposed by Greece, Serbia, and Montenegro, who were soon joined by Roumania, which had not taken part in the first war. Turkey also seized the opportunity of hitting back against her immediate neighbour, Bulgaria, which was thus surrounded on all sides. As was only to be expected, Bulgaria was defeated, and when peace was made by the Treaty of Bucharest (August 1913) she was a heavy loser. Serbia secured northern and central Macedonia, and Greece obtained southern Macedonia, with the port of Salonika. Roumania obtained from Bulgaria small concessions adjoining the Dobrudja. By a separate arrangement Turkey regained Adrianople, but Bulgaria retained her outlet to the Ægean Sea.

The Balkan Wars created a situation with an obvious bearing upon the outbreak and the course of the First World War. The Central Powers (Germany and Austria) were now cut off from direct contact with Turkey, where German influence was still strong. Among the Balkan states Serbia, which had gained over a million inhabitants, was flushed with success, and relations between her and Austria (the ruler of millions of Slavs, the robber of Bosnia-Herzegovina, and the creator of Albania) were nearly at breaking-point. Behind Serbia lay the might of Russia. As for Bulgaria, she licked her wounds in angry resentment and plotted revenge against the other Balkan states.

Sarajevo (June 1914)

During the years 1913 and 1914 Serbian agitation against Austria was at fever-heat, both inside Serbia itself and in the Serbian parts of the Austrian Empire. The Serbian Press, which was largely uncensored, preached hatred; student-bodies, as often on such occasions, were to the fore in the agitation; secret societies like the famous Black Hand advocated methods of violence and terrorism. After several unsuccessful attempts had been made on the lives of Austrian rulers, the heir to the Austrian throne, the Archduke Francis Ferdinand, was murdered, together with his wife, in the streets of Sarajevo, the capital of Bosnia (June 28, 1914). With the existing tension between Austria and Serbia, with Russia ready to act the part of 'big brother' towards her fellow-Slavs in Serbia, and with the mili-

THE BALKAN PENINSULA IN 1914

tary alliances dividing the European powers into two armed camps, the whole situation was fraught with explosive possibilities, and needed the most careful handling. This the Austrian government deliberately failed to observe.

The Archduke's murderer was a Bosnian Serb, and thus a subject of Austria-Hungary. But he had just come from Belgrade, the capital of Serbia. Inside Austria were those who regarded war with Serbia at some time as inevitable, and thought that the sooner it occurred the better. There was no evidence then (nor has any been produced since) to show that the Serbian government was directly concerned in the crime; though this does not rule out the possibility that some of its members might have known an attempt was imminent, and failed to warn Austria. The Austrian government, however, accused Serbia of direct complicity in the crime, and nearly four weeks after the event (July 23) delivered an ultimatum to the Serbian government with only forty-eight hours allowed for a reply. The demands of the ultimatum were severe in the extreme, including an apology for anti-Austrian propaganda, the publication of a list of errors as drawn up by Austria, and the dismissal of all officials distasteful to Austria. Serbia accepted many of these demands, and offered to submit disputed points to arbitration. A few hours before this reply Serbia had begun mobilization—a precaution from one angle, but a provocation from another. Germany, which had hitherto backed up her Austrian ally, now counselled moderation, but Austria took no heed, and on July 28 declared war. Russia mobilized to assist her Slavonic brethren, and Germany took steps to assist her Austrian ally.

Within a week Europe was at war. The Sarajevo incident had provided the spark, but the full conflagration can be understood only in the wider setting described in Chapter 7.

Chapter 6

THE EXPANSION OF EUROPE (1870–1914)

European Colonization before 1870

CONQUEST and colonization are among the most recurring themes in human history. What has distinguished European man from his predecessors has been his vastly superior arms and means of communication, which have enabled him—till recent years, at any rate—to regard the whole world as his domain.

The expansion of Europe began with the Age of Discovery round about 1500. It has been the result of many motives: sheer love of adventure, the lust for conquest, missionary and humanitarian zeal, and the desire to control places of strategic or economic advantage. Economic factors have themselves included such diverse motives as human settlement, overseas investment, and the control of valuable markets or sources of raw materials. Economic imperialism has resulted in those international rivalries which have played a large part in producing the wars of modern times.

In the sixteenth century Spain and Portugal divided the world between them. In the seventeenth century Holland, France, and Britain entered the colonial struggle. In the eighteenth century Britain ousted France from North America and India, and also extended her interests to Australia and New Zealand. The Napoleonic period and its aftermath saw an extension of British power and the loss by Spain and Portugal of their possessions in the New World. The Monroe Doctrine of 1823 closed the whole American continent to further colonization. From then on only Africa and parts of Asia remained as fields for further European expansion.

Africa

Broadly speaking, only parts of the African coastline had come under foreign control by 1870. Portugal retained possessions on the east and west coasts dating from the sixteenth century. Britain and France in the eighteenth century had acquired trading-stations along the Guinea coast of West Africa. In 1815 Britain obtained the old Dutch settlement of Cape Colony, whence twenty years later many Dutch Boers made their Great Trek inland to found the Boer republics of the Orange Free State and the Transvaal. The North African coast was nominally part of the Turkish Empire; in practice it was largely independent, with rulers like the Khedive of Egypt, the Beys of Tunis and Algeria, and the Sultan of Morocco owing little real allegiance to Constantinople. In 1830 France had begun the conquest of Algeria, which she completed in the next fifteen years or so. France had also for a long time shown a lively interest in Egypt, but had always been checked by Britain, anxious to protect the Eastern Mediterranean approaches to India.

In the 1870's new influences appeared to quicken European interest in Africa. Mungo Park (about 1800), followed by David Livingstone, and H. M. Stanley were only the most prominent of many explorers whose work laid bare many secrets of the "Dark Continent." After 1870 defeated France, triumphant Germany, unified and poverty-stricken Italy, trade-hungry Britain, were all soon to take an active interest in African affairs. A convenient starting-point for the new era came in 1869, with the opening of the Suez Canal.

The Suez Canal was built by the French engineer Ferdinand de Lesseps, who leased the territory from the Khedive of Egypt and formed a company for the construction and maintenance of the new waterway. De Lesseps was friendly towards Britain, and desired British capital to contribute a share towards the project, but British statesmen regarded the scheme as a French device for obtaining a foothold in Egypt and threatening our Eastern possessions. They consequently opposed the whole idea, and when the canal was opened in 1869 not one penny of British capital had contributed towards its construction.

But the Khedive Ismail of Egypt was a spendthrift, and in 1875, finding himself in financial difficulties, offered to sell his shares in the Canal (176,602 out of a total of 400,000). Disraeli, Prime Minister of Britain, realized their importance more than his Liberal predecessors, and even than some of his own colleagues. With the support of the Queen, and with £4,000,000 hastily borrowed from the Rothschilds, he snapped up the shares. Financially the move proved profitable; but events soon showed the diplomatic consequences to be even more far-reaching.

By 1876 Egyptian finances again bordered on bankruptcy. European investors from many countries feared for their money, and Britain and France stepped into Egypt to control the national finances. Thus was established the Dual Control, which in course of time found itself interfering in the whole administration of Egypt. The British representative, Evelyn Baring—better known as Lord Cromer—soon began an era of reform which earned him the title of "the Great Pharaoh of Modern Egypt."

In 1879 the powers persuaded the Sultan to replace Ismail by the Khedive's son Tewfik, who soon became little more than a puppet in the hands of the real rulers of Egypt, the Anglo-French commissioners. The inevitable nationalist reaction followed. An Egyptian military officer, Arabi Pasha, raised the cry of "Egypt for the Egyptians." He forced himself into the Egyptian government, and in 1882 the passions he had aroused found vent in a rising in Alexandria in which fifty Europeans were killed. While the great powers were discussing possible lines of action, and while France with frequent governmental changes was reluctant to commit herself to any definite policy, Britain decided on speedy action. In 1882 the British Fleet bombarded Alexandria and restored order. Later in the same year a British force defeated Arabi at Tel-el-Kebir. When France wished to resume her share in the Dual Control Britain informed her that by failing to take action at the critical moment she had forfeited her rights. France felt humiliated and defrauded, and

Anglo-French tension over Egypt remained a permanent factor in international politics till the Entente of 1904.

Occupation of Egypt soon involved Britain in the affairs of the Sudan, where a religious fanatic, calling himself the Mahdi, or promised Messiah, appeared with the object of expelling all foreigners, Egyptian and British. In 1883 the Mahdi defeated an Anglo-Egyptian force under General Hicks, and in the following year General Gordon was sent to the Sudan to report on the situation with a view to evacuation. Gordon stayed on, and was soon besieged in Khartoum. Gladstone's government delayed too long in sending help, and when British forces sighted Khartoum in January 1885 they were two days too late. The Mahdi had stormed the city, and Gordon had been killed. For the time being Britain abandoned the Sudan, but Egypt remained in her hands as a base for future operations.

FRANCE, ITALY, AND TUNISIA

In the 1880's the great powers indulged in the so-called 'scramble for Africa.' To the east of Algeria, which as we have seen was colonized by France in the years after 1830, lay the country of Tunisia. Like Egypt, it was nominally subject to the Sultan, but actually ruled by a viceroy called the Bey. Like Egypt, too, it was heavily in debt to European bond-holders, particularly French, whose governments had for some time exercised a certain control over its administration. Situated close to the island of Sicily, and containing many Italian settlers, it was coveted by Italy as well as by France. In 1878 at the Congress of Berlin Germany and Britain privately hinted to France that she might annex it as compensation for Britain's acquisition of Cyprus. In this way Bismarck wished to divert French attention from the loss of Alsace-Lorraine to overseas affairs; he wanted also to sow seeds of discord between France and other powers, and thus to isolate her among the nations of Europe. France and Britain were soon to become estranged over Egypt, where Bismarck encouraged Britain's forward policy for this very reason. Similarly, Tunisia might divide France and Italy. In 1881 French troops invaded Tunisia and forced the Bey to sign a treaty acknowledging French overlordship. Bismarck's calculations proved correct.

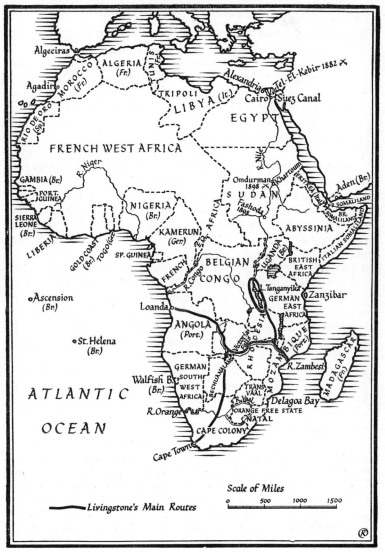

EUROPEAN COLONIZATION OF AFRICA TO 1914

In 1882 Italy joined up with Germany and Austria, whose Dual Alliance of 1879 now became the Triple Alliance.

The acquisition of Tunisia provided a further stimulus for that extension of French power from the North African coast across the Sahara which was taking place in the 1880's; but the next important moves in the 'scramble for Africa' were made by Germany.

GERMANY'S COLONIAL GAINS (1884–85)

Because of her late unification Germany found herself lagging far behind other European powers in the struggle for colonies. Indeed, for some time after 1870 she appeared content to let other countries forge ahead. Bismarck often asserted that he was 'no colony man,' his prime object being to consolidate the power of the new German Empire in Europe, rather than to engage in overseas adventures which might bring disturbances in their train. But feeling in Germany proved too strong for Bismarck. German explorers like Baron von der Decken, who first surveyed Mount Kilimanjaro in 1860, deplored the absence of German colonies in Africa. Germany's rapid industrialization after 1870 created a need for raw materials, markets, and fields of investment that colonies promised to fill. The rapid growth of population led to considerable emigration, mainly to the Americas, where the majority of emigrants, as even Bismarck deplored, were soon lost to the Fatherland. A German Colonial Society was formed which conducted an elaborate Press campaign for the acquisition of colonies. The result was that inside two years, 1884–85, Germany advanced from scratch to the position of the third European power in Africa.

In 1884 she established a protectorate over South-west Africa, taking in the coastline from Portuguese Angola in the north to Cape Colony in the south—with the exception of Walfisch Bay, which was already in British hands. Germany then deceived Britain as to her intentions in the Gulf of Guinea, and, while the British consul was on holiday, annexed the coastline of the Cameroons as well as Togoland. By 1885 she had also annexed German East Africa (now Tanganyika).

Farther afield, in the islands north of Australia, Germany acquired during these same years the north-eastern part of New Guinea (later known as Kaiser Wilhelm's Land), as well as the Bismarck Archipelago.

In general Germany's gains excited little opposition, although Britain felt aggrieved at her methods in seizing the Cameroons, and friction resulted from the division of New Guinea. It was in connexion with South Africa that most tension occurred. For long Germany wooed the Dutch Boers, under their leader, Paul Kruger, and made several attempts to establish a foothold in the south-eastern tip of Africa in order to link up with the Boer republics. British sea-power effectively scotched these plans.

In truth Germany's African empire was less valuable than its size indicated. It was vigorously exploited by capitalists and merchants, and provided a useful field of operations for German scientists. But climatic reasons prevented it from absorbing German settlers; by 1914 there were more Germans living in Paris than in all the German colonies put together! Her most valuable possession, strategically and in man-power and raw materials, was Tanganyika. But when she looked around she found Britain in control of most of the strategic points, of three of the four great river-systems of Africa (the Nile, Niger, and Zambezi—the Congo being controlled by Belgium), and of the only parts capable of large-scale white settlement. Germany remained dissatisfied, and her desire for further 'places in the sun' contributed to the catastrophe of 1914.

THE BELGIAN CONGO AND THE BERLIN CONFERENCE

The exploration of the Congo basin was carried out by H. M. Stanley, with the financial assistance and encouragement of King Leopold II of Belgium. Leopold acted more in his personal than in his royal capacity, and formed a Congo Association to exploit the rubber, ivory, and other valuable products of the region. It was largely to regulate the activities of this Association that the Berlin Conference of the leading colonial powers was held in 1884–85.

The Berlin Act (1885), which resulted from the work of the Conference, covered a wider field than the Congo, however, and was the first serious attempt to regularize the colonization of Africa. It laid down rules for the treatment of native populations, and attempted the suppression of slavery and the slave-trade. It established the procedure to be adopted in any future annexations, and provided for the free navigation of the Congo and the Niger. Leopold's newly acquired territory was formed into the Congo Free State, with provisions for free trade and equal access to raw materials on the part of all the powers.

The intentions were praiseworthy, but the practical results fell far short of the high-flown phrases of the Act. In particular Leopold flouted the regulations concerning the Congo. Other countries were excluded from sharing in its wealth, and the treatment of the native population was so scandalous that towards the end of the century the 'Congo atrocities' became a byword. In 1908 Leopold formally transferred the Congo to the Belgian State. He died in the following year, and his successor, Albert, happily did much to reform the administration of what was now known as the Belgian Congo.

ITALY, GERMANY, AND BRITAIN

After being thwarted by France over Tunis Italy turned her attention to the Red Sea coast of Africa. By 1890 she had succeeded in establishing her power in Eritrea, and in Italian Somaliland farther south. By a treaty made with Menelek, Emperor of Abyssinia, she believed herself to have acquired a protectorate over Abyssinia as well. Menelek thought differently, however, and when Italian forces advanced into his country he inflicted a severe defeat upon them at Adowa in 1896. The Italian government fell (see page 47), and Italian forces were withdrawn. Italy nursed her sense of grievance till forty years later Mussolini made another attempt to conquer Abyssinia.

In 1890, just after Bismarck's fall, Lord Salisbury for Britain concluded an important agreement with Germany. Frontier questions between German East Africa and adjacent British colonies were settled. Germany recognized the British protectorate over Zanzibar, and Britain returned the island of Heligoland, at the mouth of the Elbe, which she had held since 1815.

THE EXPANSION OF BRITISH POWER IN AFRICA

Towards the end of the century British power in Africa was consolidated and expanded. In 1877 Britain had attempted to annex the Boer republics of the Transvaal and the Orange Free State; but after her defeat at Majuba Hill in the First Boer War of 1880–81 she restored their independence to the Boers. Thereafter several British trading companies proceeded to open up widely separated parts of Africa. In the late 1880's the Imperial British East African Company began the exploitation of Uganda and Kenya; the Royal Niger Company in its search for palm-oil pushed inland from the Guinea Coast to form British Nigeria. In both these regions Captain (later Lord) Lugard, one of our greatest African administrators, came to play a large part. The British South African Company, under the inspiration of Cecil Rhodes, pushed northward from Cape Colony to form Northern and Southern Rhodesia, which prevented the Portuguese from linking up in one east-to-west block their old coastal settlements of Angola and Mozambique.

Rhodes's ambition was to create a line of British colonies stretching from the Cape to Cairo, and he was associated with the next moves against the Boer Republics. The discovery of gold in the Transvaal led many British fortune-hunters to invade Boer territory. There they were excluded from political and civil rights, and were treated as outcasts by the Boer President, Paul Kruger. In 1896 Dr Jameson, with the encouragement of Rhodes (now Prime Minister of Cape Colony), raided the Transvaal with a body of horsemen to help the Uitlanders, as the Boers called the British settlers. The raid was a failure, to the embarrassment of the British authorities and the satisfaction of our enemies. The German Kaiser sent the famous 'Kruger telegram' congratulating the Boer President on having "preserved the independence of his country against foreign invasion"—an act which, coupled with Germany's previous attempts to curry favour with the Boers and promote her own interests in South Africa, produced strained relations between the two countries.

Events moved rapidly towards the Second Boer War (1899–1902). After initial reverses Britain defeated the Boers, and by the Treaty of

Vereeniging (1902) the two Boer republics were annexed, though Britain compensated them for the losses they had suffered during the war. In 1906 a bold act of statesmanship granted them self-government, and in 1909 the four South African states (Cape Colony, Natal, the Orange Free State, and the Transvaal) were incorporated in the Union of South Africa.

ANGLO-FRENCH RIVALRY IN THE SUDAN: FASHODA (1898)

The 'scramble for Africa' in the 1880's had settled the main features of European control over the African coastline. But there still remained difficult frontier questions in the interior. Over the Sudan a serious clash occurred between Britain and France.

After General Gordon's death in 1885 the British had retreated from the Sudan to Egypt, where Lord Cromer was busy reorganizing the finances and administration of the country, and General Kitchener was creating a strong Egyptian Army. The Sudan, meanwhile, fell under the control of the Dervishes, the warlike followers of the Mahdi. About 1896 General Kitchener began preparations for the reconquest of the Sudan. After advancing cautiously up the Nile valley, he routed the Dervishes at Omdurman (September 1898) and re-entered Khartoum, the scene of Gordon's tragic death. In the same month Major Marchand hoisted the French flag at Fashoda, some three hundred miles south of Khartoum. France had never reconciled herself to the British occupation of Egypt, and in 1896 Marchand had left France for the French Congo. Thence he undertook his perilous march across Central Africa, bringing him to Fashoda at the very moment when Kitchener was re-establishing British power in the Sudan. France and Britain were soon on the verge of war. The Sudan had for long been regarded as subject to Egypt, which we now administered. Moreover, through the upper waters of the Nile it could control the very life of Egypt. The British Prime Minister, Lord Salisbury, took a firm stand. France withdrew her forces, and the Sudan came under the joint rule of Britain and Egypt.

Fashoda proved a turning-point. From then on Anglo-French relations gradually improved, and soon after the turn of the century remaining differences were smoothed out and the Entente of 1904 was concluded. Africa still remained a source of trouble in international politics, Germany casting envious eyes on the growing French power in Morocco. But the details of the Anglo-French Entente and the Moroccan crises of the early twentieth century link up with the wider issues that precipitated the Great War of 1914, and will be treated more fully in Chapter 7.

Asia

THE POSITION IN 1870

By 1800 there were certain well-established colonial 'preserves' in Asia. Since the sixteenth century Spain had possessed the Philippine Islands, and at the beginning of the seventeenth century most of the old Portuguese possessions in the East Indies had passed into the hands of Holland. In the eighteenth century Britain became predominant in India. The chief interest of the nineteenth century lies in the so-called 'opening-up' of China and Japan by western nations, and in the expansion of Russian power across the Asiatic land-mass.

In 1800 China and Japan were still practically unknown to the West, and untouched by western influences. In 1793 a British government mission under Lord Macartney, desirous of establishing trade and diplomatic relations with China, met with a haughty refusal from the Chinese Emperor:

> The request that your merchants may store and trade their goods in Peking is also impracticable. My Capital is the hub and centre around which all the quarters of the earth revolve. Its laws are very strict, and no foreigner has ever been allowed to trade there. This request is also refused.

In 1819 Sir Stamford Raffles obtained the island of Singapore for Britain, and an impetus was given to the trade with Canton, the only Chinese port where a limited amount of trade was allowed. Soon British merchants from India were pushing the sale of opium through Canton, despite the prohibition of the Chinese government at Peking. This led to the Opium War of 1839–42, which resulted in a victory for British arms; by the Treaty of Nanking (1842) Britain obtained the island of Hong Kong, while other Chinese ports were opened up for trade. China also granted legal and tariff privileges to the foreigner. This was the first of many 'unequal treaties' forced upon a helpless China. A further war in 1858 extended these privileges, together with the right of diplomatic representation at Peking.

Britain's interests lay in trade; she had no desire to establish colonies. With France it was different. Expelled from India on the one hand, and prevented by British sea-power on the other from interfering north of Hong Kong, France concentrated on the south-eastern tip of the Chinese Empire, and, beginning in 1860, built up a number of colonies in Indo-China.

Meanwhile two other western powers were appearing on the scene.

In 1854 Commodore Perry, of the United States Navy, forced Japan to grant certain trading rights to the foreigner. But the sequel in Japan was far different from that in China. Japan was sufficiently adaptable to take from the West what suited her, and by reforming her government and copying western arms was soon able to treat with the foreigner on equal terms.

As early as the seventeenth century Russian expansion across Siberia had reached the Pacific coast. In the Caucasus Russia also encroached on the Turkish Empire to reach the borders of Persia, and through Turkestan she reached the same country on the far side of the Caspian Sea. By extending her boundary to Afghanistan she threatened the north-western approaches to India. In the 1850's she took advantage of China's weakness to obtain the Amur Province, which brought her to the boundaries of Manchuria. In 1860 she founded Vladivostok, her most southerly Asiatic port, but still ice-bound for some months of the year.

FURTHER DEVELOPMENTS TO 1900

Russian expansion towards Persia and Afghanistan had long excited British apprehensions, and in 1885, when Russia seized Penjdeh, a village on the frontiers of Afghanistan, relations between the Lion and the Bear were severely strained. Gladstone's government acted with unusual vigour in backing up its protests with war-like preparations. An agreement was made which, while leaving

KARL MARX (1818–83)

Father of modern Communism; author of the *Communist Manifesto* (1848) and of *Das Kapital* (1867).

"Picture Post" Library

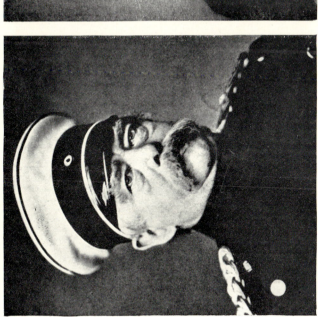

PRINCE OTTO VON BISMARCK (1815–98)

Prussian Chancellor, 1862–71; German Chancellor, 1871–90; founder of Imperial Germany.

"Picture Post" Library

BENJAMIN DISRAELI (1804–81)
(Sir John Millais)

Prime Minister of Britain, 1868 and 1874–80. Opposed
Russian designs at the Congress of Berlin, 1878.

Penjdeh in Russian hands, secured for Afghanistan control of an important pass and made it clear that Russian advance must now halt. The scene soon shifted once more to the Far East, where after 1890 two important developments occurred—the construction of the Trans-Siberian Railway and the growing strength of Japan.

The Trans-Siberian Railway stretching from European Russia to Vladivostok was built in the 1890's. It brought Russian power to the back door, as it were, of China, and outflanked British sea-power, which controlled the front door. As such it signified a threat to British interests, and opposition to Russian power in the Far East became henceforth a dominant motive in British foreign policy. Furthermore, Russia's interest in Manchuria was now increased, as Northern Manchuria provided a shorter route for the last stages of the railway than the detour along the Amur Valley. Manchuria also led to Port Arthur, coveted by Russia as a warm-water port.

Japan was quick to imitate the West where it suited her. Discarding many of her old feudal customs, she proceeded to develop modern industries and to build an Army and Navy modelled on those of Germany and Britain. Above all, she soon joined in the scramble over the prostrate body of China. Across the narrow Straits of Tsushima which divided her from the mainland lay Korea, nominally subject to China. Rivalry over Korea led in 1894 to the Sino-Japanese War. The Chinese fought with bows and arrows, and their two battleships were said to have had only three shells between them. Japan was victorious, and the Treaty of Shimonoseki (1895) awarded her a large indemnity, proclaimed Korea independent, and gave Japan Formosa, the Pescadores, and the Liao-tung Peninsula, with Port Arthur.

Japan's entry into the circle of imperialist powers was too sudden to be universally welcomed, and within a week of the treaty Russia, France, and Germany forced her to restore to China the Liao-tung Peninsula with Port Arthur. Japan smarted under the humiliation, especially as in the next few years China was still further dismembered by the European powers. In 1898 fresh concessions, technically in the form of leases, were extorted from China. Russia obtained Port Arthur; Germany Kiaochow, which dominated the valuable Shan-tung Peninsula; Britain Wei-hai-wei; and France Kwangchow, in

F

Southern China. A scramble also took place for railway concessions, especially on the part of Russia, in Manchuria. Small wonder that in 1900 China attempted in the Boxer Rebellion to throw off foreign domination. When she failed, the bonds of servitude were still further tightened.

In 1898 the U.S.A. engaged in her first overseas war, the results of which affected to some extent Far Eastern affairs. For some time she had watched with concern the cruelties of Spanish rule in Cuba. At length she forced Spain to promise reforms, but when the American warship *Maine* blew up mysteriously in Havana harbour the U.S.A. declared war on Spain (1898). Two naval battles in the Caribbean and in Far Eastern waters resulted in the destruction of the Spanish fleet. By the terms of peace the U.S.A. obtained the Philippines and the West Indian island of Porto Rico, while Cuba became independent under American protection. In the same year the United States annexed the Hawaiian Islands in mid-Pacific, which had long been under American influence. The Spanish-American war, fought in two oceans, demonstrated the need for a canal through Central America. It has been described in Chapter 1 how French efforts had failed. In 1902 Panama (with American encouragement) revolted against Colombia, and declared herself independent. She then granted the U.S.A. a ten-mile-wide zone, through which the latter proceeded to construct the Panama Canal, which was completed in 1914.

THE RUSSO-JAPANESE WAR AND THE NEW CHINESE REPUBLIC

Continued British fear of Russian designs led her to seek an ally in the Far East, and in 1902 she concluded an alliance with Japan, whereby each signatory promised the other assistance if attacked by more than one power. Russo-Japanese rivalry in Manchuria and Korea came to a head in 1904, when war between the two countries broke out. Japan was prepared and on the spot; Russian Tsardom was incompetent, and the Trans-Siberian Railway inadequate to solve problems of communication. The Anglo-Japanese Treaty prevented France from assisting Russia, even if she had wished. In 1905 the Japanese defeated the Russian Army at Mukden and the Russian

THE FAR EAST

Navy in the Straits of Tsushima. By the Treaty of Portsmouth (1905) "Jap the Giant-killer" reaped his reward. Russia gave Japan the southern half of the island of Sakhalin and her rights over the Liao-tung Peninsula and Port Arthur, while Japanese supremacy over Korea was recognized.

This first defeat of a European power by a 'coloured race' had profound results, particularly in Asia. We have seen in Chapter 3 how Russia's defeat produced revolution at home and the experiment of the Dumas. The sequel in China was even more important. Revolutionary and reformist bodies were increasingly demanding an end of the old Manchu Empire, which had failed to protect China from the claws of the foreigner. Prominent among these was the Chinese Nationalist Party, or Kuomintang, founded by Dr Sun-Yat-sen. In 1910 Japan annexed Korea outright. In 1911 rebellion broke out in China—an event commemorated till recently as the 'Double Ten,' from October 10, when the revolt started. Early in 1912 the last Manchu emperor was deposed, and China became a republic. But she was to know no peace or settled government. Rival factions warred for leadership, and when the First World War in 1914 diverted the attentions of the Western powers to Europe, Japan was left undisturbed in the Far East to press further claims upon China. The 'coloured races,' though disunited among themselves, were beginning to assert their independence of the white man.

Chapter 7

INTERNATIONAL RELATIONS (1870–1914)

The Great Powers in 1870

INTERNATIONAL relations arising from Balkan and colonial questions have been considered in previous chapters. We must now bring together these and other strands of foreign policy to see how the pattern of alliances and counter-alliances of the pre-1914 years was built up. The position of the leading European powers in 1870 will form a convenient starting-point.

GERMANY

The new German Empire was the strongest power on the Continent, and its military strength was unchallengeable. For the next twenty years Bismarck dominated the European stage as Metternich had done in the years after 1815, and the story revolves mainly around his personality.

FRANCE

Defeated by Germany in 1870, France had to submit to the Treaty of Frankfort (1871), by which she lost Alsace-Lorraine and was saddled with an indemnity of £200,000,000 and a German army of occupation. Her reactions to this humiliating situation were summed up by the ardent republican Gambetta: "To think always of *revanche* [revenge], but never to speak of it." Franco-German hostility is the supreme and most constant factor in international relations from 1870 to 1914.

AUSTRIA-HUNGARY

It has been described in Chapter 4 how the Austrian Empire, after its expulsion from Germany in 1866, became the Dual Monarchy of Austria-Hungary in 1867. Relations with Germany were naturally somewhat strained, but Bismarck had treated her leniently, and blood-ties and political interests combined to heal the wounds. Austria remained neutral during the Franco-German War of 1870, and gradually drifted into the German orbit. Under Bismarck's encouragement she sought expansion into the Balkans—the *Drang nach Osten*. This increased the hostility of the Balkan races, especially the Serbs, already estranged because of the treatment of fellow-Slavs inside Austria-Hungary. It also produced a conflict of interests with Russia, which had her own Balkan ambitions, and her Slavonic sympathies. Austro-Italian relations were also strained on account of the continued subjection of Italians in the Trentino and Istria to Austrian rule.

RUSSIA

Checked in the Crimean War (1854–56), Russia turned her attention eastward, towards Persia, Afghanistan, and China, where, as we have seen, she fell foul of British interests. But she did not renounce her Balkan ambitions; Constantinople, the Straits, and the Eastern Mediterranean were put aside for the moment, always to be brought out (as during the Bulgarian atrocities of 1875–76, or the Balkan Wars of 1912–13) as opportunity offered. In 1870 she denounced the clauses of the Treaty of Paris (1856) demilitarizing Sebastopol and the Black Sea. As the largest Slavonic power in the world, she encouraged the Pan-Slav movement intended to give the Slavonic races of the Balkans and of Austria-Hungary some sort of political cohesion. The details were vague, but the broad aim was clear: to form a Slavonic bloc in South-eastern Europe under Russia's leadership. The international consequences were far-reaching. Britain's hostility to Russia's Mediterranean thrust was traditional; but now Austria-Hungary was closely concerned, as Russian policy not only conflicted with her *Drang nach Osten*, but also increased those racial aspirations of Czechs, Croats, and Serbs which threatened to disrupt her own empire. Just as Franco-German rivalry is the dominating factor in Western Europe, so Austro-Russian rivalry dominates the situation in South-eastern Europe.

ITALY

The year 1870 saw the completion of Italian unification; but the new Italy was far from strong. With few natural resources, with a poverty-stricken and largely illiterate population, and with a Parliamentary form of government beyond her capacity to work satisfactorily, she was the weakest of the six leading powers. None the less, her Mediterranean coastline and her guardianship of the Alpine passes gave her considerable strategic value. The legacies of the wars of unification continued to exercise an important influence on her foreign outlook. She had fought two wars to expel the Austrians from Lombardy and Venetia, but the Austrians still held Trieste and Fiume on the Adriatic coast, and the Trentino district (*Italia Irredenta*, or "Unredeemed Italy"), which she regarded as rightfully hers. Towards France Italy felt no gratitude for the assistance given by Napoleon III in 1859; Napoleon had made peace with Austria behind Piedmont's back; he had later exacted his 'pound of flesh' (Savoy and Nice); and till 1870 French troops had guarded Rome against Italian efforts to seize it. Even after 1870 the French Clericals averred their desire to restore the Pope's temporal power. Thus Italian feelings towards Austria and France were far from friendly. But towards Britain, which had afforded refuge for Italian exiles, and whose governments and people had shown every sympathy for Italian aspirations, the new kingdom felt gratitude and affection.

BRITAIN

To defend her overseas empire and safeguard her commerce Britain possessed the most powerful navy in the world. Her repeated warnings to Russia, arising from Russian expansion, her interference in Egypt, and later her naval race with Germany—all these showed her readiness to take action where her vital interests were concerned. But European politics as such (unless they involved a Louis XIV or a Napoleon spreading his tentacles over the whole Continent) did not greatly concern her. First under the peaceful-minded Gladstone, and later under Lord Salisbury, with his policy of 'splendid isolation' Britain stood aside from the Continental game of alliance and counter-alliance, and was eventually drawn into the arena only by the force of circumstances.

Principles of Bismarck's Foreign Policy (1870–90)

Bismarck, as we have seen, dominated European politics till his downfall in 1890. What, then, were the guiding principles of his foreign policy? With the defeat of France in 1870, and the proclamation of the German Empire in 1871, Bismarck declared himself "satiated." No more aggression, no more conquests; henceforth consolidation of what he had achieved. This seems genuinely to have been his desire—witness his reluctance to embark on naval or colonial ventures which might offend Britain. But unification had not been achieved without creating enemies. Denmark, defeated in 1864, was a minor power which could safely be ignored. Austria, defeated in 1866, and expelled from the German Confederation, was in a different category; but Bismarck, with an eye to the future, had treated her leniently, and from the moment of her defeat had successfully wooed her, so that she remained neutral in 1870. To take Austria's mind off German affairs Bismarck encouraged her expansion into the Balkans, the *Drang nach Osten*. In 1879 the two German powers formed an alliance.

There remained France, whom he had defeated and humiliated in 1870–71. France he could never win to his side, and if he wished to preserve his Empire he must above all keep France weak and isolated. Therein lies the key to his foreign policy in the next twenty years. His general method (the details will appear in the sequel) was to prevent France from obtaining Continental friends or allies. To that end he gladly saw her adopt a republican form of government, as being less likely to commend her to the crowned heads of Europe. He encouraged French colonialism, to take her mind off *revanche* for Alsace-Lorraine, and to embroil her with other powers, as with Britain over Egypt or with Italy over Tunis. He sought to catch as many countries as possible upon the complicated web of alliances he skilfully spun from his Chancellery at Berlin. This was no easy task when we recall Austro-Russian rivalry in the Balkans, or Austro-Italian rivalry in the Adriatic. But Bismarck was undaunted, and, to adopt his own Emperor's simile, he carried on like a juggler, trying to keep five balls in the air the whole time. For twenty years the old juggler kept them going, but well before the act was closed some were obviously becoming too slippery for even Bismarck to control much longer.

From 1870 to the Dual Alliance (1879)

In pursuance of his policy of detaching other countries from France, Bismarck began soon after 1870 to cultivate friendly relations with Austria, a policy facilitated by the personal friendship existing between the German Emperor William I and the Austrian Emperor Francis Joseph. Ceremonial visits between the two Emperors were made. In 1872, when the Austrian Emperor was visiting Berlin, the Tsar Alexander II was also in the German capital, and Bismarck seized the opportunity of forming the *Dreikaiserbund*, or Three Emperors' League (1872)—a somewhat informal agreement among the three rulers to maintain the *status quo*, to work together in solving Near Eastern problems, and to present a common front against the growing threat of international socialism. Although somewhat vague, it suited Bismarck's purpose for the time being, and during the next few years further meetings of the sovereigns took place.

The rapid recovery of France under Thiers was not at all to Bismarck's liking, and in 1875 there was talk in Germany of a 'preventive' war against her old enemy. Both Britain and Russia, however, made clear their disapproval of such a course, and the scare passed.

The Russo-Turkish War of 1877, the subsequent Treaty of San Stefano, and its alteration at the Congress of Berlin (1878) had important results on the international situation (see page 62). Bismarck pretended as chairman of the Congress to be the 'honest broker,' but British and Austrian interests in the Near East clashed so much with those of Russia that it proved impossible even for the wily German Chancellor to reconcile them all. He was obliged to come down on one side or the other, and he chose the side of Austria. He acquiesced in the check administered to Russian ambitions, and in the increase of Austrian power in Bosnia-Herzegovina. Russia knew herself to have been diplomatically isolated, and Alexander II as a protest withdrew from the *Dreikaiserbund*.

The sequel will show that Bismarck did not let Russia escape from his orbit as easily as all that. None the less, he felt the need of a secure ally. Britain was too remote, and only spasmodically interested in European affairs, and so Bismarck turned to Austria. The Austrian Chancellor, Count Andrassy, held the highest cards in the negotiations that followed, for whereas Germany sought the Austrian alliance through fear of France, Austria herself had nothing to fear from France, and desired protection against Russia, whom Bismarck had just estranged. The Austro-German or Dual Alliance of 1879 reflects this situation. Each power agreed to assist the other if attacked by Russia (thus Austria definitely obtained German assistance in case of a Russian attack). If another power—*i.e.*, France—attacked either of them (and she was only likely to attack Germany), then the other party promised benevolent neutrality. Only if Russia joined France would both parties give active assistance.

The Dual Alliance was intended to be secret, and its terms were not published till 1887. But Russia knew of its existence almost before the ink was dry. For the time being her resentment against the 'honest broker' found little outward expression; but the long-term result was definitely to worsen Russo-German relations. The Alliance of 1879 was renewed periodically, till the events of 1914 brought it into operation.

The Triple Alliance (1882)

In 1881 France occupied Tunisia (see Chapter 6). This she did with the encouragement of Bismarck, desirous of diverting French preoccupations over Alsace-Lorraine into other spheres, and also of embroiling France with Italy, which had her own ambitions in Tunisia. The result fully justified his expectations. Feeling herself isolated, Italy entered the Austro-German camp, and the Dual Alliance of 1879 was converted into the Triple Alliance of 1882. Germany and Austria agreed to aid Italy if Italy was attacked by France; Italy agreed to aid Germany under similar circumstances; a joint attack by France and Russia upon any one of the signatories would bring the other two to its assistance.

By these terms Bismarck was now assured of the assistance of another power if France alone attacked Germany—a contingency not covered in the Austrian alliance. As for Italy, she was glad to enter the circle of the great powers and to safeguard herself against French attack. But her position in the Alliance—periodically renewed to 1914 —was somewhat shaky. From the outset she stipulated that the treaty was in no case to be directed against Britain. As time went on, moreover, her grievances against Austria over *Italia Irredenta* would be sure to strain her loyalty to her treaty engagements.

Diplomatic Jugglery

Despite the growing estrangement between Russia and Germany, Bismarck never despaired of keeping on friendly terms with Russia. In his overriding aim of preventing a link-up between France and Russia he was prepared to indulge in any amount of 'diplomatic jugglery' to keep open, as he said, the "private wire" between Berlin and Petersburg, even if the "public telegraph" were broken.

The accession in 1881 of a new Tsar, Alexander III, possessed of a strong dislike of the French Republic, played into his hands. In that year the League of the Three Emperors was revived for a period of three years; in the event of war by any one against a fourth power the other two agreed to remain benevolently neutral. In 1884 the agreement was renewed.

In 1887, when Austro-Russian relations in the Balkans were particularly strained, Bismarck made a secret Reinsurance Treaty with Russia alone. Certain Russian interests in the Balkans were recognized, and it was agreed that, if either power were involved in war with a third country, the other power was to remain benevolently neutral. Despite a provision to the effect that the treaty was not to apply if Russia *forced* a war on Austria-Hungary, it was difficult to see how Bismarck could altogether reconcile his new commitment with his promises to Austria in the Dual Alliance of 1879. No wonder the old Emperor compared Bismarck with a juggler! No wonder, too, that the crafty performer wished to conceal from Austrian eyes the new ball he was trying to keep in the air alongside the old ones!

The Dismissal of Bismarck

In 1888 the Kaiser William I died. His son, Frederick, reigned only three months. Frederick's son, a young man of twenty-nine,

now ascended the throne as William II. Disagreements between
William II and Bismarck soon arose. The new Kaiser disapproved
of Bismarck's repression of the socialists, of his cautious colonial and
naval policy, and of his courtship of Russia at the risk of offending
Austria. In 1890 the Reinsurance Treaty, due for renewal, was
allowed to lapse, and in the same year the old Chancellor, who had
dominated the European stage for thirty years, was dismissed.

Germany's New Master

William II was a man of restless ambition, for himself and for his
country. In character he was at times headstrong and impulsive,
qualities that ill suited the ruler of a powerful state. It was *his* will,
and not that of his successive chancellors, which henceforth determined his country's policy. Unlike Bismarck, who, with unification
completed, had regarded Germany as a 'satiated' power, and had in
consequence pursued a cautious foreign policy, William II soon
embarked on schemes to enhance Germany's prestige and power,
recking little the offence they might give to others. He pressed
colonial claims to their utmost, demanding for Germany "a place in
the sun." He planned a large expansion of the Navy, remarking that
otherwise "we shall hold our colonies only by the permission of
England." He offended Russian susceptibilities even more blatantly.
Not only was the Reinsurance Treaty allowed to lapse, but Austrian
ambitions in the Balkans were openly encouraged. In the early years
of his reign he visited Constantinople (for over a century the objective of Russia's ambitions), and declared that Germany regarded herself as the protector of the Moslem world. Practical application of this
new rôle soon followed when he announced plans for the construction of a railway from Berlin to Bagdad. German capital and engineers would in consequence penetrate the Ottoman Empire; Germany
(and Austria) would dominate the Balkans; Russia would be cut off
from Constantinople, and her sea-passage through the Straits im-
peded; British sea-power and the Suez Canal route would be by-
passed; and German power would extend to the Indian Ocean.

William II directed German affairs for the next thirty years (1888–
1918). His policy is often summed up as *Weltpolitik*—an interest in
world-politics, which other nations feared would result in Germany

becoming the master of the world. Although other rulers and nations cannot escape a share of the blame for the catastrophe of 1914–18, a large measure must undoubtedly rest with the Kaiser William II.

The Dual Alliance (1895)

The first-fruits of Germany's new policy were soon apparent. Bismarck had with increasing difficulty maintained friendly relations with Russia, and it must be doubted whether the old Chancellor could have maintained them much longer. But William's policy tipped the scales down with a bang. France, of course, was anxious for a Continental ally, which, with the existence of the Triple Alliance, left only Russia. The autocratic Tsar Alexander III still looked with misgiving upon republican France as a possible ally, but Germany's aggressiveness wore down his scruples. In 1891 the French fleet paid a friendly visit to the Russian naval base at Kronstadt. Two years later the visit was returned. Military agreements were made, and loans to Russia were floated in Paris. The accession of Nicholas II in 1894 was followed in 1895 by the public announcement of the Dual Alliance. France and Russia agreed to come to each other's assistance in the event of an attack by Germany. Thus what Bismarck had spent his life trying to prevent had now come to pass. Furthermore, Europe was henceforth divided into two armed camps, making the localization of any future conflict almost impossible.

Which Side Britain?

Britain alone of the great European powers was uncommitted to either side—and for very good reasons. Both geographically and by tradition, she was aloof from the Continent, and her Prime Minister, Lord Salisbury, boasted of his policy of 'splendid isolation' from European quarrels and entanglements. Furthermore, Britain had her differences, colonial and commercial, with most European powers, and it was hard to see which group she could readily join. In the early 1890's she was attracted more towards the German combination than to the Franco-Russian. In 1890 the Anglo-German agreement over Heligoland and Zanzibar removed one source of friction. The Kaiser William II had a genuine affection for his grandmother,

Queen Victoria, and paid a number of visits to this country. More-over, at this juncture Anglo-French differences over Egypt were acute, and in the Far East the construction of the Trans-Siberian Railway was increasing Britain's fear of Russia. Nothing definite resulted, however, to bring Britain and Germany more closely together, though the possibility still remained open.

As the decade wore on 'splendid isolation' began to lose its splen-dour, and to acquire at times a nasty-looking tarnish. Anglo-French relations nearly reached breaking-point over the Fashoda incident of 1898 (see page 78), though the subsequent French withdrawal from the Sudan opened up the possibility of happier relations in the future. In the Far East the Russian menace took definite shape with the com-pletion of the Siberian Railway, the seizure of Port Arthur in 1897–1898, and the penetration of Manchuria by branch railway lines under Russian control.

But it was the German menace which was eventually to prove decisive, though it took many years before its full implications were realized. Germany's military predominance was evident; step by step she slowly, but surely, unfolded her intention of becoming also a top-ranking nation in commerce, colonization, and sea-power—matters which touched Britain to the quick. The Kaiser perceived that sea-power lay at the basis of his ambitions, and made no secret of his plans. "I will never rest until I have raised my Navy to a position similar to that occupied by my Army" was a recurring theme in many of his public utterances. In 1895 the Kaiser Wilhelm, or Kiel, Canal was opened, increasing the mobility, and hence the effective strength, of Germany's existing fleet. Two years later the German Navy was placed under the control of Admiral von Tirpitz, a fanatical 'Navy man' determined to challenge Britain's leadership. The Boer War (1899–1902) increased Anglo-German tension, and emphasized the decisive rôle of sea-power. Already in 1896 the Kaiser had offended Britain by his congratulatory telegram to President Kruger on sup-pressing the Jameson Raid "without calling in the help of friendly powers." With the outbreak of the war itself not only Germany but France and other nations expressed open satisfaction at Britain's early reverses, and but for Britain's obvious naval supremacy a European coalition might have been formed against her.

Britain abandons Isolation: Anglo-French Entente (1904)

In 1902 the Anglo-Japanese Treaty ended, in a startling manner, Britain's isolation in the Far East. Faced with Russian ambitions, Britain made an alliance with the rising Asiatic power of Japan, whereby each promised the other assistance if attacked by more than one foreign power. The resulting Russo-Japanese War (1904-5) and its far-reaching consequences have already been described in Chapter 6.

In Europe Britain's course of action was still not clear at the turn of the century. Differences with France and Russia still led her to desire an agreement with Germany, but although advances were made nothing came of them. A major obstacle was Germany's fear that she might be used as a catspaw to fight Britain's quarrel on the Continent, while Britain profited by picking up French and Russian possessions overseas. Soon after the turn of the century events occurred to bring Britain and France more closely together. In 1901 Queen Victoria was succeeded by Edward VII, whose gay, pleasure-loving way of life attracted him to France rather than to Germany. In a visit to Paris in 1903 he captivated the hearts of his French hosts, and although as a constitutional monarch his influence upon governmental policy must not be exaggerated, he undoubtedly established those friendly personal contacts which facilitated agreement on wider issues. France herself, steadfast as ever in her hostility to Germany, was becoming increasingly desirous of a settlement of Franco-British differences. Her Foreign Minister, Delcassé, had already in 1900 made an agreement concerning North Africa with Italy, thus weakening the Triple Alliance. His desire to add Britain to his list of friends was stimulated by the sight of his only ally, Russia, engaged in a distant war in the Far East—*and* not doing too well.

In 1904 Lord Lansdowne (British Foreign Secretary) and Delcassé concluded the Anglo-French Entente. It was an agreement designed to settle in a peaceful manner outstanding differences throughout the world. By its most important terms France recognized the British occupation of Egypt, while Britain recognized the French penetration of Morocco which had been proceeding for some years. (By another agreement immediately afterwards Delcassé settled differences with Spain over *their* respective spheres in Morocco.) Other clauses included: adjustment of colonial claims in West Africa; boundary agreements between Siam and French Indo-China; settlement of disputed fishing rights off Newfoundland which had existed since the Treaty of Utrecht in 1713; and an agreement concerning the New Hebrides.

It must be emphasized, as it was at the time, that this 'understanding' was in no sense an alliance with military commitments. Britain held it up as a model agreement, and expressed her willingness to conclude similar agreements with other nations. All this is true. None the less, it marked a turning-point. Germany was suspicious. Britain and France, as friendly nations, were henceforth morally obliged to give each other certain *diplomatic* support. It paved the way to a similar entente with France's ally, Russia, in 1907 (see pages 97–98). By 1914 the entente still remained an entente and not an alliance; but before then further understandings had created additional moral ties which would make neutrality still more difficult in the case of open conflict.

Morocco: Algeciras Conference (1906)

Germany soon decided to test the strength of the new entente, as well as to assert afresh her right to a "place in the sun." She found her opportunity in Morocco, where France was continuing to press her claims upon the Sultan. In March 1905 the Kaiser, on a cruise in the Mediterranean, landed at Tangier and made a provocative speech in which he proclaimed the sovereignty of the Sultan, and Germany's support against any attempts to undermine it. The defeat of France's ally, Russia, at the hands of Japan emboldened Germany in her demands. She forced upon France the resignation of Delcassé for the part he had played in the recent Anglo-French Entente. She went on to demand an international conference to settle the Moroccan question, and the Sultan of Morocco, encouraged by Germany's support, echoed the demand. France resisted, but eventually consented, and early in 1906 twelve nations met at Algeciras, close to Gibraltar, to discuss Morocco.

If the summoning of the conference itself was a victory for Ger-

KAISER WILLIAM II (1859–1941)

German Emperor, 1888–1918. Shown here with his troops
in the First World War.

96

GEORGES CLEMENCEAU (1841–1929)

French statesman; Prime Minister, 1906–9 and 1917–20,
and French delegate to the Versailles Peace Conference,
1919.

Photo Sport and General

97

many the proceedings and the outcome were quite the reverse. Only Austria-Hungary supported the German point of view; even Italy, the third member of the Triple Alliance, was lukewarm. But Britain, Spain, Russia, and to a less extent the U.S.A., backed up France. The decisions of the conference were wrapped up in fine phrases proclaiming the sovereignty of the Sultan, while subjecting his territories to an appearance of international control. An international police force was created, a State Bank established, the 'open door' in commerce proclaimed. But in reality, and as the event proved, France was the dominant power in these arrangements, and in a position to mould them to her own purposes. Germany had suffered a moral defeat, not only by the outcome over Morocco itself, but also by the fact that the Anglo-French Entente had withstood the strain and emerged stronger than before.

The Anglo-Russian Entente (1907)

Other events during this period were serving to widen the gap between Britain and Germany, and also to narrow the gap between Britain and Russia. By repeated Navy Laws Germany planned to expand her Navy, and a race in the construction of new and powerful battleships, the dreadnoughts, developed between Germany and Britain. The latter was determined to maintain her naval supremacy, which Germany was equally determined to challenge. In these circumstances proposals for a 'holiday' in naval construction, made by Britain on several occasions down to 1914, were rejected by Germany. On the other hand, France's ally, Russia, had supported the British viewpoint at Algeciras. Since her defeat by Japan in 1905 she appeared a less formidable threat to Britain's Mediterranean and Asiatic interests. Her Parliamentary experiment with the Dumas (see Chapter 3) tempered, albeit in a small degree only, the absolutism of her Tsars, and made her more acceptable as a friend. Moreover, German persistence in the Berlin to Bagdad Railway alarmed both countries.

In 1907 an entente was signed, clearing up (as in the case of Britain and France in 1904) points of dispute between the two countries. Both agreed to keep out of Tibet, and respect the overlordship of China in that vast area. Russia acknowledged Afghanistan as within

G

the British sphere of interest, provided its integrity were observed and it was not used to foster anti-Russian designs. Most important, Persia was divided into three zones: a northern, under Russian influence; a southern, likewise under British influence; and a neutral zone in between. At the same time Persia's integrity was proclaimed, though one may reasonably doubt how far this was consistent with her division into spheres of interest.

Like the Anglo-French Entente, this agreement was in no sense an alliance. Indeed, Britain continued to suspect Russian designs, especially in the Balkans, and Sir Edward Grey, Britain's Foreign Secretary, was criticized for giving Russia too much power in Persia. A cartoon at the time showed him in the Russian Bear's embraces, but with a look of fear on his face lest he be hugged to death. None the less the two countries *had* come to an agreement, and the Triple Alliance of Germany, Austria-Hungary, and Italy was henceforth countered by the Triple Entente of Britain, France, and Russia— with the two latter countries bound by their own Dual Alliance. The European armed camps were complete, and Germany complained of being encircled.

"Milestones to Armageddon"

Beginning with the Moroccan affair of 1905–6, Europe experienced one crisis after another—"milestones to Armageddon," as they have been aptly named. Efforts to check the drift to war, as at the Hague Conferences of 1899 and 1907 (see Chapter 8), proved unavailing. Two storm-centres stand out, the Balkans and Morocco; but the whole sky was threatening. The Balkans have received detailed treatment in Chapter 5, and will receive only brief mention here to fit them into the general picture.

In 1908, following the Young Turk revolution, Austria-Hungary annexed Bosnia and Herzegovina, which she had protected since the Treaty of Berlin in 1878. Serbia was angered at seeing more of her fellow-nationals come under Austrian rule. Russia protested strongly at this advance of Austrian power; but Germany backed up her ally with, as the Kaiser boasted, her own "shining armour." Not daring to risk a conflict, Russia accepted the situation—but with an ill grace.

Agadir (1911)

The next crisis occurred over Morocco, where, since the Algeciras Conference, French power had been steadily increasing. When French forces occupied the capital, Fez, on the pretext of maintaining order Germany protested at this alleged violation of the Act of Algeciras. She sent a gunboat, the *Panther*, to the Moroccan Atlantic port of Agadir in order, she maintained, to protect German lives and property. France was indignant; but it was Britain's reaction that was probably decisive. German sea-power in the Atlantic, with the danger that Germany might annex Agadir and turn it into a base, was more than Britain would stand. The Foreign Secretary, Grey, protested, but above all Lloyd George in a speech at the Mansion House asserted, in language as blunt as any the Kaiser himself had used, that peace on Germany's terms "would be a humiliation intolerable for a great country like ours to endure." Germany climbed down. A new agreement, while maintaining the open door commercially, gave France increased powers in Morocco, enabling her in the following year to declare Morocco a French protectorate. By way of compensation Germany received some French Congo territory to be added to the German Cameroons; but all the world recognized this as the sugar-coating to the bitter pill she had been forced to swallow.

To consolidate her newly gained powers in Morocco France sent to Fez General (later Marshal) Lyautey. With distinguished service behind him in Indo-China, and along the Algerian-Moroccan frontier, Lyautey set about his task with remarkable ability. A well-organized and efficient government was established which stood the strain of the First World War. The name of Lyautey, inseparably connected with Morocco for many years afterwards, is perhaps the greatest name in French colonial history.

A sequel to Agadir was the arrangement made in 1912 whereby France concentrated her fleet in the Mediterranean, and Britain hers in the North Sea and English Channel—with the understanding that each country would safeguard the other's interests. The continued assertion, still true in strict theory, that no alliance existed was wearing very thin indeed.

The Balkans Again

· The years following Agadir witnessed events in the Balkans which precipitated the First World War.

In 1911–12 Italy joined in the attack on the Turkish Empire, and seized Tripoli and the island of Rhodes. In 1912 the Balkan League (Greece, Serbia, Montenegro, and Bulgaria) attacked the remaining Turkish possessions in Europe, and won speedy and unexpected successes. The First Balkan War (1912–13) was ended by the Treaty of London, dictated partly by the great powers. Turkey in Europe was reduced to Constantinople, and her Balkan territories divided up. Most important, in view of what happened later, Austria insisted on the creation of an independent Albania to prevent Serbian access to the sea. Quarrels between the members of the Balkan League over the division of Macedonia produced in 1913 the Second Balkan War, in which Bulgaria was assailed by her previous allies, plus Roumania, plus also Turkey. By the Treaty of Bucharest (1913) the Balkan powers profited at Bulgaria's expense. Turkey also recovered Adrianople. The results of the Balkan Wars may be summarized as follows: Bulgaria full of resentment against her neighbours; Serbia flushed with victory, angry with Austria for her annexation of Bosnia in 1908, and her creation of Albania; similarly, Austria alarmed at the expansion of Serbian power; Germany and Austria now cut off from direct contact with their friend, Turkey.

It was in this atmosphere that on June 28, 1914, the Austrian Archduke, Francis Ferdinand, and his wife were murdered at Sarajevo in Bosnia by a Bosnian Serb. Alleging Serbian complicity in the plot, the Austrian government, with German support, delivered a stiff ultimatum. When Serbia, while accepting some demands, rejected others, Austria declared war (July 28). Efforts made by Sir Edward Grey to localize the conflict proved unavailing, though at one stage he did meet with a favourable response from Germany. But Europe was too sharply divided into its armed camps, and nothing short of a miracle could have stopped the conflagration from spreading.

When Russia began preparations to assist Serbia Germany demanded that she cease mobilization. On Russia's refusal Germany declared war (August 1). Similarly, when France took steps to assist Russia, Germany declared war on her (August 3). Italy, for long a lukewarm member of the Triple Alliance, announced her neutrality. What would Britain do?

The "Scrap of Paper"

Sir Edward Grey, under the agreement of 1912, was prepared to defend the north French coast from German naval attack; but Britain had no definite obligations on this or any other score, and it did not follow that Grey would carry the government or the country with him over this. What brought Britain into the war was the question of Belgian neutrality, guaranteed by the great powers under the Treaty of London (1839) when Belgium won her independence from Holland. This treaty had been signed, among others, by Prussia and Austria (there being then no Germany); but in 1870 Germany, along with France, had confirmed it. Grey now asked for further assurances, which were readily given by France, but refused by Germany. When the German Chancellor, Bethmann-Hollweg, was told that Britain would go to war if Belgian neutrality were violated, he retorted, " So England is going to make war on us for a mere scrap of paper." In the afternoon of August 4 German troops crossed the Belgian frontier. By midnight the British ultimatum for their withdrawal expired, and Britain was at war.

Causes of the 1914 War: A Summary

The war was the result of so many interwoven factors that it might be useful to attempt a brief disentanglement, under the following headings:

GENERAL CAUSES

Although other countries were not guiltless, especially in their imperialism, Germany must bear a large share of the blame: the general suspicion that her doctrine of *Weltpolitik* aimed at world domination; her militarism; her philosophy that Might is Right; the Kaiser's repeated provocative speeches.

Europe's armed camps: to some extent these merely reflected existing tensions; but they also increased them by emboldening their members—*e.g.*, France over Morocco, Austria over Bosnia and Serbia; they also made well-nigh impossible the localization of any conflict.

PARTICULAR CAUSES

France and the Triple Alliance. French desire to avenge 1870 and to recover Alsace-Lorraine;

Conversely Germany's intention of keeping France weak and if possible without allies;

Franco-German differences over Morocco;

France had only minor differences with Italy—*e.g.*, over North Africa.

Russia and the Triple Alliance. Russia's main differences were with Austria, due to their rival interests in the Balkans—*e.g.*, Russian affinities with Slavonic peoples and her ambition to reach Constantinople;

Austria's seizure of Bosnia (1908) and her attitude towards Serbia (1914);

Russia viewed with alarm the Austro-German project of the Berlin–Bagdad Railway and Germany's championship of Turkey and the Moslem world.

Britain and the Triple Alliance. Britain's differences were almost entirely with Germany;

Germany's colonial ambitions—*e.g.*, attitude during Boer War, Morocco; but remember that the German overseas empire was small owing to her late start;

Berlin–Bagdad Railway threatened to bypass the sea-route to the Indian Ocean;

Commercial rivalry: German skill and industry threatened British markets—*e.g.*, in South America—with articles 'made in Germany';

Naval rivalry: extremely important in view of British traditions and overseas interests, and the fact that Germany was already the strongest *military* power in the world;

German invasion of Belgium in 1914 an immediate cause only, important for revealing Germany's unscrupulousness and for bringing into action the deeper-seated causes above.

Chapter 8

INTERNATIONAL CO-OPERATION BEFORE 1914

The Growth of Internationalism

BY the summer of 1914 nationalism had once more triumphed over the various movements towards internationalism which had appeared during the previous half-century.

Europe had a tradition of unity dating back to the Roman Empire —a tradition continued thereafter by the Catholic Church. The Protestant Churches of the Reformation were, it is true, more national in character, but missionary and other activities had often given them an international influence. None the less, the Christian Churches have repeatedly failed to prevent war even among their own members.

Modern means of travel and communication were fast making national frontiers meaningless. Economically, too, nations were becoming more inter-dependent, and war would be likely to impoverish victor as well as vanquished. But economic rivalries often outweighed economic co-operation, and after 1850 most nations (Britain being a notable exception) began to erect tariff and other barriers against their neighbours.

Learning and culture, like the Christian religion, were traditionally international. The Swedish scientist Alfred Nobel (who incidentally discovered dynamite, and thought it so devastating that it would henceforth make wars unthinkable!) left his fortune, on his death in 1896, to provide many prizes open to men and women of all nations; among them was the Nobel Peace Prize. In 1887 Dr Zamenhof of Warsaw invented an international language, Esperanto, in an attempt to overcome language barriers.

Sport and games have also brought the nations more closely together. In 1896 the Olympic Games of the ancient Greeks were

revived. In 1908 Lord Baden-Powell founded the Boy Scout movement. It spread rapidly throughout the British Empire, and into
foreign countries, and when the first international jamboree was held
in London in 1920 Scouts from twenty-seven different countries
attended.

The International Postal Union

A wide variety of topics, such as telegraphs, weights and measures,
patents and copyrights, railways, and shipping have called for international agreements. One of the most important of such agreements
is the International (or World) Postal Union.

As postal services developed agreements between one country and
another over such obvious questions as charges, weight, and transport
became necessary. By the nineteenth century there were hundreds of
such agreements in existence, resulting in much overlapping and
confusion. In 1863 the U.S.A. suggested a conference to co-ordinate
existing arrangements. This was held at Paris, and useful principles
were drawn up; but the American Civil War delayed further action.
Germany, with long-standing experience of such problems, based
upon its own inter-state regulations, took the initiative, and in 1874
a conference was summoned at Berne. This led in 1875 to the International Postal Convention, signed by over twenty nations, mostly
European, except for the U.S.A. In course of time other countries
joined, the last important one being China in 1914.

The Postal Union thus established has its headquarters at Berne,
and it deals with all the complicated questions obviously involved in
the ease with which correspondents can dispatch mail from any one
country to any other. A permanent bureau at Berne manages day-to-
day work, the relatively small costs being shared by the constituent
countries in agreed proportions. Every six years or so a full conference is held of delegates from over the whole world, each country
possessing one vote no matter what its size or importance. In 1951 the
colours of the British stamps were altered in accordance with agreements made by the Union.

The International Red Cross

The desirability of some form of international law is obvious if nations are to regulate their dealings with one another on a satisfactory basis. Unfortunately, so long as nations remain sovereign, there is no certain method of enforcing such law. The Red Cross was created to obtain international agreement at any rate over the alleviation of suffering caused by war.

The Crimean War (1854–56) and the War of Italian Unification (1859) witnessed bloodshed and misery on an unprecedented scale. In particular the battle of Solferino, in North Italy (1859), left thousands of unattended wounded on the battlefield. Swiss humanitarians came to their aid, and three years later Henri Dunant, of Geneva, published *Un Souvenir de Solférino*, suggesting that

> the leaders of the military art of different nationalities agree upon some sacred international principle, sanctioned by convention, which, once signed and ratified, would serve as the basis for the creation of societies for the aid of the wounded in the different European countries.

Out of this suggestion grew the Red Cross. In 1863 a preliminary international meeting was held at Geneva to lay down principles and agree upon a plan of action. This was followed in 1864 by the Geneva Conference, at which twenty-six governments were represented. Here the Red Cross was born. The first Geneva Convention was agreed upon concerning the treatment of wounded prisoners of war. The red cross on a white background (the Swiss flag with the colours interchanged) was adopted as the recognized symbol, and, by the Convention, granted immunity from acts of war. The pattern of organization was for each country to form its own national Red Cross Society—a course of action soon followed by the leading states—and for the co-ordination of their work and the observance of the Convention to be in the hands of the International Red Cross Committee at Geneva. In 1906 a revised Geneva Convention was drawn up, which the second Hague Conference (see p. 107) adopted and extended to include naval as well as land warfare.

The two World Wars of the twentieth century have proved the inestimable value of the Red Cross. 'Total war' has also extended the scope of its activities. Formed originally to look after the sick, wounded, and prisoners of war, it has had in modern times to concern itself with many other questions, such as famine, disease, destitution, and the resettlement of refugees and displaced persons.

The Hague Conferences (1899 and 1907)

In 1898 the Tsar Nicholas II, influenced by the growing cost of armaments among the great powers, and impressed by a book on international law he had been reading, suggested the summoning of a conference to consider matters of international concern. The proposal was taken up on all sides, and in 1899 the first conference, attended by twenty-six states, met at The Hague. Three main topics engaged its attention:

First, the reduction, or, at any rate, stabilization, of armaments. While some countries, notably the U.S.A. and Britain, were inclined to favour such a proposal, most others either opposed it outright or raised insuperable difficulties. In particular, Germany regarded disarmament as an interference with her national pride and sovereignty. In face of widespread opposition nothing was achieved, and the armaments race continued unabated to the catastrophe of 1914.

Secondly, the mitigation of the laws and customs of war. A little was achieved in this direction, though it is always doubtful how far nations will obey the 'rules of war' when it comes to the point. Hopes had originally been entertained by the Tsar of outlawing new weapons and explosives and prohibiting the use of submarines. This proved impossible; as well might Canute try to stem the tides.

Thirdly, the settlement of international disputes by arbitration instead of by war. This method had already been successfully applied in about a hundred cases. A notable instance had been Gladstone's reference to arbitration of the *Alabama* dispute between the U.S.A. and Britain in 1872. Again, in 1895 a dispute over the boundary between Venezuela and British Guiana had been settled in the same way. The Hague Conference now debated whether to make a regular practice of what had hitherto been occasional; a compulsory practice of what had been optional; a practice applying to major as well as to minor disputes. This was to aim too high in existing circumstances, and it soon became clear that only by leaving arbitration optional could any agreement be reached. With this limitation, however, all the twenty-six nations signed the Convention for the Pacific Settlement of International Disputes. Therein the signatories agreed to "use their best efforts to assure the pacific settlement of international differences." To this end mediation on the part of a neutral power might be offered. Even more important, a permanent Arbitration Tribunal was to be established at The Hague to which disputing powers could have recourse. Here we have the origin of what has since developed into the International Court of Justice, one of the organs of the United Nations. A notable case of arbitration occurred a few years later, when in 1904 the Russian fleet, steaming to the Far East, fired on some British fishing-smacks in the North Sea, thinking they were Japanese torpedo-boats. Britain set a good example by referring the question to an international commission set up under the terms of the Hague Convention.

The first Hague Conference had thus only a limited success; but it was a beginning, and the intention was expressed of holding similar conferences every seven years. In 1907 the second Hague Conference met, attended this time by forty-five states. The same topics engaged its attention as before; but by now the international sky was much darker, and the armaments race much faster. Attempts to limit armaments or to make arbitration compulsory were widely opposed, Germany being particularly outspoken in her objections. The only achievement on this occasion lay in the adoption of certain rules intended to 'humanize' the conduct of war, including, as we have seen, the revised Red Cross Geneva Convention of 1906.

International Labour and Socialist Movements

The working-classes also had their international contacts, which in the second half of the nineteenth century received an impetus from the teachings of Karl Marx.

Marx (1818–83) was born in Germany, the son of a converted Jew. After a university career in Berlin he took up journalism, and soon formed a friendship (which was to last a lifetime) with Friedrich Engels. In 1848 Marx and Engels published their *Communist Manifesto*, a book brief in compass but containing the essential features of their doctrines. The European reaction following the failure of the 1848 revolutions forced Marx to seek refuge in England, where he spent the rest of his life. He worked for years in the British Museum collecting material for his great work, *Das Kapital*, whose first part was published in 1867. This book has been aptly called the "Bible of Marxist Communism." Human history, according to Marx, is actuated, not by motives of idealism, religion, or self-sacrifice, but by economic forces—in particular by the struggle between those who possess the means of production and the vast masses of the proletariat, who, without any property of their own, have to sell their labour on terms which in effect rob them of the produce of their toil. Hence arises the class-struggle which will eventually overthrow capitalism and establish communism. The class-division between those who possess capital (land, factories, mines, etc.) and the proletariat, which does not, is the true division of mankind, overshadowing minor distinctions of nationality or religion. "Workers of the world, unite!" was the clarion-call trumpeted forth by the new prophet. Working-class internationalism thus became a historical necessity.

In 1864 there was formed in London the International Federation of Working Men, usually termed the First International. It contained many brands of socialists, but Marx was the leading spirit. Several international congresses were held, and practical evidence of working-class solidarity was shown when strikers in one country were financially helped by workers in others. The excesses and failure of the Paris Commune of 1871 brought discredit on the First International, which, although it had not as a body organized the Commune, included among its members some of those who had. After a bitter quarrel between Marx and the Russian anarchist, Michael Bakunin, the First International died a lingering death in the years 1872–76.

At Paris, on July 14, 1889—exactly a century after the fall of the Bastille—a Second International was organized. This differed considerably from the First in the looseness of its structure and the variety of its member-bodies. It provided little more than an opportunity for socialist and reformist societies of many nations to meet together in congresses, which they proceeded to do down to 1914. Extreme Marxists, like the Russian Lenin, condemned it as too mild, and too concerned with the varying national circumstances of its members. As international tension mounted its interest in peace increased, and at Basle in 1912 resolutions were passed demanding that governments should stop the drift towards war. The most outstanding member of the Second International was the French socialist Jean Jaurès. Jaurès was a great scholar who held a professorship at Toulouse University, but his strong sense of justice led him into politics. In the various crises confronting from time to time the Third French Republic—the Panama scandal, the Dreyfus case, the struggle against the power of the Church—Jaurès appeared on the side of enlightenment and reform. Although advocating arbitration as a means of settling international disputes, he was an intense patriot who made it clear that in the last resort he would defend France by force of arms against the German menace. Towards the end of July 1914 he was in Brussels, attempting with socialists from other countries to avert the impending catastrophe. His efforts were misunderstood in some quarters as treachery, and a half-wit assassinated him on July 31, 1914.

A few days later most of Europe was at war. International labour had failed equally with other international bodies to find the key to world peace. The Second International still clung to life. It survived till well after the First World War, but by then it was faced with the rival Third Communist International (the Comintern) founded by the Russians in 1919.

Chapter 9

THE FIRST WORLD WAR (1914–18)

1914: Germany's Attacks Held

FACED with a war on two fronts, Germany aimed at disposing of one before turning seriously to the other. She reckoned that Russia would be slow in mobilizing, and that a small German army in the east, together with the forces of Austria-Hungary, would be sufficient to stop the Russian 'steam-roller' from getting going. Meanwhile she would be able to paralyse France by capturing Paris, and neutralize Britain by capturing the Channel ports. As early as 1905 Count Schlieffen, then German Chief of Staff, had worked out his famous plan for accomplishing these ends. Regarding the French frontier from Switzerland to Luxembourg as too heavily defended by fortifications, as well as protected by the Vosges and other mountains, the Schlieffen plan envisaged a wide-sweeping movement through Belgium and Luxembourg, with the German fortress of Metz as its pivot. The outermost right wing would take in the Channel ports and, sweeping southward, approach Paris from the west and south. In this way not only Paris, but the French armies, would be caught in a net and forced to surrender. Unfortunately for Germany, the younger Moltke, a later Chief of Staff, modified the plan by strengthening the pivot at Metz and weakening the right wing. This, together with other factors which will appear in the sequel, explains the German failure to capture Paris in the first month.

The Belgians put up a heroic resistance, and the defence of Liège in the first week of the War slowed up the German advance. Similarly, their defence of Antwerp, which did not fall till October, diverted valuable German units from the main objective. None the less, before the end of August both Brussels and the fortress of Namur were in German hands. General Joffre, in supreme command

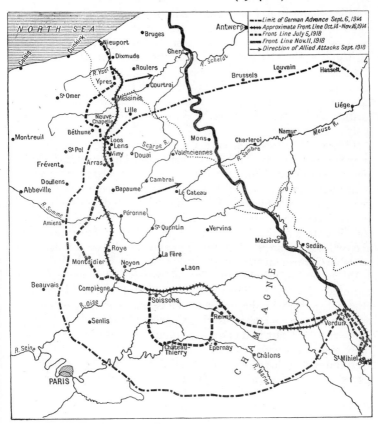

THE WESTERN FRONT, 1914-18

of the French forces, was obliged to withdraw his troops nearer to
Paris to mass them for a supreme effort. The small British expedition-
ary force, 'contemptible' in the eyes of Germany, conducted its
famous retreat from Mons at the end of August. At the beginning of
September the battle of the Marne was fought, with Paris as the
prize. For a week the two sides were locked together, the French even

rushing troops from Paris by taxi-cab. At length the Germans withdrew to the river Aisne, and Paris was saved. The Marne can truly
rank as one of the decisive battles of the world. A month later the
British won the first battle of Ypres, and saved the Channel ports.
By the end of the year both sides were digging themselves in, and
before the first winter was over trenches ran from the Swiss frontier
to the Channel coast. Thereafter, till the very last weeks of the War,
neither side shifted the other by more than thirty miles, and then
only after enormous casualties.

Events on the eastern front had contributed to the defeat of German plans in the west. Austria-Hungary shaped badly against Serbia,
and when the Russians, contrary to German expectations, attacked
East Prussia as well as Austrian Galicia things began to look serious
for Germany. On August 28 von Hindenburg and von Ludendorff
inflicted a severe defeat on the Russians at Tannenberg, followed ten
days later by a further blow at the Masurian Lakes. The threat from
the east was countered, but only by depriving the western front of
valuable German units.

By the end of October the Central Powers had secured another
useful ally in Turkey. The traditional enmity between Turkey and
Russia, together with the long-standing German courtship of Turkey
and the latter's hope of recovering Cyprus and Egypt from Britain,
all played their part in Turkey's decision. Germany now controlled
the Straits, and possessed communications through to the Persian
Gulf and Indian Ocean. To safeguard the Suez Canal Britain declared
Egypt a British protectorate, with Turkish overlordship at an end.

1915: Western Trenches and Eastern Adventures

The year 1915 saw little change on the western front, where the
opposing armies were too strongly entrenched. Long and costly
battles were fought, but they achieved little. In the spring the second
battle of Ypres failed to dislodge the British, and thus threaten the
Channel ports. It was inevitable that both sides began to think more
in terms of the eastern front, or rather fronts, where the position was
more fluid. In directing her main effort in 1915 against Russia, Germany was influenced by the turn of events in Italy, and her desire to
help Austria-Hungary deal with a new foe.

We have seen how Italy had for many years been a somewhat unreliable member of the Triple Alliance. In 1914 she declared her neutrality on the grounds that she had not been consulted over the Austrian Note to Serbia, and that her allies had embarked on an aggressive war which freed her from her obligations. Early in 1915 the Entente Powers played upon Italy's ambitions against Austria, and won her to their side. They were aided by an Italian socialist, Benito Mussolini, who in his newspaper, *Il Popolo d'Italia*, advocated Italian intervention. By the Treaty of London (April 1915) the Allied Powers promised Italy valuable rewards in return for her aid. She was to obtain the Trentino and the southern Tyrol up to the Brenner Pass; also Adriatic territories including Trieste, Istria, Dalmatia, and a number of islands; her possession of the Dodecanese, which she had seized from Turkey in 1911-12, was confirmed; she was to receive a share of the Turkish Empire in Asia Minor, and of the German Empire in Africa. Although she promised concessions, including Fiume, to Serbia, the latter was ill-pleased with this treaty; it merely exchanged King Log (Austria) for King Stork (Italy) in the Adriatic. In May Italy declared war on Austria-Hungary; her pressure diverted Austrian forces from elsewhere, but otherwise made little difference.

Anticipating Italian intervention, Germany began early in 1915 an all-out attempt to clean up the eastern front. A powerful offensive broke the Russian line, and by the late summer the Russians were driven completely out of Poland. Germany was now free to turn against Serbia. The Balkan situation was, as ever, very complicated. At the moment Bulgaria held the stage. Smarting at the loss of Macedonia to Serbia and Greece during the Balkan Wars of 1912-13, she was anxious for revenge. The pro-Ally Greek statesman, Venizelos, tried unsuccessfully to persuade his king to give Bulgaria compensation, and thus keep her, like Greece itself, neutral. German victories against Russia and Allied failures at Gallipoli decided Bulgaria to join the Central Powers in September. By the end of the year Germany and her allies had crushed Serbia. In October Allied forces violated Greek neutrality by occupying Salonika in a vain attempt to save Serbia.

The entry of Turkey into the war towards the end of 1914 also

H

gave the Allies scope for eastern campaigns. A force from India occupied Basra, at the head of the Persian Gulf, and proceeded to advance into Mesopotamia. But General Townshend met superior forces, and was obliged to retreat to Kut, where he was besieged for five months (December 1915 to April 1916). His surrender was followed by the shameful maltreatment of his troops.

A more spectacular, but equally unsuccessful, effort was made to capture Constantinople. This would indeed have been a valuable prize. Access to the Black Sea would enable the Allies to send equipment to Russia, and receive grain from her in return. It would also cut the enemy communications from the Balkans to the Middle East. In the early months of 1915 the Navy bombarded fortifications and attempted to force the Dardanelles; but the latter were too heavily defended. It was decided, therefore, to make a land-attack from the sea. At the end of April the first landings were attempted—British and Anzac (Australian and New Zealand Army Corps) forces on the Gallipoli peninsula, and French forces on the Asiatic mainland. For the rest of the year the struggle continued; but in face of stout Turkish resistance under German leadership the Allies could win little more than their original foothold. By December the Allied troops had been successfully withdrawn. The campaign had failed; the 'Easterners' in Britain (Lloyd George and Winston Churchill) were somewhat discredited; Russia remained isolated from her allies. Her subsequent defeat, and the Bolshevik revolution, spring partly from the failure of the Gallipoli campaign.

The Rôle of the Navy: Jutland (1916)

As the war spread from one continent to another, and as, with the passage of time, it developed into a war of exhaustion, the rôle of the Navy became increasingly important. The combined Allied fleets were vastly superior to those of the enemy, who tried to make up in submarines what was lacking in surface vessels. For the most part the German fleet was bottled up in the Kiel Canal, and only one large-scale naval engagement, the battle of Jutland, occurred. But the work of the Navy was incessant and vital, the responsibilities of our naval commanders unique. As Winston Churchill later wrote of the Commander-in-Chief of the British Battle Fleet: "Jellicoe was the

only man on either side who could lose the War in an afternoon."
An analysis of the Navy's work will throw light upon its many
activities.

With some half a dozen theatres of war, and with the widely
scattered nature of the British Empire, one obviously important task
was the transport of men and materials. After the entry of the U.S.A.
into the War in April 1917 this assumed increasing importance,
though the work was henceforth aided by the powerful American
fleets as well.

Next, the Navy, as always, protected our shores and our overseas
possessions from invasion. German warships made a few tip-and-run
raids on the east coast, but these did nothing to affect the course of
the War. Conversely, the German Empire lay at our mercy. British,
French, and South African forces captured enemy territories in
Africa; Australians and New Zealanders those in the South Pacific;
the Japanese those in the Far East and mid-Pacific. Well before the
end of the War Germany had lost every square inch of overseas
territory.

Most important of all, the Navy (both Royal and Merchant) had
to ensure the continued supply of foodstuffs, raw materials, and
equipment from overseas upon which the very life of these islands
depended. Overseas commerce was the Achilles heel of Great
Britain, and the Germans spared no effort in their attacks. In February 1915 they declared Britain in a state of blockade; Britain retali-
ated by declaring a blockade of Germany. The Central Powers were
less vulnerable than Britain to this form of attack; but none the less
they *were* vulnerable, and the British blockade was more effective
than the German. The slow, but sure, strangulation of Germany
played an important part in producing her downfall. On both sides
the blockade, involving interference with neutral shipping, provoked
incidents with the U.S.A., which under President Wilson endeavoured in the early years to pursue a policy of neutrality.

To carry out its tasks the Navy had obviously to clear the seas of
enemy ships, and by constant patrol to keep them clear. The main
part of the Home Fleet was stationed at Scapa Flow, in the Orkneys,
and guarded the North Sea exit to the Atlantic. Fast destroyers were
based upon Harwich to watch the North Sea itself. The Dover

Patrol was responsible for the English Channel. Throughout the War the main German fleet was bottled up in the Kiel Canal; but certain units were at large when war was declared. Two German cruisers, the *Goeben* and *Breslau*, were in the Mediterranean; they sought refuge in the Dardanelles, and Turkey's refusal to surrender them hastened her entry into the War. Another German warship, the *Emden*, did great damage to merchant shipping in the Indian Ocean, till it was caught by the Australian *Sydney* in November 1914. From August to December 1914 attempts to clear the seas produced a few small engagements. Beatty sank three German cruisers in Heligoland Bight. In the South Pacific Admiral Cradock suffered defeat when attacking a superior German squadron under von Spee at Coronel, off the coast of Chile. Von Spee's fleet was later annihilated off the Falkland Islands by a force specially sent under Admiral Sturdee (December 1914).

Henceforth Germany concentrated upon submarine warfare, with special attention to the Atlantic approaches to Great Britain. On May 7, 1915, occurred one of the most blatant acts of German 'frightfulness' in the whole war. The Cunard liner *Lusitania* was torpedoed off the Irish coast, and sank in eighteen minutes. Over a thousand civilian lives—men, women, and children—including over a hundred Americans, were lost. American wrath reached unprecedented heights, and although Wilson kept his country neutral for another two years, this barbarous act prepared American opinion for the eventual declaration of war.

A year later (May 31, 1916) occurred the battle of Jutland, the biggest naval encounter of the War. The German fleet emerged from Kiel, and was sighted by Beatty's scouting cruisers off Jutland, where the main battle-fleets of Jellicoe and von Scheer joined issue. Counting all the different types of warships concerned, there were 145 British ships against 110 German. As a battle it was only a partial and inconclusive affair, and controversy exists as to which side was victorious. The British fleet suffered considerably larger casualties in men and tonnage; but the German fleet hurried back to harbour, and never really put to sea again till its surrender at the end of the War.

At the beginning of 1917 Germany declared unrestricted submarine warfare against all ships, belligerent or neutral, in British waters or their approaches. The U.S.A. protested, and broke off diplomatic relations with Germany. British shipping losses mounted terrifically; at one time about one-quarter of all the ships leaving British ports failed to return. The food situation became serious. The courage and skill of both the Royal and Merchant Navies eventually warded off this new threat. Enemy exits were mined, and 'mystery' or Q-boats disguised as tramp-steamers lured German U-boats to destruction. Above all, the convoy-system was introduced, in which convoys consisting of many merchant vessels sailed under naval protection. The submarine menace diminished, but was still serious, and on St George's Day (April 23), 1918, a detachment of the Dover Patrol made a daring raid on the enemy submarine-base at Zeebrugge, and sealed its exit with sunken block-ships. A similar raid on Ostend was less successful.

The Allied blockade of Germany and her allies played a large part in achieving final victory. By the end of the War Germany was short of all kinds of food and materials. At the beginning of November 1918 the German crews at Kiel mutinied when ordered to put to sea on what would have been a 'death-cruise.' When the War ended on November 11 the German fleet surrendered to Great Britain, and later scuttled itself at Scapa Flow.

The Western Front (1916–17)

We must now return to the various land-fronts to review briefly the course of events. Early in 1916 the Germans began massive attacks on the French fortress of Verdun. For five months the French resisted, and, although they suffered enormous casualties, they vindicated their boast, "*Ils ne passeront pas*." In July the British under Sir Douglas Haig began the long battle of the Somme. After five months of bloody warfare little had been achieved, and the Germans retired for the winter to their well-prepared Hindenburg line. It was during the Somme battle, on September 15, that tanks—so called to keep their purpose a secret, even from the workers constructing them—were first used.

In 1917 further costly and fruitless attempts were made to break through on the western front. A third battle of Ypres, fought amid indescribable conditions of mud round Passchendaele, was launched in an attempt to capture the German U-boat base of Ostend. Later in the year tanks were first used on a large scale at Cambrai. On the Austro-Italian front the disastrous rout of the Italians at Caporetto in October nearly gave the enemy control of the north Adriatic coastline; but British and French troops, transferred from the western front, helped to seal the gap.

1917: Enter the U.S.A.; Exit Russia

The most significant events of 1917 occurred well away from the western front, where stalemate still continued.

In 1914 President Wilson had urged his country to remain neutral in thought as well as in action. Safely surrounded (as she thought) by two vast oceans, and with a century's preoccupation with the many problems involved in filling up her own continent, the U.S.A. viewed European wars with a detachment mingled with contempt. While many Americans sympathized with the Allied course, others could not overlook the fact that the Allied camp contained autocratic Russia and imperialist Japan among its members. Millions of Americans were immigrants, or near descendants of such, from countries in both camps, and intervention on one side or the other would raise difficult questions of loyalty. The blockade, too, created cross-currents of opinion in America. Whereas German submarines at times sank defenceless passenger or merchant-vessels, with losses of life or property to America, the British Navy interfered with American shipping on the plea that it carried contraband of war, or that the goods, even if intended in the first place for neutral countries, were destined ultimately for our enemies. In November 1916 Wilson won his second presidential election as the man who had kept his country out of the War. But the logic of events was soon to prove stronger than traditions of neutrality.

At the end of 1916 Britain began to raise loans on the American market, thus giving their subscribers an interest in Allied victory. Far more important, German activities gave increasing offence to the U.S.A. German agents promoted strikes, and even sabotage, to deprive the Allies of American goods. German sinkings aroused stronger passions than did Allied seizures of merchant ships. The *Lusitania* (May 1915) has been previously mentioned. So too has

German unrestricted submarine warfare, beginning on February 1, 1917; the U.S.A. immediately broke off diplomatic relations with Germany. Shortly afterwards British Intelligence agents intercepted and handed to the U.S.A. a telegram from the German Foreign Secretary, Zimmermann, promising Mexico German support in any war against the U.S.A. to recover lost Mexican territories. In mid-March Germany's unrestricted sinkings began. On April 6, 1917, the U.S.A. declared war upon Germany. "The world must be made safe for democracy," declared Wilson in his address to Congress. The American fleet was an immediate gain to the Allies, but it took time before her immense industrial and human resources made their influence felt.

News of the overthrow of the Tsarist autocracy in March 1917 had done something to reconcile American opinion to the Allied cause. The Tsarist régime had broken down under the stress of war, and in March the Tsar Nicholas II was forced to abdicate. The Russian Revolution is more fully described in Chapter 11; here we shall note only its relationship to the War. A moderate government under Prince Lvov and Kerensky took over and continued to prosecute the War. Germany cunningly allowed the extreme Bolshevik revolutionary, Lenin, to pass from Switzerland to Russia in the hopes that he would create further trouble and paralyse the Russian war-effort. Her hopes were amply fulfilled. In October-November 1917 the second revolution took place, and Lenin and Trotsky assumed control. The War, in their view, was an imperialist war on both sides; the sooner they could back out of it the sooner they could commence their real job of communizing Russia. After long negotiations, in which the exorbitant German demands surprised the Russian peacemakers, led by Trotsky, the latter reluctantly agreed to the Treaty of Brest-Litovsk (March 1918). Russia ceded to Germany vast territories including Russian Poland, Lithuania, Courland, Livonia, and Esthonia. To Turkey she gave Ardahan, Kars, and Batum in the Caucasus region. She had to recognize the independence of Finland, Georgia, and the Ukraine—the latter to become, in effect, a German granary. Reparations payments were also exacted. By a single treaty Russian gains over several centuries, going back to Peter the Great and Catherine the Great, were wiped out.

The German triumph was as short-lived as it was spectacular. But for the Russian Revolution and the consequent peace, the War might have ended in 1917. As it was, before 1918 was out Germany was as prostrate before the Allies as Russia was now before herself.

The Balkans and the Near East (1916–18)

In 1916 Roumania, anxious to secure Transylvania from Austria-Hungary, entered the War on the side of the Allies. Despite initial successes, she was soon driven back by German armies, and the collapse of Russia in 1917 sealed her fate. The Treaty of Bucharest (May 1918) gave the Central Powers control of Roumania's oil and wheat and a right-of-way through to the Ukraine. Like the Treaty of Brest-Litovsk, it was short-lived. Elsewhere in the Balkans the most important event was the abdication of the pro-German King Constantine of Greece (1917), forced upon him by the Allies and the Greek opposition party of Venizelos. The latter returned to power, and Greece joined the Allies. In 1918 successful campaigns were waged from Salonika against Bulgaria and Turkey.

The Ottoman Empire was crumbling under assaults from all sides. In Mesopotamia the Allied surrender at Kut (April 1916) was avenged by British advances in the next two years to Bagdad and beyond. From his Egyptian base General Allenby advanced into Palestine, and in December 1917 captured Jerusalem. Early in 1918 he established contact with Arab forces from the south whose revolt against their Turkish overlords had been inspired by the Oxford archæologist, Colonel T. E. Lawrence. The Turkish Empire was on the verge of collapse.

1918: Finale

With large German armies set free by the defeat of Russia and Roumania, and with the disquieting prospect of growing American aid to the Allies, Germany decided on a supreme effort on the western front early in 1918. On March 21 the spring offensive of Hindenburg and Ludendorff began, and soon the Allies were in retreat. The usually silent Haig issued his famous "backs to the wall" order to the British forces. The French general, Foch, was appointed generalissimo over the whole western front, an office that should have been created much earlier in the War. By May the Germans were at the Marne again, though never so close to Paris as in 1914. Then on July 18, three days after Ludendorff's final effort to break through, Foch ordered the counter-offensive. Superior for the first time in military equipment, and heartened and helped by American troops, the Allies soon had the enemy in retreat. August 8, when British forces drove the Germans across the old Somme battlefield, was in Ludendorff's words "the black day of the German Army." In September the Hindenburg Line was pierced. Germany's allies were falling like autumn leaves: Bulgaria in September, Turkey in October, Austria at the beginning of November. German morale crumbled as the certainty of defeat dawned upon a starving nation. The German fleet at Kiel mutinied, the Kaiser William II abdicated (November 9) and fled to Holland, and the last Imperial Chancellor yielded his powers to the socialist Ebert. Germany asked for an armistice, and at 11 A.M. on November 11 the fighting ceased. Dying embers of war continued to flicker in parts of the east for several years; but these will be more conveniently considered in connexion with the peace treaties.

The causes of Germany's defeat are to be found scattered throughout the foregoing narrative. In summary they can be stated as follows: the failure of the Schlieffen plan in 1914 by reason of the staunch Allied resistance and the weakness of the German right-wing; the long-term effects of Allied naval power in defeating the submarine menace and in sapping Germany's physical and moral strength by the counter-blockade; the weakness of Germany's allies, which British naval power made it possible to exploit; German provocation of the U.S.A., whose vast material and human resources turned what might have been stalemate into certain victory—so long, as was in fact the case, the Allies continued to control the Atlantic shipping-routes.

Chapter 10

THE PEACE TREATIES AND THE LEAGUE OF NATIONS

The Armistice and the Fourteen Points

BY the terms of the Armistice the fighting ceased and Germany laid down her arms; but it was not unconditional surrender. In January 1918 President Wilson in a speech to Congress had laid down Fourteen Points as the basis for peace. In October, when Germany's defeat was imminent, the last Imperial Chancellor, Prince Max of Baden, had agreed with Wilson to accept these points. Wilson then approached the Allies to obtain their consent. The Allies, it is true, did not accept the points outright. The British government insisted on its own interpretation of the 'freedom of the seas' (which involved the right of blockade); furthermore, it was insisted that reparations be widely defined to include all damage done "to the civilian population of the Allies and to their property by the aggression of Germany by land, by sea, and from the air." In some respects, therefore, the Fourteen Points constituted a somewhat vague starting-point.

Any summary of the points is obviously fraught with the dangers of compression and distortion; but a brief statement of their principal contents will show their main intentions.

Point 1 urged the end of secret diplomacy.

Point 2 provided for freedom of navigation on the high seas.

Point 3 urged the removal of barriers to international trade.

Point 4 urged a large measure of disarmament.

Point 5 dealt with the problem of colonies.

Point 6 provided for the evacuation of Russian territory and the right of Russia to choose its own form of government.

Point 7 provided for the restoration of Belgium.

Point 8 provided for the evacuation of French territory and the restoration to her of Alsace-Lorraine.

Point 9 provided for the readjustment of Italian frontiers according to nationality.

Point 10 recognized the right of the peoples of Austria-Hungary to self-determination.

Point 11 recognized a similar right to the peoples of the Balkan peninsula.

Point 12 recognized a similar right to the peoples of the Ottoman Empire, and guaranteed freedom of passage through the Dardanelles for all nations.

Point 13 provided for the establishment of an independent Poland with access to the sea.

Point 14 provided for the formation of an association of nations safeguarding great and small states alike.

The Paris Peace Conference (1919)

On January 18, 1919, the peace conference was opened at Paris, and continued till the summer months. Its task was the biggest that had ever faced such a gathering, involving as it did the fate of four empires (Germany, Russia, Austria-Hungary, and Turkey), together with that of Bulgaria, and having repercussions upon every continent. Its work was conditioned by many factors: the Fourteen Points; secret treaties and other arrangements made under the stress of war; the accomplished facts of national revolts in the Austro-Hungarian and Ottoman Empires; the continuing war-fever and hatred of Germany; and, finally, the nations represented, and the personalities of their leaders. Altogether over thirty victor powers were represented. Notable absentees were Russia (still in the throes of revolution, and with the Bolsheviks abhorrent to many Allied statesmen) and the ex-enemy states, who were still regarded as 'outside the pale.' The Germans and others were allowed at a certain stage of the proceedings to make written observations upon the proposed terms, which the Allies then considered without any oral negotiation at all. When completed the various treaties were then 'signed on the dotted line' by the enemy powers concerned.

Only six full meetings of the conference were held. Most of the work was done by commissions, and major decisions taken by the leading statesmen. Among the latter a Big Four soon emerged: Woodrow Wilson, of the U.S.A.; Georges Clemenceau, of France;

Lloyd George, of Britain; and Vittorio Orlando, of Italy. After the latter's protests and retirement at what he considered the unjust treatment of Italy, the remaining Big Three dominated the proceedings.

President Wilson was an ex-Professor of History and Political Economy, with the good qualities, as well as the defects, of the academic mind. He was a man of the highest ideals, with two objects uppermost in his mind: democratic self-determination for oppressed peoples, and the establishment of a League of Nations. His almost puritanical faith, and the immense power of the country he represented, led him to be regarded by many millions of war-weary Europeans as the saviour of mankind, a *deus ex machina* from a continent which seemed to have solved the problems of democracy and nationality which still beset the Old World. But he lacked the political ability to translate his ideals into practice—or did much of the fault lie with those others who lacked his idealistic outlook? Although the Republicans had beaten Wilson's Democrats in the Congressional elections of November 1918, he did not include any Republicans in his delegation, or make any serious attempt to conciliate his political opponents at home. With a single-track mind, he proved incapable of the give-and-take in negotiation that the work of the conference demanded. As his shining ideals became tarnished in the dusty debates of the conference he took refuge in his conception of the League of Nations. So long as that were born it would live, he thought, to right any wrongs now being done. Through his influence the Covenant of the League was one of the first-fruits of the conference; through his influence it was incorporated as an integral part in every one of the peace-treaties.

Clemenceau acted as chairman of the conference. Born in 1841, he was now seventy-eight years old, with half a century of political work behind him. He was a staunch republican and radical, who had opposed the Boulangist movement, championed Dreyfus, and supported the separation of Church and State. Before the War he had proved a strong minister, as when he used the military to break a miners' strike. He was a burning patriot, alive to the German danger long before it broke, and fiercely critical of the shortcomings of French ministries before and during the early years of the War. In

1917, at the age of seventy-six, he formed his 'Victory Cabinet,' determined to prosecute the War with the utmost vigour. He strongly supported the appointment of Foch as generalissimo of the Allied armies. He was cast in a different mould from Wilson. He had lived through two German invasions of French soil, and his dominant passion was to destroy the German menace by the most direct and straightforward methods: by keeping her disarmed, by dismembering her, and by exacting heavy reparations for the wrongs she had committed. His fighting spirit and tenacity had earned him the nickname of "Tiger." He urged the creation of a buffer-state in the Rhineland, somewhat reminiscent of Napoleon's Confederation of the Rhine. In face of opposition he gave this up, but only after Wilson and Lloyd George had promised to guarantee France in the post-war years. When the American Senate later refused to honour Wilson's promise, and Britain in consequence backed out, Clemenceau and France felt they had been tricked. Clemenceau's political work ended with the conference. He had led France to victory, but with the hand of a dictator, and early in 1920 his ministry was defeated and he retired from active politics.

David Lloyd George, like Clemenceau, had become Prime Minister during the War (1916) because of his vigour and inspiring leadership. Unlike Clemenceau, he remained in power for several years afterwards. In December 1918, in the flush of victory, he held a general election, and was returned with an overwhelming majority. The election had inevitably produced a crop of anti-German speeches, and promises had been made from many a platform to "hang the Kaiser" and to "squeeze Germany till the pips squeaked." In the midst of the conference, when it was thought in Britain that Lloyd George was becoming too moderate in his attitude towards reparations, 370 M.P.'s sent him a telegram demanding stronger action. Of Lloyd George himself it can be said that he combined a nimble mind with an outlook on Germany somewhere between Wilson's idealism and Clemenceau's fanatical hatred.

On June 28, 1919, two somewhat obscure German delegates were ushered in silence into the Hall of Mirrors at Versailles—the very room where in 1871 the German Empire had been proclaimed. After signing the German treaty they were, in the words of a British diplomat present on the occasion, "conducted like prisoners from the dock, their eyes fixed upon some distant spot on the horizon."[1] The Treaty of Versailles dealt only with Germany, and after its completion the conference drew to an end. Treaties with the other ex-enemy powers were framed by the chief Allies in council, and consisted of the following:

The Treaty of Saint-Germain with Austria (September 1919).
The Treaty of Neuilly with Bulgaria (November 1919).
The Treaty of Trianon with Hungary (June 1920).
The Treaty of Sèvres with Turkey (August 1920), which, for reasons described later, was replaced by the Treaty of Lausanne (July 1923).

The Treaty of Versailles (1919)

The chief territorial changes affecting Germany were as follows. Alsace-Lorraine, which Germany had taken from France in 1871, was now restored. No plebiscite was held; but its restoration was one of Wilson's Fourteen Points. By restoring this Germany lost about 40 per cent. of her iron ore. Two small districts, Eupen and Malmédy, on the Belgo-German frontier, were transferred to Belgium. This followed a plebiscite in which the conditions of voting made it very difficult to vote in favour of Germany. The Saar coalfield was given to France to compensate her for the damage to her own north-eastern coalfields during the War. It was, however, to be administered by the League of Nations, which after fifteen years was to hold a plebiscite to determine its final fate. (The plebiscite, held in 1935, resulted in its return to Germany by an overwhelming majority—see page 218). In Schleswig, one of the two duchies taken from Denmark by Bismarck in 1864, a plebiscite resulted in the northern part being returned to Denmark and the southern remaining German. Germany was forbidden to unite with Austria without Allied consent through the League.

Germany's eastern frontier presented many difficult problems because of the intermixture of Poles and Germans. Poland, which had disappeared from the map in the eighteenth century, was now

[1] Harold Nicolson, *Peace-making, 1919* (Constable, 1933).

CENTRAL AND EASTERN EUROPE AFTER 1918

re-created from parts taken back from her former robbers: Prussia (Germany), Austria, and Russia. She was represented at the peace conference by the world-famous Polish pianist, Paderewski. Germany was made to yield to the new state parts of East and West Prussia, of Posen and of Silesia. The coal and industrial area of Upper Silesia was very mixed in population, and the holding of a plebiscite there was the only important point gained by Germany in the written observations she was allowed to make during the peace conference. The resulting plebiscite gave roughly 60 per cent. votes in favour of Germany and 40 per cent. for Poland, but with many districts strongly on one side or the other. The Allies gave the League of Nations the difficult task of dividing Upper Silesia between the two countries. As a result Poland obtained most of the coal-mines, and what was really one industrial region was now shared by two antagonistic countries. Nearer the Baltic the Polish-German frontier presented not only the usual difficulty of mixed populations, but two special problems. One was the existence of a fairly solid block of Germans, including the Prussian Junkers, or landowners, in East Prussia; the other the promise in the Fourteen Points to give Poland access to the sea. An awkward compromise attempted to reconcile the conflicting interests involved. Germany retained East Prussia; in two adjoining regions, Allenstein and Marienwerder, plebiscites were held, and resulted in Germany's favour. Poland was given an outlet to the sea through Danzig—the famous Polish Corridor, fifty miles wide, separating Germany from East Prussia. Danzig itself was almost entirely German in population; yet it was Poland's natural outlet through the river Vistula! In the result it was made into a Free City under a Commissioner appointed by the League of Nations, but it was to be in customs union with Poland, which was also to control its foreign policy. Across the other side of East Prussia to the east the port of Memel was taken from Germany and held by the Allies till it was forcibly seized by Lithuania in 1923.

Outside Europe Germany lost all her colonies, which later on were given as League mandates to the following countries: German South-west Africa to the Union of South Africa; East Africa (Tanganyika) to Britain; the Cameroons and Togoland, part of each to Britain and to France; German Samoan Islands to New Zealand; German New

Guinea and Bismarck Archipelago to Australia; German rights in Kiaochow (China) and islands in North Pacific (Marshall and Caroline Islands, etc.) to Japan.

Stringent measures were taken to prevent a revival of German militarism. Her navy was limited to six light battleships with supporting craft, her army to 100,000 soldiers. The General Staff was dissolved; military and naval aircraft, tanks and submarines altogether prohibited. The Rhineland, by which was meant all German territory to the west of the Rhine, and a zone thirty-two miles to the east of the river, was to be demilitarized for ever; no troops or fortifications were henceforth allowed. An Allied army was to occupy this area for the next fifteen years, withdrawing in stages as Germany fulfilled her treaty-obligations.

In the famous 'war-guilt' clause the treaty-makers referred to "the war imposed upon them by the aggression of Germany and her allies." This, and alleged German war-crimes, provided the Allied justification for war-trials and reparations. At Leipzig twelve Germans were later tried for crimes, of whom six were convicted. The Dutch government refused to hand over the Kaiser for trial. Reparations proved one of the thorniest problems of the treaty-makers, and of successive statesmen over the next twelve years. Germany made immediate delivery of coal, ships, and other goods; but this left the main questions unanswered. How much *should* she pay; should, for instance, the cost of war pensions, lost merchant shipping, and every other conceivable item be included? How much *could* she pay, having regard either to her own capacity or to the possible harmful effects that payments might have upon the recipients themselves; might not, for instance, deliveries of German coal and ships put British miners and ship-builders out of work? Fantastic and widely different answers were given to such questions by so-called experts, as well as by politicians; France, as might be expected, put forward the highest figures. In the end the treaty left the final amount and other details to be worked out by an Inter-Allied Reparations Commission by May 1, 1921. In the interim, however, Germany was to pay on account the sum of £1,000,000,000.

The Treaties of Saint-Germain (1919), Neuilly (1919), and Trianon (1920)

These treaties with Austria, Bulgaria, and Hungary respectively contained many features similar to the Treaty of Versailles: inclusion of the League Covenant, disarmament, dictation by the Allies, reparations from Austria (which in practice it was found impossible to exact). The territorial provisions were the most important, and for convenience the Austrian and Hungarian treaties will be considered together. To a large extent these treaties registered accomplished facts, as towards the end of the War the old 'ramshackle empire' had disintegrated through revolts into its component national parts. The Hapsburg monarchy, in the person of Charles I, who had succeeded the aged Emperor Francis Joseph in 1916, also came to an end.

The new map of Europe showed Austria and Hungary as two completely separate states, shorn entirely of their previous possessions, and containing only Austrian Germans and Magyars respectively. To the north lay the 'succession' state of Czechoslovakia, formed out of Bohemia, Moravia, Slovakia, and part of Ruthenia, and inhabited by the Slavonic Czechs and Slovaks, but with considerable racial minorities. To the south lay another Slavonic 'succession' state, Yugoslavia; this was composed of pre-war Serbia and Montenegro, together with large areas of the old Austro-Hungarian Empire, notably Croatia, Bosnia-Herzegovina, and Slovenia. Important districts were also transferred to other countries. The new Poland obtained Galicia. Italy at long last obtained *Italia Irredenta*—the Trentino district and the Istrian peninsula, with Trieste; north of the Trentino she also obtained South Tyrol, inhabited by a quarter of a million Germans, to bring her frontiers to the strategic Brenner Pass. She also obtained the port of Zara, on the Dalmatian coast. Roumania obtained the large district of Transylvania, inhabited mainly by people of her own stock.

As for Bulgaria, which has made a habit of 'backing the wrong horse,' she had lost so much, especially in Macedonia, as result of the Second Balkan War of 1913 that there was not much more she could lose. However, she had to make minor frontier adjustments in

Yugoslavia's favour; more important, by ceding Western Thrace to Greece she lost her outlet to the Ægean Sea.

The Peace Treaties: An Appraisement

Final settlements involving Russia and Turkey were concluded only after several years, following further military activities. They will be deferred for the moment while a brief appraisement of the above-mentioned treaties is attempted.

The treaty-system as a whole had many good features. The new national boundaries for the first time gave self-determination to the different racial groups in Europe. Only about 5 per cent. of Europe's population henceforth lived on the wrong side of the frontier, and in some cases this was inevitable; minorities treaties, signed soon afterwards, guaranteed subject-races full rights. Condemnation of aggression, trial of war-criminals (albeit on one side only), the promise of general disarmament, above all the creation of the League of Nations —all these represented steps towards a happier world. That the goal was never reached was as much the fault of subsequent statesmen and of their peoples as of the treaty-makers themselves.

Nevertheless, the treaties themselves cannot escape a measure of blame. They were drawn up too hurriedly in the atmosphere of war-fever still prevailing. It was psychologically unsound to dictate terms to enemy countries without any negotiation or co-operation at all; Germany could later protest that she was not bound by the *Diktat* of Versailles. The war-guilt clause was too sweeping a summary of complicated historical processes. Figures regarding reparations were often vindictive and fantastic; it was because of this that the British economist J. M. Keynes wrote at the time his *Economic Consequences of the Peace*, prophesying the very disasters that reparations later produced. It was possible to argue that the Fourteen Points had not been faithfully observed regarding, for instance, some of the territorial arrangements, or the colonial settlement. Territorially, as mentioned above, the new Europe was more just than the old—and this cannot be over-emphasized. But even here there were black spots. Some of the newly created minorities were almost impossible to avoid: over 3,000,000 Germans in the Sudetenland of Czechoslovakia; the mixtures in the Polish Corridor and adjacent areas. But in other cases, such as Eupen-Malmédy and, to a less extent, Upper Silesia, plebiscites had not been fairly conducted. Some minorities could not easily be justified. About 3,000,000 Hungarians now lived in Czechoslovakia, Roumania, and Yugoslavia. A quarter of a million Austrian Germans in the South Tyrol were now under Italy. The new Austria was a top-heavy state of just over 6,000,000, with 2,000,000 of these living in Vienna; she was forbidden to unite with Germany. In fact, the break-up of the Austro-Hungarian Empire (accomplished by the peoples themselves before the treaties were drawn up) destroyed what had once been a natural economic unit in the Danubian basin and substituted a number of small, antagonistic states. Here, as elsewhere, *national* self-determination had triumphed, when the world's overriding need was for *international* co-operation. Would the new Europe be capable of combining the two to get the best out of both?

Dying Embers of War: (1) Eastern Europe

In Eastern Europe the situation remained very confused for several years to come. It should be recalled that after the second Russian revolution, in October-November 1917, the Bolsheviks had taken Russia out of the War, and concluded the Treaty of Brest-Litovsk with Germany in March 1918. To Russia's western allies it spelt desertion, and gave Germany the opportunity to launch her western offensive in the spring of 1918. In the circumstances it is not surprising that Russia was not represented at the Peace Conference, especially as at the same time she was in the throes of civil war, in which the ex-allied powers joined.

The Civil War and the Wars of Intervention occupied most of the period from the end of 1918 to the end of 1920. They sprang from a variety of motives. Representatives of the old Russian régime naturally attempted to oust the new rulers, and organized forces of 'white' Russians to attack the 'reds.' (These politically 'white' Russians must not, of course, be confused with the race of White Russians adjoining the Polish frontier.) Ex-Allied countries, at one time reaching fourteen in number, joined in. Some were actuated by a dislike of revolution and of communism; some by the fact that Tsarist debts had been repudiated; some by the wish to avenge the Bolshevik desertion; some, especially Russia's neighbours, by a desire to seize new territories. In many cases, as often, motives were mixed. The White Generals Denikin and Wrangel were aided in South Russia by British and French forces; British, French, and Americans co-operated with Whites from Murmansk and Archangel in the north; in Siberia Kolchak received aid from Japanese, Americans, and Czech ex-prisoners of war. Poles, Roumanians, and the newly liberated Baltic peoples attacked Russia from the west. To Trotsky, who was appointed Commissar of War, fell the main task of organizing Russian resistance on as many, at one time, as sixteen different fronts. Trotsky accomplished his task with energy and genius. He trained and organized armies of peasants and factory-workers; he used those officers of the old Imperial Army who were willing to co-operate, despite the opposition of some of his colleagues; he visited the different fronts to inspire his soldiers and co-ordinate their efforts. In short, he laid the foundations of the later Red Army. The struggle ebbed and flowed; when it ended Russia had to acknowledge certain losses, but she was still intact, and, above all, the Bolshevik government still in command.

Out of the confusion Finland and the Baltic states of Esthonia, Latvia, and Lithuania emerged as independent. Roumania had successfully asserted her claim to Bessarabia. The case of Poland is less simple.

We have already seen how the Paris Peace Conference re-created the Polish state from territories previously owned by Germany, Austria, and Russia. Before her partition in the eighteenth century Poland had been a vast state comprising many non-Polish races—Lithuanians, White Russians, and Ukrainians mostly. At the conference Polish delegates, including the pianist Paderewski, pressed for the old, historic Poland again. This offended Allied susceptibilities, and a committee of experts was appointed to draw the fairest possible racial boundary between Poland and her eastern neighbours. The result was the Curzon Line, named after the British statesman Lord Curzon. But for the Wars of Intervention, the Curzon Line would have remained as Poland's eastern frontier. As it was, the wars gave Poland a chance to push farther east. Marshal Pilsudski, head of the Polish state, even dreamed of annexing the Ukraine. His troops reached Kiev, but were then driven back to within six miles of Warsaw. The French, who wished for a large and strong Poland to act as an eastern counterpoise to Germany, rushed supplies to

Poland, and dispatched their brilliant General Weygand to advise the Polish leaders. In August 1920 the tide again turned; by a battle later referred to as the 'miracle of the Vistula' Warsaw was saved, and the Russians again repulsed. In 1921 the Treaty of Riga between Russia and Poland gave the latter a frontier about 100 miles east of the Curzon Line. In the confusion of the previous two years Poland had also annexed Eastern Galicia, once part of the Austro-Hungarian Empire. By her gains thus acquired, against the wishes of Britain and the U.S.A., territories predominantly non-Polish were incorporated in the new state.

The fate of three towns will complete the story of this part of Europe. With Czechoslovakia Poland disputed the possession of Teschen, a coal-mining centre adjoining Upper Silesia; Poland eventually obtained the town, but Czechoslovakia obtained the mines (1920). In the same year a dispute with Lithuania over Vilna was settled when a semi-independent Polish force seized the city two days after the Polish government had agreed to renounce its rights; the Polish government then changed its mind. In 1923 Lithuania awarded herself compensation when she took Memel, which French troops were still holding on behalf of the Allies, who were intending to place it, like Danzig, under the League of Nations.

Dying Embers of War: (2) Turkey

When Turkey surrendered to the Allies at the end of October 1918 it seemed at long last as if 'the sick man of Europe' were really dead. In the Balkan Wars preceding 1914 Turkey had lost most of her European possessions; the few still left in Thrace were now under Allied control. Her North African empire, for long shadowy, was now completely gone. The Arabs, with the assistance of Lawrence of Arabia and Allenby, had successfully revolted, and their independence only awaited legal recognition. Even Constantinople had been promised by secret treaty to Russia (though this would obviously not now be fulfilled), and other secret treaties had promised large parts of Anatolia (Asia Minor) to Italy and France. But if the old Turkey were dead, she was soon to produce a very substantial ghost to haunt the Allies.

Because of Allied preoccupations with other countries, the Treaty of Sèvres with Turkey was not ready till early 1920. Before then important developments had taken place. The Greek Prime Minister, Venizelos, viewed with alarm the possible extension of Italian power in Asia Minor and the Eastern Mediterranean. He persuaded the Allies to allow Greek forces to occupy part of the west coast of Asia Minor, where a considerable Greek population already lived. In May 1919, with the help of Allied fleets, Greek troops landed at Smyrna (Izmir). This provoked a Turkish nationalist reaction, and raised the 'ghost' of the dead Turkey in the shape of Mustapha Kemal.

Kemal was a native of European Turkey, having been born at Salonika of Turkish parents in 1881—a fact which might partly explain his later Western outlook. He had joined the Young Turk Party, and taken part in the revolt of 1908. During the War he had distinguished himself as a soldier in the Gallipoli fighting of 1915. In defiance of his own sultan he now proceeded to organize national resistance to the dismemberment of his country, making Angora (Ankara), in Anatolia, his headquarters. His party was victorious in the elections, and in January 1920 issued a National Pact embodying their programme. Briefly, while willing to relinquish the Arab territories, the Nationalists refused to surrender any of their homeland in Asia Minor or Thrace; they outlined certain reforms, and demanded equality with other nations. The Allies occupied Constantinople, and the pliant Sultan outlawed the Nationalists. The latter continued at Angora to act in defiance of both.

In May 1920 the terms of the Treaty of Sèvres were announced, which the Sultan signed three months later. Like the other treaties, it was dictated without negotiation, and contained clauses dealing with reparations and disarmament. The Arab territories received their independence, which they had in fact already won; Greece was to obtain Eastern Thrace (she had already obtained Western from Bulgaria); the straits were to be internationalized, with Constantinople under Allied control; Italy was to obtain part of Asia Minor; and the Greeks were to stay in Smyrna and district for five years, after which a plebiscite was to be held.

Kemal's Nationalists rejected most of these provisions, and war immediately broke out between themselves and the Greeks. In September 1921 Kemal defeated the Greeks at the Sakaria river. A year later he had driven the Greeks from Asia Minor and massacred the Greek population. He now turned to Constantinople (September 1922). At Chanak, on the Asiatic side of the Dardanelles, a small Allied force barred the way. When the French and Italian detachments were withdrawn on orders from their governments only a few hundred British troops remained. The British Prime Minister, Lloyd George, was for fighting; a strong body of opinion in Britain and the Dominions opposed him. Kemal acted with commendable restraint, hostilities were avoided, and in October 1922 an armistice signed. The Chanak incident was partly responsible for Lloyd George's downfall, which occurred soon afterwards. Kemal, now in undisputed command of his country, abolished the sultanate and declared Turkey a republic.

The Treaty of Sèvres was now smashed to smithereens, like a broken article of the porcelain-ware for which its factories are world-famous. A new treaty was signed at Lausanne in July 1923. Although the loss of her Arab and African empires (which the Kemalists had always accepted) was confirmed, Turkey retained Anatolia intact. Constantinople was freed from Allied control, but the straits were to be demilitarized. Eastern Thrace, with Adrianople, was returned to Turkey. Greece retained Western Thrace (which she had obtained from Bulgaria by the Treaty of Neuilly), and the Italian possession of Rhodes and the Dodecanese (seized in 1911-12) was confirmed. Apart from these somewhat doubtful places, the Turks now possessed their rightful homeland. Furthermore, mention of reparations and other punishments was now omitted.

The Treaty of Lausanne proved the most successful of the post-war treaties—maybe because it was concluded when the passions of war had subsided, and was negotiated between near-equals, and not just dictated.

The Covenant of the League of Nations

Visionaries had long looked forward to the time when, in Lord Tennyson's words,

> . . . the war-drum throbbed no longer, and the battle-flags
> were furled,
> In the Parliament of Man, the Federation of the World.

Now, for the first time in history, a serious attempt was made to turn the dream into a reality.

We have already seen that President Wilson's Fourteenth Point envisaged an international organization. Other minds too, notably in Britain and France, were occupied with this idea well before the War ended. The South African statesman General Smuts contributed a valuable paper to the problem. At the Paris peace conference Wilson insisted that the matter should receive priority; also that when the Covenant, or Constitution, of the League was approved it should be incorporated in each of the peace-treaties.

The Covenant consisted of twenty-six articles, preceded by a preamble which stated the objects of the League: "to promote international co-operation and to achieve international peace and security." Herein is indicated the twofold and closely interrelated approach to world peace which permeates the Covenant and the subsequent work of the League, and which must always be adopted in any similar schemes. Peace and security must be ensured by stopping aggression and the resort to war; but nations must also co-operate to build a just and fair world to remove, or at any rate diminish, the temptation to resort to force. More easily stated than achieved—especially when one considers the complexity of world-problems, and the fact that, where interests genuinely conflict, no solution will appear just to all. It is this reflection that makes the *will* to peace, on the part of peoples as well as their leaders, perhaps even more important than the elaborate machinery devised by statesmen from time to time.

The League's headquarters were to be at Geneva, and the original membership was forty-two states, with provisions for adding others. The chief organs were to be an Assembly, a Council, and a Secretariat. The Assembly may be likened to the Parliament of the League; it met normally once a year, and every member-state, no matter what its size, had only one vote, although it could send three delegates. The Council was somewhat like a Cabinet. It was originally to consist of five permanent members (Britain, France, Italy, Japan, and the U.S.A.) plus four (later raised to six) non-permanent members selected from the other states by the Assembly; it met three or four times a year. The Secretariat was the Civil Service, drawn from different nationalities, and working full-time at Geneva; the first Secretary-General was Sir Eric Drummond, a British Foreign Office expert.

Several articles dealt with the question of disputes. Every member undertook, not only to respect, but also to preserve, the territory and independence of other members. In the event of war or threat of war the League, possibly on the advice of the Council, was to take any action it thought fit to preserve the peace. Disputes between members were to be settled by arbitration, or by a judicial decision or by inquiry on the part of the Council; no member was to resort to war until three months after an award by whichever of the three methods was chosen. Provision was made for non-member states to use these facilities. If they refused both they and member-states were subject to Article 16, the famous article dealing with sanctions, or methods of bringing a recalcitrant country to heel. This article stated that an act of war in defiance of the Covenant was an act of war against all members. The latter undertook to impose immediate economic and diplomatic sanctions by breaking off trade and other relations with the offending state. Furthermore, the Council was to recommend to members what forces they should contribute to enable the League to apply military sanctions.

Many diverse matters were included in other articles, intended to promote greater international justice. A general reduction of armaments was planned, to accomplish which the international regulation of the traffic in arms was looked forward to. Out-of-date treaties were to be revised; this would prevent the perpetuation of injustices due to changing circumstances. Undesirable forms of trade—*e.g.*, in dangerous drugs or in slaves—were to be put down. Two important bodies, although not strictly part of the Covenant and the League, were soon established in connexion with League activities, and may, for practical purposes, be considered as part of its machinery. The International Labour Organization, or I.L.O., was created to deal with social and labour problems on an international basis; to establish, for instance, fair working conditions in all countries, and thus prevent labour unrest and the dumping of cheaply produced articles abroad. Its first director was the Frenchman Albert Thomas, and it drew its representatives from employers' and employees' organizations as well as from governments. The Permanent Court of International Justice, or the World Court, was created to provide a permanent international body of judges to deal with judicial disputes between nations. It sat at The Hague, where the conference of 1899 had created a similar though less permanent Arbitration Tribunal.

With regard to ex-enemy colonies, the Covenant instituted the system known as mandates. The colonies had been transferred to the Allies, who had disposed of them among themselves. The mandates system was the work of the League. The complete arrangement was therefore a joint responsibility. Article 22 laid it down that the ex-enemy colonies should be administered to promote the well-being and development of their inhabitants. To ensure this the ruling powers or mandatories had to render an annual report to the League, which later established a Mandates Commission to consider such reports. Recognizing the differences in development and status between the different colonies concerned, the article divided the mandated territories into three groups:

Group A covered certain ex-Turkish territories where the natives were fairly well advanced, and where the mandatory power was to act in an advisory capacity till such time as full independence was granted.

Group B covered Central African colonies, which were less advanced, and where the mandatory power was to exercise fuller authority, subject to giving equal trade opportunities to other members of the League.

Group C covered South-west Africa and the Pacific Islands, which by reason of their small size or population and their backwardness could be regarded by the mandatory powers as integral parts of their territory—though they still had to render the annual report to the League.

Allied apportionment of the colonies in conjunction with the League mandates system resulted in the following arrangements:

Under Group A France obtained Syria, and Britain obtained Iraq, Transjordan, and Palestine; the mandate for the latter made Britain responsible, by reason of certain promises contained in the Balfour

Declaration of 1917, for establishing in Palestine "a national home for the Jewish people."

Under Group B Britain obtained practically all of Tanganyika, and divided with France the Cameroons and Togoland.

Under Group C the Union of South Africa obtained German South-west Africa, while Australia, New Zealand, and Japan shared out Germany's Pacific islands.

The League of Nations: Criticism

It is easy to criticize the League, especially in view of its now known failure to prevent another world war. But for a first attempt at a permanent international organization it embodied many worthy features. It performed much extremely valuable work during its lifetime, some of which is described later in Chapter 14.

None the less, it possessed serious defects, perhaps the most important being that for various reasons it appeared at times to be a league of the victors against the vanquished, designed to perpetuate the Versailles and other treaties. At the beginning Germany and other ex-enemy countries were excluded from membership, although they were later admitted (*e.g.*, Germany in 1926). Russia was excluded (till 1934) because of her revolution and the confusion it produced. The U.S.A. backed out at the start. In consequence it was most of the time only half a league. Of the seven great powers of the world (Britain, France, Italy, Japan, Germany, Russia, and the U.S.A.) only the first four were members during the early years. It has been argued also that it was a mistake to embody the Covenant in the dictated treaties. Possibly too it was a mistake to associate the League (as then constituted) with the disposition or administration of disputed territories such as the Saar, Upper Silesia, or Danzig. The League failed to promote disarmament, or to prove effective in revising treaties. All this, it must again be emphasized, tended to make it appear an instrument for maintaining the *status quo* to the disadvantage of Germany.

On a larger view it can be maintained that the League was wrong in conception because it still allowed each nation too much power, including the control of its own armed forces. Under the Covenant practically every decision had to be unanimous, so that one country could hold out against the rest. A country could even wage war after the 'gap' of three months following a decision of which it disapproved. Article 16, the sanctions article, made economic measures against an offender immediate and automatic; but military action was a recommendation only. The French had wanted an international army under League control, but this had been turned down. In pointing out that the League failed to curb national powers, or to subordinate them to a truly supranational organization, we must be fair to the statesmen who designed it. The people they represented were not ready in 1919 for such a jump—nor were they again in 1945, when the United Nations, successor to the League, was born.

The U.S.A.: Isolationism and the Washington Conference

It remains to record the policy of the U.S.A. in the immediate post-war years. President Wilson had taken no steps to associate his Republican adversaries with his actions at the Paris Peace Conference; both his policy and his personal attitude aroused much opposition back home. Under the American Constitution a two-thirds vote of the Senate is necessary for the ratification of treaties. The Treaty of Versailles, and in particular the League of Nations Covenant which formed part of it, was bitterly attacked. For the U.S.A. to undertake the commitments contained in the Covenant, in particular that of Article 10 guaranteeing the integrity of all member-states, was too much for isolationist America to swallow. Wilson by now was a sick man, soon unable to champion in person the cause nearest his heart. In November 1919 the Senate voted 55 for and 39 against ratifying the Treaty—a majority, be it noted, indicating the strength of pro-League opinion in America, but not the necessary two-thirds majority required by the Constitution. The U.S.A.'s absence from the League during the inter-war years was a tragedy of incalculable consequence. At the same time the Anglo-American promise to assist France in case of attack also fell through, and France felt herself cheated.

By tradition the U.S.A. was more actively interested in Pacific than in European affairs, with a 'soft spot' towards China, and a lively suspicion of Japanese designs. The preoccupation of the western powers with the European war had left Japan with a free hand in the

Far East. China was still a prey to warlords following her revolution of 1911, and was in no position to resist Japan. In 1915 the latter had presented China with Twenty-one Demands which were calculated to increase the Japanese stranglehold. As one of the Allies Japan had seized German territories in the Pacific, and at the end of the War she was confirmed by the Treaty of Versailles in their possession. These included not only Pacific islands, but also German conces-sions in Kiaochow and the Shantung Peninsula, one of China's richest provinces. The U.S.A. was determined to reach a settlement more to her liking. She summoned the Washington Conference (1921–22) of the leading powers, though for various reasons Russia and China were not represented. Japan was obliged to surrender her special rights in Kiaochow and Shantung. A nine-power treaty guaranteed the integrity of China and equal trading rights for all nations. The four major powers (Britain, the U.S.A., France, and Japan) undertook to consult together regarding Pacific problems in the future—an agreement which in effect ended the Anglo-Japanese alliance dating from 1902. After much discussion over naval arma-ments it was agreed that Britain, the U.S.A., and Japan could build battleships according to a tonnage-ratio of 5:5:3 respectively. Britain and the U.S.A. agreed not to fortify Hong Kong and the Philippines; this left Singapore and Pearl Harbour as their nearest naval fortifica-tions. In other words, Chinese integrity depended henceforth mainly upon Japan's good behaviour, and when in 1931 she invaded Man-churia the western powers were unable or unwilling to resist her. Events showed that the Washington Agreement was a poor substitute for a strong League of Nations.

Chapter 11

THE NEW EUROPE: SOVIET RUSSIA

Introduction: Post-war Dictatorships

PRESIDENT WILSON, in a memorable phrase, had once told his countrymen that the War was being fought to "make the world safe for democracy." Democratic forms of government and individual liberty had spread steadily, though at different rates in different countries, throughout the nineteenth century. The most advanced democratic countries, Britain, the U.S.A., and France, had won the War. Yet the post-war years soon saw the emergence of personal dictators in many of the countries of Europe: Lenin and his Bolshevik associates in Russia; Mussolini in Italy; Mustapha Kemal in Turkey; Primo de Rivera in Spain; and lesser imitators in some of the small countries of Central and Eastern Europe. Even the German democratic experiment of the Weimar Republic ended after a dozen years in the victory of Nazi-ism and the dictatorship of Adolf Hitler. What is the explanation of this seeming paradox?

There is no single explanation, and factors which apply to one country might not apply with the same force to another. In Italy, for instance, Parliamentary government was already largely discredited before the War. Or, again, in Soviet Russia the communist leaders believed in the dictatorship of the proletariat, which they interpreted as the dictatorship of themselves. But some causes are of more general application. In most of the dictator countries democracy had really made little headway before the War. Parliaments had existed, it is true, but usually with very limited powers. Sometimes, as in Russia, Turkey, or Spain, the royal family had proved incapable of its task; its place was then taken by a dictator, whose novelty lay not so much in his powers as in the ruthless efficiency with which he applied them. Furthermore, the War had given governments greater powers to enable them to wage the life-and-death struggle in which they were engaged. This was true even of the western democracies, where a Lloyd George or a Clemenceau had wielded unprecedented powers. In Britain, France, and the U.S.A. the democratic elements were strong enough to reassert themselves at the conclusion of the War; in many other countries they were not. To quote an authoritative book: "Among the causes making for dictatorships after the war the experience of dictatorships during the war is one of the most important."[1] Conditions after the War contributed to the same end. For four years men had been trained to get their way by force; they were not likely to put aside these habits at a moment's notice and embrace democratic methods with their give-and-take compromises and their apparent slowness. Peace and contentment did not come with the Armistice and the treaties. There were still wars to be fought, boundaries to extend, existing gains to consolidate; economies had been shattered, and there was much distress. It was a jungle world, man against man, nation against nation. Parliamentary debates and individual liberties stood in the way of strong and speedy action. Only the powerful leader, it appeared, could give his country orderly government and champion his country's rights against the encroachments of greedy and unscrupulous neighbours. Such an atmosphere bred dictators as naturally as the jungle breeds the lion.

The First Russian Revolution (March 1917)

Tsarist Russia had entered upon the war in 1914 with a vigour which had surprised her enemies, and although she was defeated at Tannenberg before the end of August, her attempted invasion of Prussia had diverted German troops from the western front and contributed to the Allied victory at the Marne. For the next two years the Russians fought desperately against the better-equipped and better-organized German armies and suffered enormous casualties. Under the stress of war the Tsarist régime began to crack. Her western allies failed to force the Dardanelles. A few supplies could be sent to the White Sea ports of Murmansk and Archangel when they were not frozen up; or along the thousands of miles of the Trans-Siberian

[1] A. J. Grant and H. Temperley, *Europe in the Nineteenth and Twentieth Centuries* (Longmans, 1940).

Railway, which was quite inadequate for such a purpose. In June 1916 Kitchener sailed in the *Hampshire* for Archangel, to examine Russia's military situation, but the ship struck a mine, and nearly every one, including Kitchener, was drowned. Slowly but surely Russia was smitten by a creeping paralysis. Her armies lacked equipment, clothing, food, medical supplies—in fact, everything needed to keep them in the field. War-weariness, desertions, and eventually mutiny appeared. At home the people were starving. In a last desperate effort the Tsar, Nicholas II, took over control of the armies himself; but only a miracle could have saved the situation. The Russian Duma, or Parliament, bitterly attacked the government, which was now more than ever under the control of the Tsarina and the disreputable monk, Rasputin. At the end of 1916 Rasputin was assassinated. In March 1917 strikes occurred in Petrograd, and crowds paraded the streets asking for bread. The soldiers fired half-heartedly on the people, then shot one of their own officers and mutinied. Both Duma and Army demanded the Tsar's abdication, which took place on March 15, 1917. The Romanov dynasty, rulers of Russia for three centuries, was ended. Nicholas II and other members of his family were murdered over a year later.

The revolution was the final crumbling of a rotten edifice, and not the work of any of the revolutionary parties or their leaders. Maybe the regiment which had mutinied at Petrograd, and in a sense leaned on the toppling structure, can claim to have produced the final collapse. A provisional government was soon formed with Prince Lvov as its head, but with a young and energetic labour leader, Kerensky, as its guiding spirit. The new government drew support from Liberal elements as well as from hastily formed soviets, or councils of factory-workers and soldiers. The Menshevik section of the Social Democrats (Marxists who believed in gradual and constitutional methods—see page 41) also gave their support. The general intention was to build up a democratic system of government somewhat after the western model, and arrangements were made for a Constituent Assembly to meet early in 1918. Before then the Kerensky government was itself overthrown, two main factors producing its early death.

The first was the government's determination to continue the war against Germany. This was contrary to popular wishes and popular needs. Distress and starvation were too widespread and deep-seated to be relieved under conditions of war. In any case, the soldiers themselves were settling the issue by mutiny and desertion; they made their way home to help their families and to seize lands from noble and priest. In Trotsky's vivid phrase, they "voted with their feet."

The second factor was the appearance on the scene of a new wave of revolutionaries. As a vacuum will attract winds from all quarters, so the collapse of Tsardom attracted exiles from all directions: Lenin and Zinoviev from Switzerland, Trotsky from the U.S.A., Stalin from Siberia—all determined men, with clear ideas as to what they wanted, and ready to promise Russia the 'bread and peace' for which she yearned.

The Second Russian Revolution (November 1917)

Lenin (or, to give him his real name, Vladimir Ulyanov) was born in 1870, and came of the smaller Russian provincial gentry. His elder brother was put to death for attempting the life of Alexander III, an event which deeply affected Vladimir. For his own early revolutionary activities he was exiled to Siberia for several years. On release he went abroad, and, like his idol, Marx, spent much time studying at the British Museum. At the London Conference of Russian Social Democrats in 1903 he associated himself with the Bolshevik, or majority, wing which advocated violent methods to achieve a wholesale revolution. He revisited Russia during the revolution of 1905, but was soon in exile again in Switzerland. There he was when war broke out in 1914—a war which he denounced from the beginning, and which he publicly hoped would bring about the downfall of Tsarist Russia. When the first revolution of 1917 only produced another war-minded government the Germans allowed Lenin to pass through their country in a sealed railway carriage in the hope that once in Russia he would add to the confusion among their enemies. Lenin reached Petrograd in April 1917. He was soon joined by other like-minded colleagues, among them being Leon Trotsky, a Russian-born Jew, who had lived in exile in many countries and was then in the U.S.A. Trotsky had been, and still was, a Menshevik; but he soon went over to Lenin's Bolshevik party.

On his arrival Lenin startled the moderate Social Democrats who were supporting Kerensky's government by his strong denunciations of their actions. He immediately ordered his followers to attack the moderate Kerensky government, and for six months a bitter struggle ensued. After a premature attempt in July the Bolsheviks carried through a successful *coup* on November 7, 1917. Red soldiers seized strategic points in Petrograd, and the guns of a red-controlled warship threatened the city. Kerensky fled, and Moscow was taken with little effort. Within a few days a new government was formed, with Lenin at its head.

Lenin establishes Control

The Bolshevik revolution of November 1917 was the work of a small minority of determined men without the active support of the vast majority of their countrymen. When the Constituent Assembly, whose election had been arranged by the previous government, assembled in January 1918 only about one-fifth of its members were Bolsheviks. After sitting continuously for a day and a half, it was dispersed by force. Despite internal distress and discontent, open revolt, the intrigues of the old order, civil war and foreign invasion, the Bolsheviks retained their power during these critical early years. What is the explanation?

It must be borne in mind that the vacuum existing on the downfall of the Tsarist régime had by no means been filled by Kerensky's weak government. Chaos and dissatisfaction continued. The circumstances were ideal for agitators who knew exactly what they wanted, and were unscrupulous as to the means they employed. Such were the Bolsheviks. Lenin in particular was wonderfully clear-minded, with the gift of changing his tactics to suit different circumstances without losing sight of his ultimate goal. He promised to grant the two most crying needs of the people—bread and peace. The peasantry, who formed the bulk of the population, cared more for land than for Marxist doctrines, even if they knew anything about the latter! They had already seized much land in the confusion since March. One of Lenin's first acts was a decree giving the land to the peasants. Wholesale seizure was now legalized, and went forward with all its attendant acts of indescribable violence. Peasant ownership of land was not part of Lenin's Marxist creed; nor did it produce immediate bread for starving Russians. But the peasantry were now his supporters, and could be fitted into the 'system' later, when Bolshevik power was consolidated.

As for the other need, peace—Lenin's desire was as strong as that of the ordinary person. Only freedom from the stress of war would enable him to strengthen his position and tackle the urgent problems that beset Russia. The War, in any case, as he had consistently preached since 1914, was an imperialist war contrary to the needs of the proletariat. An armistice was signed with Germany, and Trotsky was given charge of the negotiations for a peace-treaty. The terms of the Treaty of Brest-Litovsk (March 1918) have already been described on page 119. Their stiffness nearly caused Trotsky to break off the negotiations; but Lenin was more far-sighted, and, as on other occasions, was prepared to take one step backward in order at some later time to take two steps forward.

Though relieved of the German menace, Russia knew no peace for several years, being a prey to civil war and intervention on the part of her ex-allies (see pages 132–133). That these wars did not unseat the Bolsheviks may be attributed to several factors. The White armies were the forces of reaction, their officers often the old squires in uniform. Their triumph would have meant retribution and the loss of the peasants' newly acquired land; the peasants naturally rallied round their Bolshevik rulers to prevent this. Nor must we overlook Trotsky's inspiring organization of Bolshevik resistance, and also the national unity that foreign invasion usually promotes no matter what the circumstances. Finally, as an important factor in the endurance of the Bolshevik revolution, we must remember that Russia had centuries of autocracy behind her, and that the Bolsheviks ruthlessly continued this tradition with whatever means came to hand. Many members of the old Tsarist secret police, the Okrana, were used to establish a new secret police, renamed the Cheka—a name which was itself later discarded for others without altering the essential nature of its task. Other means also (food discrimination in conditions of famine, the taking of hostages, large-scale execution of malcontents) enabled the Bolsheviks to rivet their régime on a weakened and war-weary nation.

Russia till the Death of Lenin (1924)

Tremendous tasks faced Russia's new rulers as peace slowly returned. Most important of all was the problem of providing a mere physical existence for a nation numbering 140,000,000. The communist doctrines of Karl Marx had so far existed on paper only. Marx had argued that the ownership and control of the means of production and distribution—*i.e.*, of land, factories, mines, banks, transport, etc.—should be transferred from the capitalist few to the workers, or proletariat, and used henceforth for the benefit of all who contributed through their labour to the common good. But no one knew the answers to the hundred and one questions that were bound to arise when practice took the place of theory. The Russian communists themselves have given different answers at different times, while keeping their broad objectives fixed. Abnormal difficulties existed from the start. Marx had believed that his theories would be first applied in the advanced industrial countries of the west. Russia was 90 per cent. agricultural; her industries small and concentrated in a few areas; her people poor, uneducated, and by every standard backward. She was just emerging painfully from a war and its aftermath, which had produced bankruptcy, starvation, disease, anarchy, and death on an unprecedented scale.

In the first few years after 1917 the government commandeered everything it wanted—if it could find it! In particular, agricultural produce was confiscated from the peasant to feed the town-worker and the soldier; the peasant by contrast could obtain very little from the town in return, and only at the scarcity prices then obtaining. The peasant protested in the only way open to him; he hid his food, or (more effective still) ceased to produce it. A drought in 1921 added to Russia's troubles. Famine stalked the land, and the Russians themselves quoted 3,000,000 as having died of starvation. Lenin, though opposed by some of his colleagues, decided on one of his temporary steps backward as a prelude to later advance. In 1921 he introduced the New Economic Policy, or N.E.P. While the government still controlled the nationalized banks, transport, and heavy industry, 'capitalistic' concessions were made to the peasantry and the small tradesmen. After the peasant had paid a tax on his produce he was allowed to market the rest to his own advantage; middlemen, or 'nepmen' (from N.E.P.), could engage in small-scale industry and trade, though they might still find themselves subject to the competition of government and co-operative enterprises. The Russian government also began to open up trade relations with other countries, and to push on with the schemes of electrification, in which Lenin had immense faith. Slowly conditions began to improve.

Among other features of Lenin's Russia we may note the discouragement of religion, which although still often permitted was subject to many restrictions. Marriage-ties were loosened, and divorce made easy. By 1923 a Constitution had been drawn up. Lenin had referred to Tsarist Russia as a "prison-house" of the different nationalities comprising it: Ukrainians, White Russians, Georgians, Armenians, and many others, who were subordinated to the Russians proper. This the new Constitution proposed to rectify by allowing each main racial group to form its own republic, with control over its own local affairs, and with its own language and traditions safeguarded. The different republics (whose number had increased from the original seven to sixteen in 1940) were then federated to form the Union of Socialist Soviet Republics. Government was based upon the local soviets, or workers' councils, of town and village; from them a pyramid-like structure was built up of soviets for the larger regions, till at the apex the Congress of Soviets was supposed to represent the whole country. But under the 1923 Constitution certain classes were excluded from the vote—namely, 'nepmen,' priests, and others identified with the old order. Furthermore, the peasantry were given only one-fifth of the votes that their numbers really entitled them to. More important than even these limitations was the fact that the whole machinery of government was dominated by the Communist Party, which at this time numbered less than a million.

Stalin v. Trotsky

Lenin's death in 1924 led to a struggle for power between Trotsky and Stalin. Trotsky, the Russian-born Jew, who had lived in many countries before 1917, had an international outlook. In character he was brilliant and versatile, with at times that inattention to detail that often accompanies brilliance. As Lenin's right-hand man, he had negotiated the Treaty of Brest-Litovsk, and had organized victory in the civil wars following the Revolution. He was now Commissar of War. His rival was Joseph Stalin (an assumed name meaning 'man of steel'—fortunately much easier to handle than his real name, Jugashvili!). Stalin was born in 1879 in Georgia. The son of a cobbler, he was intended for the priesthood; but he soon changed to revolutionary activity. He played a minor part in the 1917 revolution, but a greater part in the civil wars, when his defence of Tsaritsin caused that town to be renamed Stalingrad. In character Stalin was patient, methodical, and calculating. As General Secretary of the Communist Party he had gathered the reins of power into his own hands, and built up a body of supporters devoted to their 'comrade.' In contrast to Trotsky, he had hardly ever been abroad, and throughout his life his outlook was Russian rather than international. This difference was reflected in matters of high policy. Trotsky, more in line, perhaps, with the original doctrines of Marx, urged the importance of world revolution; only when this was achieved could Russia push on with her communist experiment. Stalin thought otherwise; Russia was sufficiently large and powerful to advance well along the road to full communism independently of the rest of the world. It was largely a question of tactics, for it can be disputed whether Stalin intended to renounce world revolution completely or was merely putting it in cold storage for the time being.

As Secretary of the Party Stalin held most of the high cards, and knew exactly where the others lay. Within the next few years Trotsky was relieved of his post as Commissar of War and expelled from the Communist Party. In 1929, as he refused to go into exile, he was taken to the frontier and pushed across. He was on his travels again, and eventually finished up in Mexico, where he was assassinated by a Russian agent in 1940. He had spent his exile denouncing Stalin as the "betrayer of the revolution." With Trotsky and other rivals disposed of, Stalin proceeded to put his ideas into practice.

The Five-year Plans

Stalin's economic policy found expression in the Five-year Plans, the first of which was launched with tremendous enthusiasm in 1929. Their object was to harness the productive forces of the country over a period of four or five years towards those ends which the planners thought best suited to the needs of the country. In theory the workers, through trade unions and other organizations, shared in the formulation of the Plan; in practice the main decisions were taken by a central planning authority called Gosplan, though the workers could express opinions over details affecting their own factories and workshops. The first plan concentrated upon the provision of capital equipment such as hydro-electric power-stations, iron and steel industries, and machine-tool factories. It was inevitable that in this period ordinary consumer goods, such as clothing and household articles, would be scarce; the Russian was obliged, as it were, to tighten his belt for the sake of better times ahead. The first plan also included the collectivization of agriculture, which will be considered more fully in the next section. The second plan laid emphasis upon the development of Russia's transport system, and the production of more consumer goods; but with each successive year the threat of war was now increasing, and more and more of the nation's resources had to be diverted towards military ends. So it went on, and it must have seemed to the unfortunate Russian that it was never "jam to-day," though always "jam to-morrow."

The very idea of the plans presupposed that the State controlled the means of production and distribution. Even under Lenin's New Economic Policy the State had controlled the basic industries. This was now extended to include practically everything, though control might be exercised through subsidiary bodies such as the separate republics, municipalities, collective farms, or co-operative societies. In consequence the last remaining nepmen died out. Private property was, of course, allowed; but—and this forms an essential part of Soviet communism—no one was allowed to use his wealth in order to employ others to work on his behalf. Industries were formed into trusts or combines under skilled management which were responsible for producing their share of the plan at fixed prices. If an undertaking failed to produce its quota the management might be dismissed; if it produced more the workers would share the surplus with the State in the form of increased amenities, such as social services, canteens, playing-fields, etc. The collective farms were responsible for their quota of food production. It is not surprising, and in itself is no condemnation of the system, that plans on such a vast scale sometimes went wrong, that shortages or bottle-necks occurred.

A few of the more important aspects of Soviet planning may be mentioned. How did the ordinary worker fit into the scheme? In the first flush of enthusiasm after 1917, experiments had been made with workers' control of their own industries, and with equal rewards for all. These had proved impracticable, and had very soon been discarded. Through their trade unions the workers helped in such tasks as distributing sick or accident benefits or in keeping their fellows up to the mark. At times, too, they might criticize the management; but the latter was ultimately responsible for the control of production. Unlike their counterparts in capitalist countries, the Russian trade unions do not engage in strikes; the reason is disputed between supporters and critics of the Soviet system. The problem of getting the worker to give of his best has been tackled in a variety of ways, including competitions between different groups or factories, or the award of the title of Stakhanovite for outstanding effort (so called after Stakhanov, the Donbas miner who performed prodigious feats of coal-hewing). Most important over the whole scene has been the widespread use of piece-work rates, and of different levels of wages and other privileges for different types of work. Higher rewards were often given to attract workers to development areas beyond the Urals, or to other remote spots. When this failed to attract the necessary number of workers, other, less desirable means were employed. In particular, forced labour was exacted (and according to many sources still is) from 'undesirables' such as wealthy peasants, or *kulaks*, from those associated with the old régime, and from those many others who were accused of opposition to the government. Whatever the methods employed, the Plans have resulted in the opening up of vast and remote areas which in Tsarist days were neglected. Among many evidences of success in this respect may be mentioned the heavy industries of Magnitogorsk, the Kuznetzk coalfield, the Stalingrad tractor works, the Dnieper Dam, and the Turkestan-Siberian Railway.

The Collectivization of Agriculture

The countryman everywhere is difficult to fit into a system; he is conservative by nature, attached to and jealous of his land, and distrustful of the townsman, who usually knows all too little of the processes of nature. Stalin's first Five-year Plan set about the difficult task of incorporating the peasantry into his system.

It has been estimated that during the Revolution the peasantry increased their holdings by about 20 per cent. They suffered in the early years from government confiscations of food, but under the New Economic Policy they had been given greater freedom in marketing their produce. Many had grown rich, and had bought up the lands of their less fortunate neighbours; these well-to-do peasants were called *kulaks*, from the Russian word for a fist. In the main, however, the Russian countryside in 1929 presented most of the features obtaining before the Revolution. The peasant owned his land, his agricultural methods and implements were primitive, and he still worked in co-operation with his fellows in the old Russian *mir*, or village. Beginning in 1929, government and party agents descended upon the countryside to impose a new pattern upon it more in keeping with communist philosophy. Resistance on the part of the kulaks was punished by 'liquidation'—a convenient word covering a multitude of fates. Many were put to work on the Leningrad-White Sea canal, or sent to develop areas beyond the Urals. Nor was resistance confined to the kulaks. The smaller peasants, too, refused to co-operate, and slaughtered their livestock rather than have them confiscated. Stalin, anxious for the nation's food-supply, wrote his famous article "Dizziness from Success," accusing the government agents of being over-zealous in their work. The pace was in consequence slackened, but not stopped. By 1933–34 collectivization had been achieved. In the process millions had been liquidated, millions probably had died of starvation, countless others had been shot.

Under the new system a small proportion of the countryside was organized into large state-farms run by officials with hired labour; on these a great deal of useful experimentation was conducted. The vast bulk of the cultivated land, possibly over 90 per cent., was organized into collective farms. These naturally varied in size and nature according to circumstances, but they all conformed to a general pattern laid down by government regulations. On each collective farm the peasants pool their land, after reserving up to about five acres for their own private use. The farm is then run co-operatively under the direction of an elected committee of management. Brigades of workers (mainly the peasants and their families) perform their tasks on the farm as a whole without regard to individual poolings of land, and all work done is credited, according to its amount and its skill, to every individual worker. The harvest is later shared out among the various interests involved. Part goes to the government at a price well below the market-price; this may be regarded as rent for the land, which legally belongs to the State, though the peasant's use of it is guaranteed. Part goes to the local machine tractor station; this is for services rendered in the way of research and the hire of machinery, and is an indication of the mechanization of agriculture which has accompanied collectivization. Part is reserved for future sowings, and part is used to finance village amenities such as halls, libraries, or recreation-grounds. The remainder is then divided among the peasantry in proportion to the number of work-days performed over the past year.

The combined result of many factors has been a tremendous advance in agricultural production and a marked improvement in the amenities of village-life. Yet it would be idle to pretend that difficulties no longer exist. Whenever, for any reason, government vigilance is slackened the peasantry is still apt to push its individual interests beyond the limits laid down in the regulations. Examples occurred during the turmoil of the Second World War, when peasants falsified their number of work-days, or increased their own private holdings over the legal maximum of five acres.

The Stalin Constitution (1936)

By the middle thirties Stalin judged the time ripe for a new Constitution, replacing that of Lenin in 1923. On the assumption that a classless society now existed, certain features of the earlier Constitution were discarded. Every man and woman aged eighteen or over was given the vote; this ended the previous discrimination against the peasantry and the disfranchisement of priests, nepmen, and other 'misfits.' Instead of the old system of voting by show of hands, the secret ballot was introduced; the remarkable advance in literacy accomplished by the Soviet educational system facilitated this change. Furthermore, instead of a pyramid of soviets with the bottom layers electing those above, the various soviets, high and low, were now directly elected by the voters. Stalin retained, however, the federal nature of the state. There were still the Union Republics and other smaller units representing the different racial groups and possessing limited powers over their own affairs, and as before these were federated into the all-embracing Union of Socialist Soviet Republics, or U.S.S.R. Every Union Republic elected its own soviet; municipalities and country districts had their councils too. For the whole country there was a Supreme Soviet composed of two Houses: the Soviet of the Union, elected in roughly equal constituencies, like the British House of Commons; and the Soviet of Nationalities, for which every Union Republic, no matter what its size (and this varied enormously), elected twenty-five members. The Supreme Soviet elected from among its members a Praesidium, or standing committee, to perform its functions when it was not sitting; the President of this Praesidium is usually known as the President of the U.S.S.R., and is the titular head of the state. The actual work of government was in the hands of commissars, or ministers, each one being in charge of a department such as War or Finance or Foreign Affairs; they had to be approved by the Supreme Soviet, which from time to time had the chance of judging their policies.

Such in outline has been the Soviet system of government from 1936 to the present day. But it would be misleading to leave it at that. In practice the Communist Party rules Soviet Russia—or, rather, that section of the party that can assert its power over its rivals. The Constitution guarantees the individual many freedoms: of speech, of conscience, of assembly. He is guaranteed also the right to work, and holidays with pay. The constituent Republics have the theoretical right to leave the Union if they wish. The Russian worker has, it is true, been free from the nightmare of unemployment that has at times haunted his counterpart in the west. But most of his 'constitutional' freedoms exist on paper only, or in ways which, while they might seem proper to many Russians, are quite out of tune with western democratic ideas. The Communist Party is the only political party allowed; it numbered in 1954 about 6,000,000 out of a total population of about 200,000,000. It has sections for the young: the Pioneers for those up to fifteen years, the Komsomol for those up to twenty-five. At elections there is only one candidate for each constituency. He (or she) is chosen as candidate after consultations between local organizations; he need not be a member of the party, but must be approved by it. The voter can signify disapproval by not voting or by crossing out the candidate's name, but he cannot put forward any opposition candidate. All key-positions in the state are held by the leaders of the party. Supreme power really resides in the Political Committee of the party, the *Politburo*, composed of about a dozen leaders.

If the Communist Party rules the state, who rules the Communist Party? Lenin held an all-party congress every year; Stalin extended the interval to four or even more years. The struggle between Stalin and Trotsky was not decided by methods familiar to western democracy. In the very year of the new Constitution, and again in 1937 and 1938, an astonished world witnessed the trials of several score of Bolshevik leaders on charges of Trotskyism, sabotage, treason, and similar offences. The accused included veterans of the Revolution like Zinoviev and Kamenev, as well as eight Russian generals. They were found guilty, and for the most part executed. The real ruler of Russia was Stalin, General Secretary of the Communist Party, though this is not to deny that probably the vast majority of Russians supported his rule. In the circumstances there is no sure way of finding out.

Soviet Achievement

The Russian lives under a totalitarian system which fashions his thoughts and restricts his contacts with other countries. He is also subject to the vast bureaucracy inherent in a planned state, and in some respects the privileges and rewards of those at the top are more marked than in the west.

But there is another side to the picture. Apart from the fact that the Russian has never experienced western democratic methods, and is therefore apt to view things differently from ourselves, Soviet Russia has numerous worthwhile achievements to its credit. A semi-feudal agricultural country has been modernized and industrialized.

An illiterate country has been made literate. The rights of the sub-ject-nationalities have received greater recognition than ever before. There is far more equality of opportunity than in Tsarist days. The people have been given a new sense of purpose. If their standard of living still falls short of that in the west, it is much higher than it was half a century ago.

Chapter 12

THE NEW EUROPE: GERMANY, ITALY, AND FRANCE

GERMANY

GERMANY A REPUBLIC

On November 9, 1918, the Kaiser William II abdicated and fled; his example was followed by about twenty princes of the separate German states. The last Imperial Chancellor, Prince Max of Baden, transferred his powers to Friedrich Ebert, an ex-saddler by trade, and leader of the Social Democratic Party. By the next day the socialists had formed a provisional government, and a republic had been proclaimed.

The new government concluded the armistice for November 11, and was faced with the usual varied tasks involved in the transition from war to peace. Over and above these, it had to maintain law and order, and as soon as possible establish a regular form of government. Germany was in a state of turmoil. The older parties of the Right, representing the industrialists, the large landowners or Junkers, the militarists, and others, were discredited. The Social Democrats themselves were divided into the more moderate majority section (to which Ebert belonged) and the left-wing independent socialists. More extreme still were the communists, intent on seizing power by violence and establishing a soviet system after the Russian model. Ebert's provisional government took stern measures against the forces of disruption. The Berlin communists, or Spartacists (from Spartacus, leader of a slave-revolt in ancient Rome), staged a revolt early in January 1919. It was suppressed, and the Spartacist leaders, Karl Liebknecht and Rosa Luxemburg, were brutally shot by the police while on their way to prison.

Meanwhile the government had arranged for elections to be held on January 19, 1919, for a National Assembly to draw up a permanent

Constitution. In February the assembly met at Weimar, a picturesque, old-world town in Central Germany, associated with Goethe and Schiller.

THE WEIMAR CONSTITUTION

The Weimar Assembly was composed largely of moderate socialists and middle-class democrats. It deliberated from February to late summer in circumstances of extreme difficulty. Germany was still torn by strikes, and by risings from the Left and the Right; the continued Allied blockade, largely due to the German government's refusal to use its own money and ships for imports, produced undernourishment and starvation; the Treaty of Versailles, published in May and signed in June, was regarded as a national humiliation. Despite these obstacles the assembly went ahead, guided largely by a Professor of Constitutional History named Preuss, and on July 21, 1919, the Weimar Constitution received its final assent.

Under the new Constitution the individual German was guaranteed such rights as liberty of speech, conscience, association, and writing. Despite the wishes of Preuss and others, Germany was to continue as a federal state composed of eighteen separate *Länder*, as they were now called. Prussia was easily the largest—larger, in fact, than the rest put together; Bavaria, Württemberg, and Saxony may be mentioned as illustrating the others. Like Germany as a whole, every component state had to adopt a republican and democratic form of government, and the powers left to the states were small and somewhat vague.

The titular head of the Reich—*i.e.*, of the all-German federation—was to be the President, elected directly by universal suffrage (men and women over twenty years of age,) and by a clear majority of all votes cast. He held office for seven years, and was eligible for re-election. Normally he acted as a figurehead, but in a sudden emergency he possessed the power of suspending individual rights and ruling by decrees. The Weimar Assembly had at the beginning chosen Ebert as the first President without resort to the popular election later provided for; Ebert continued in office till his death in 1925.

The German Parliament was to consist of two Houses. The

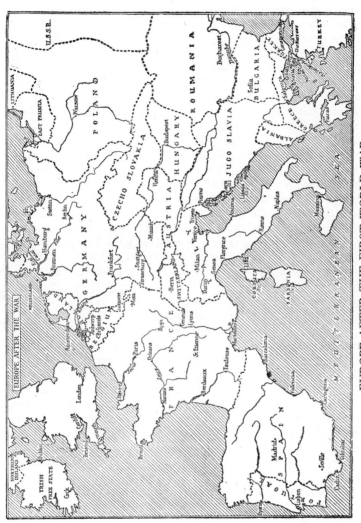

EUROPE AFTER THE FIRST WORLD WAR

Reichstag, corresponding to the British House of Commons, was to be elected every four years by adult male and female suffrage under a system of proportional representation. The country was divided into large constituencies, and each party could put forward a list of candidates; a candidate had to obtain 60,000 votes to be elected, any surplus being transferred to the second preferences on his list. In this way the Reichstag would almost exactly mirror the political opinion of the country. Unlike the former imperial Reichstag, the new body had wide powers, and was the dominant House. It controlled the finances, and, what was novel and extremely important, it controlled the government. The latter, consisting of the Chancellor and his ministers, could be called to account and dismissed by the Reichstag, in the same way as the British government is responsible to the House of Commons. The second House was the Reichsrat, which took the place of the former Bundesrat. The Reichsrat represented the various states, or *Länder*, by allowing the *government* of each state to send representatives to it. The number sent was roughly proportionate to each state's population; but to prevent Prussia from having a clear majority it was provided that no state could have more than two-fifths of the total number of seats. Although the Reichsrat was intended to act as a brake upon hasty legislation, its opposition could be overruled by a two-thirds majority in the Reichstag.

Two further features deserve mention. If a sufficient number of the Reichstag or the electorate demanded, controversial matters had to be submitted to a plebiscite or vote of the whole people; this was done, for instance, over the question of compensation to former dispossessed rulers. There was also established a National Economic Council, representing employers and employees in the major industries. Its function was to advise Parliament upon economic questions; but in practice it was one of the least successful features of the new Constitution.

Apart from the possible objection that proportional representation and resort to plebiscites might lead to weak governments by giving the people too much power, the Weimar Constitution was as good an effort as could be made to establish a democratic Germany. It remained to be seen whether, in face of the many pitfalls that beset her, Germany could make it work.

PARTIES AND GOVERNMENTS

Among the chief political parties at this time may be mentioned the communists on the extreme Left, the Social Democrats, or socialists (split into two main wings themselves), the Democrats (or Liberals), the Catholic Centre Party, and the Right-wing People's Party and National Party. There were also many smaller parties now or later; by the end of the decade there were about thirty all told. Partly for this reason, and partly because of proportional representation, most governments were coalitions, with the Social Democrats prominent at first, and with the rather more Right-wing parties prominent later on. Governments were also unstable and short-lived —an unfortunate start for the new republic. In the first twenty-one months there were four different Chancellors, and the situation saw little improvement as time went on. Only one statesman of note was thrown up in the 1920's: Gustav Stresemann, Chancellor August to November 1923, and thereafter Foreign Minister throughout many governments till his death in 1929. He was the guiding hand in Germany during his six years of office; but it is significant that even he could not hold the Chancellorship for long. Germany's failure to produce stable governments during these years was the result not only of her lack of experience in democratic methods of give-and-take, but also of the difficulties that confronted her both at home and abroad.

On the death of Ebert in 1925 the hero of the First World War, Field-Marshal von Hindenburg, was elected President. Supporters of the old order in Germany looked forward to a return of the monarchy, but Hindenburg disappointed them. He had sworn to be faithful to the republic, and he kept his word.

INTERNAL ENEMIES OF THE REPUBLIC

From the very beginning the Weimar Republic had to meet the challenge of many of its own people. The communists continued their attacks, but the chief danger was from the forces of the Right: from the militarists, from wealthy industrialists like von Thyssen, from the Junkers, and from members of the old Civil Service, including judges and teachers. The new republic was distasteful to them on two grounds. One, because many Germans were still at heart monarchists who disliked the democratic republic on principle, especially as it was controlled in the early days by the socialists. Even Stresemann, faithful to the Republic as he was, corresponded with the ex-Crown Prince in exile, and was privately a monarchist. Secondly, the Weimar Republic was associated in many German minds with the humiliations of the Treaty of Versailles which it had been obliged to accept —with war-guilt, reparations, disarmament, Allied occupation forces, and loss of territory at home and abroad. German governments in the 1920's were between the devil and the deep sea; if they tried to satisfy the Allies they were reviled by their own countrymen, but if they resisted the Allies the terms were likely to be made worse. From this angle the Allied governments themselves are not free from blame for the unpopularity and eventual collapse of the republic. In time the absurd legend grew up among Germans that their armies had never been defeated, but that they had been 'stabbed in the back' by Jews, socialists, and other traitors at home. This increased dissatisfaction with the Weimar Republic, which seemed in itself to embody many of these 'traitors.'

A few facts will illustrate the form this opposition took. In 1920 a former Prussian official, Kapp, aided by military forces which had refused to disband, seized part of Berlin with the intention of proclaiming a new government. The regular government fled to Stuttgart, where it managed to quell the rising by calling on the Berlin workers to strike. In 1922 the Foreign Minister, Rathenau, a Jew, was murdered by ex-officers of the Army. In 1923 a somewhat obscure ex-corporal, Adolf Hitler, staged a rising at Munich in favour of his National Socialist, or Nazi, Party; it was easily suppressed. The National Socialists were but one of several groups which possessed private armies to terrorize their opponents and defy the government. In government offices, in the schools, and even in the law-courts enemies of the Republic voiced their views, often with no attempt at concealment. The government took little action, partly because of its excessive belief in the virtues of free speech, and partly because it was powerless to do much about it. If it called on the military for assistance it might meet with refusal; or if the military acted the government might find itself at the mercy of its own protectors.

THE REPARATIONS TANGLE

The problem of reparations raised many difficult questions. There was the moral question of Germany's war-guilt. There were political issues, particularly the advisability of prolonging a matter which poisoned international relations and weakened the reputation of the Weimar governments among their own people. Finally, there were economic factors. How much could Germany pay, having regard to her impoverishment? In what form could she pay it? Not in gold, as there was not enough in the world; not in German marks, as these lost their value outside Germany; if, then, in goods, how could this be done without creating surpluses and unemployment in the receiving countries? Similar problems arose, incidentally, over the repayment of war-debts between the Allies themselves; France and others owed Britain much money, while Britain owed much to the U.S.A. A few years after the War the British government announced its willingness to cancel all its claims to reparations and war-debts, if other countries would join in a general settlement along these lines; but this proposal was turned down.

The Paris peace conference had left the total amount of reparations to be determined by a commission, and this body in 1921 fixed the amount at £6,600,000,000. For a year or so Germany struggled to make her periodic payments, mostly in coal, shipping, or timber; but she was sorely strained, and her currency began to lose its value through inflation—*i.e.*, excessive issues. France grew increasingly impatient, and had never given up hopes of creating a separate Rhineland state; her Premier at this time was Poincaré, in whom burned a passionate hatred of Germany. An excuse for action came when Germany committed a technical default over her supplies of timber. In January 1923 French and Belgian troops occupied the Ruhr, the main centre of Germany's coal-mines and heavy industries. The British government opposed this action; but France thought she had at last found a way of satisfying her desires. Economically, she would work German industry for her own benefit; politically, she would create a separate state under her own control. The tragic sequel upset all these calculations. The German government ordered the workers to strike, and without their assistance the French could not work the industries. It was the same with French schemes to establish a Rhineland state; although they found a few Germans willing to co-operate, the majority remained aloof. Scenes of violence, sometimes involving fatalities, inevitably occurred. The German financial situation grew fantastic as the German government printed countless notes to pay the millions of workers on strike. Prices rocketed, and the German middle-classes found their savings worthless. France too found that the military occupation and the attempts to work the Ruhr industries were costing her more than she was getting back in return.

The tragedy of the Ruhr came to a slow end. In August 1923 Stresemann became Chancellor and Foreign Minister, holding the latter office till his death at the end of 1929. Without in the least accepting the Ruhr occupation or other humiliations, he was none the less anxious for an honourable settlement. His policy was one of 'fulfilment'—*i.e.*, of meeting Germany's legal requirements under the Treaty of Versailles. He soon ended the policy of passive resistance in the Ruhr. In May 1924 France disowned Poincaré, whom a year back she had hailed, and a more conciliatory government took over. Finally a committee under the American banker General Dawes drew up a new reparations plan (1924). In November 1924 the occupation of the Ruhr ended.

The Dawes plan heralded the brightest period in the inter-war years. It was followed in 1925 by the Locarno Pact, and in 1926 by Germany's admission to the League of Nations (see Chapter 14). Reparations payments proceeded smoothly—and no wonder! For foreign countries, particularly the U.S.A., were lending Germany tremendous sums to put her on her feet again. This continued till 1929, when the U.S.A. ceased to lend money, and began to call in what she had already lent. Stresemann died in October of the same year, but not before he had negotiated the final withdrawal of Allied troops from the Rhineland, which took place in 1930, five years before the time-limit fixed at Versailles. Meanwhile a new attempt was being made by the Young Committee to reach a final settlement of the reparations question. Its arduous labours were wasted. The world was soon in the throes of an economic crisis, in which reparations and war-debts were thrown overboard. The Nazis came to power, and Germany's history underwent a remarkable change.

ITALY

A DISCONTENTED NATION

The immediate post-war years brought disillusionment and discontent to Italy. She had entered the War in 1915 in the expectation of considerable territorial gains as promised by the Treaty of London. Her forces, it is true, had been badly beaten at Caporetto in 1917, but her war-effort had been on a large scale. The peace conference proved a humiliation to her, and her Prime Minister, Orlando, quitted it in disgust. President Wilson in particular opposed Italian demands as contrary to his doctrine of self-determination. As we have already seen on page 130, Italy obtained the Trentino district and the Austrian-inhabited South Tyrol, together with the Istrian peninsula (including Trieste) and the port of Zara, on the Dalmatian coast. Other territories promised by the Treaty of London were, however, denied her. She did not obtain the rest of the Dalmatian coast; she did not obtain a protectorate over Albania; she did not obtain an acre of German Africa; she was unable to retain any of Asia Minor in face of Greek ambitions and the Turkish revival under Mustapha Kemal. With regard to Africa, negotiations were begun at the peace conference, and concluded some years later, for a few frontier adjustments. Jubaland was transferred from British Kenya to Italian Somaliland; Libya was enlarged by transferring a strip of the Sahara desert from French to Italian control.

Italian dissatisfaction found immediate vent in an unofficial attempt to seize the port of Fiume, an Istrian port inhabited largely by Italians, but which had *not* been promised Italy under the Treaty of London. In September 1919 the romantic Italian poet and airman Gabriele D'Annunzio occupied Fiume with volunteer forces of his own, defying the Allies, whose small forces had to retire, and defying his own government, which although sympathetic dared not support him. For fifteen months he staged a scene fit almost for a comic opera, were it not for its sombre background. Daily parades were held, impassioned speeches were made, and a delegate even opened up an office in Paris. Not till November 1920 did the Italian and Yugoslav governments agree that Fiume should be independent under the League of Nations. Even then D'Annunzio refused to budge, and

Italian forces were sent to eject him (January 1921). But it was the poet who had interpreted Italian national feeling; the government was despised for betraying it.

Parliamentary democracy, never very strongly rooted, was now withering. Governments were weak and short-lived, and seemed quite incapable of tackling Italy's many problems. The socialists were growing in strength in Parliament, and their left wing was increasingly seeking inspiration from Soviet Russia. Food was scarce and prices high. Strikes, accompanied by violence, were widespread. They reached their height in the autumn of 1920, when the workers of North Italy seized some six hundred factories with the object of running them themselves. They held out for over ten weeks, after which they were forced through accumulated difficulties to negotiate a settlement with their employers. The Red menace was never again so threatening. All sorts of societies were being formed, characterized by disgust at existing conditions and a determination to end them, if necessary by violence. They found ready recruits among the returning ex-soldiers. Among these societies was the *Fascio Italiani di Combattimento*, founded in March 1919 by Benito Mussolini.

THE FASCISTS TAKE OVER

Mussolini was born in 1883, the son of a blacksmith. He was to change his political colour many times before he ended up with the blackshirts of Fascism. After a short period of teaching in his native country, he went to Switzerland, where he engaged in socialist agitation. He returned to Italy and became editor of the socialist paper *Avanti*, in which he vigorously attacked the imperialism of his own country, which was just then manifesting itself in the war against Turkey (1911–12) for the possession of Tripoli. The monarchy, the Church, and Italian nationalism all came under attack. On the outbreak of war in 1914 he advocated Italy's intervention on the Allied side. This led him to part company with his socialist colleagues, to give up the editorship of *Avanti*, and to found a new socialist paper, *Il Popolo d'Italia*, in which he urged his views. He served in the Italian Army during the War, rising, like Hitler, to the rank of corporal, and was invalided out as a result of wounds sustained from an accidental explosion. The post-war turmoil provided just the right atmosphere for his ambition, and in March 1919 he founded, as we have seen, his *Fascio Italiani di Combattimento*—the Italian Union of Combatants. The word *Fascio* meant 'bundle' or 'collection,' and was later associated by the Fascists with the *fasces*, or bundles of rods, that were carried before the consuls of ancient Rome as a symbol of their authority.

For more than two years Mussolini manœuvred for power. Although posing as the champion of the workers, he denounced the socialists as dupes of communist propaganda. After the strikes of 1920 he became more violently anti-Bolshevik than ever, and soon began to draw support from the peasantry and the middle-classes. D'Annunzio's disbanded soldiers also swelled his numbers. In the spring of 1921 the Fascists, with their founder, obtained 35 seats in the Parliamentary elections, and soon afterwards Mussolini assumed the title of Il Duce, or the Leader. For the next year guerilla warfare raged throughout the land. Bands of Fascists beat up communists, socialists, and Catholics with bludgeons or dosed them with castor-oil, all in the name of law and order, which Mussolini claimed to be enforcing. He appeared, in default of strong governments, to be the one man able to save Italy from Bolshevism, and soon the big industrialists and landowners began to finance him. In September 1922 he dropped his previous republicanism, and thus won the King, Victor Emmanuel III, to his side. At the same time his attacks on the Church were toned down. He was preparing to strike. The Army leaders, likewise scornful of the weak government established by Parliament, promised not to interfere. In October 1922 the so-called March on Rome took place. Thousands of Fascists converged on the capital from all directions. When it was safely occupied their Duce came on in a sleeping-car from Milan. The Prime Minister, Facta, resigned, and Mussolini took office at the head of a coalition government. As Prime Minister, Foreign Minister, and Minister for Home Affairs, Mussolini now controlled Italy.

FASCIST ITALY: DOMESTIC AFFAIRS

Mussolini had no ready-made policy for his country, though

certain broad facts were clear. First and foremost he intended to keep himself in power. His opposition to Parliamentary methods of government sprang from this desire, and from the weakness of Parliament in recent years. In contrast to his views in early life, he now bitterly opposed, not only democracy, but socialism, pacifism, and internationalism. By converse his positive policy emphasized the following points: a strong and closely knit state in which the individual was subordinated to the common aim, as defined by Mussolini and his party; a state as self-sufficient as possible in its economy, in order to reduce Italy's dependence on foreign nations; in the international sphere an assertion of Italy's rights by the same methods of bluster and force which had won Fascism its victory in the domestic sphere. In short, his policy was one of strength for Italy, to be attained by methods of dictatorship and totalitarianism.

Mussolini retained the monarchy and Parliament, but subordinated them to his own ends. In 1923 a new electoral law assured the Fascists a substantial Parliamentary majority. A young socialist deputy, Matteotti, who protested against this law was brutally done to death by Fascists in the following year. Similar methods of force were used against all other opponents. In 1928 an entirely new electoral system was introduced, calculated to make Parliament a mere pawn on the Fascist chess-board. The various industrial and professional organizations of Italy (themselves controlled by Fascists) submitted a list of over a thousand names as possible Parliamentary candidates. From these the Fascist Grand Council, consisting of Mussolini and his henchmen, selected four hundred, who were then submitted *en bloc* to the electorate. With no alternative nominations, the electors always approved Mussolini's list. There was no freedom of speech or of the Press. Boys and girls were organized into junior branches of the Fascist party, and made to repeat such slogans as "Mussolini is always right," or taught that Italy had won the War for her allies.

In contradistinction to the communist doctrine of the class war, Mussolini developed what he called the corporate state. Fascist-controlled syndicates of workers and of employers were formed, and the local syndicates were built up to form nation-wide confederations representing the two sides in Italy's main industries—agriculture, commerce, banking, etc. Later these confederations, with other bodies representing Italy's cultural life, were formed into corporations and joined together into a National Council of Corporations. Employers had to improve working conditions in some instances, but there was no question of the workers gaining ownership or control, as in the other great totalitarian state, Soviet Russia.

Mussolini carried out many schemes of economic development. Roads, ports, schools, tenement-flats, and so on were constructed; it used to be boasted that for the first time in Italy's history the trains ran on time. The Pontine Marshes were drained, and the monuments of ancient Rome restored to remind Italy of her glorious past. To reduce Italian dependence on foreign coal hydro-electric schemes were put in hand. Great efforts were made to make Italy self-sufficient in wheat-production, and Mussolini himself was often photographed stripped to the waist working in the fields. The so-called 'battle of the grain' had been won by 1932.

One of Mussolini's most striking successes was in effecting a settlement with the Roman Catholic Church. Since 1870 the Pope had refused to recognize the Italian kingdom or to set foot outside the Vatican on territory taken from him by the 'usurper' (see page 46). Mussolini himself was not religious, and viewed such questions strictly from the statesman's point of view. The majority of his countrymen were Catholic; it was essential, therefore, in a totalitarian state to regularize the position of the Church. Quite early after seizing power he pleased the Church by suppressing freemasonry. He soon went further by introducing services, including the Mass, into public ceremonies, and also by instituting religious teaching in the schools. In this favourable atmosphere negotiations were begun with Pope Pius XI, and in 1929 the Lateran Treaty and Concordat were concluded. The Pope was recognized as temporal sovereign of the Vatican City, with its area of about one hundred acres. The Roman Catholic faith became the sole religion of the state, and its laws regarding marriage and morals were to be enforced. The Pope was also granted some monetary compensation for the territories taken from him in 1870. In return the Pope recognized the kingdom of Italy under the House of Savoy, and regarded the Roman question as "definitely and irrevocably settled."

This indeed was a personal triumph for Mussolini; but it was soon marred by a dispute regarding the training of the young. The Pope objected that the Fascist youth organizations took young people from the Church clubs and administered oaths of obedience to the Duce contrary to Catholic teaching. Mussolini retorted by closing the Church clubs, but after some time a compromise solution was reached.

FASCIST ITALY: FOREIGN POLICY TO 1930

Dictators who have successfully used gangster methods at home are inevitably prone to use similar methods abroad. Mussolini was no exception. War, he preached, provided the supreme test for human effort, and was virtuous in itself. Like most of his countrymen, he was dissatisfied with Italy's small gains following the War. His general object was to extend Italian power and influence wherever possible, even if it meant flouting the recently established peace settlement.

The Adriatic was one of the two chief scenes of Mussolini's activities in the 1920's. Italy was disappointed that she had not been given a legal protectorship over Albania. Her special rights had, however, been recognized by the Allies in 1921. By loans and missions Mussolini proceeded to apply these rights, and by 1926–27 Albania, a poor country of 1,000,000 inhabitants, was virtually, though still not legally, an Italian protectorate.

In 1923 four Italians and an Albanian were murdered while engaged in their official task of fixing the boundary between Albania and Greece. This gave Mussolini his first chance of championing Italian rights by strong-arm methods. He presented the Greek government with a note demanding an apology, an inquiry with Italian assistance, death-sentence for the culprits, and an indemnity of fifty million lire. When the Greek government rejected some of these terms Italian warships bombarded the Greek island of Corfu, killing fifteen civilians, and Italian forces then occupied the island. A complicated dispute followed in which Mussolini objected to any intervention by the League of Nations, and insisted that Greece should pay the indemnity direct to Italy. He was allowed to have his way, whereupon the Italians handed back Corfu. Altogether the incident demonstrated two disturbing facts: one, that the new dictator was completely out of tune with the ideals of the League; two, that the League was ready to take the line of least resistance in its dealings with one of the major powers.

In 1924 Italy and Yugoslavia came to a friendly agreement regarding Fiume. The Allied idea of making it into a Free State like Danzig was ignored. Instead Italy obtained the main port, and Yugoslavia obtained adjacent areas and rights of using the port. As time went on this new spirit of friendship dwindled with the growing anxiety of Yugoslavia over Italy's designs in Albania.

Farther afield, Mussolini championed those powers, like Austria and Hungary, which shared Italy's dissatisfaction with the peace-treaties. In 1924 Jubaland was officially transferred from British Kenya to Italian Somaliland. With France Mussolini's relations continued unfriendly. Quarrels occurred over the rights of the numerous Italians living in the French colony of Tunisia. Furthermore, Mussolini regarded Italy as the dominant power in south-east Europe, and resented French attempts to build up alliances with Yugoslavia and Czechoslovakia. But he was as yet not strong enough to act the bully in a large way; his chance came when the appearance of Nazi Germany weakened the relative strength of the democratic countries.

FRANCE

POST-WAR FRANCE

Unlike most of the larger Continental countries, France continued after the War with the political Constitution which had served her before the War—namely, the Third Republic, established in 1875. She emerged as one of the victor-powers and was enriched by the restitution of Alsace-Lorraine. But she had suffered heavily as a result of the War. One and a half million men had been killed, and several million wounded. One-tenth of her country, including the industrial area of the north-east, had been devastated. Reparations, which to the French meant literally 'repairs,' proved quite inadequate to make good the damage. Loans, printing of money, and other dubious methods were resorted to by French governments in their efforts to meet the cost. The Frenchman, even more than his counterpart in other countries, is averse to heavy taxation, and skilful in avoiding payment. Budgets were often unbalanced, and the franc fell seriously in value.

Politically also France continued to experience many difficulties. The Third Republic was assailed on the Right by Catholics and royalists, and on the Left by communists. The chief weakness, however, lay in the French party-system. The existence of numerous political groups meant that no single group ever possessed a complete majority. This led to coalitions, with their attendant bargaining, which at times degenerated into dishonesty or occasionally outright corruption. It also resulted in short-lived governments, making strong and efficient rule an impossibility. The Chamber of Deputies could not be dissolved till its four-year term of office was up; it was therefore able to turn out governments without the danger of risking a general election.

At no time was the fear of a German revival absent from the minds of Frenchmen. Foreign policy was therefore of major concern; but as this is bound up with the general European situation, it is reserved for a later chapter.

THE NINETEEN-TWENTIES: POINCARÉ AND BRIAND

'Tiger' Clemenceau had resigned the Premiership in 1920. The next ten years produced many Premiers and several Presidents, but two names are outstanding, Raymond Poincaré and Aristide Briand. They were sharply contrasted in many respects, though they often worked in harness. Poincaré (1860–1934) was a Lorrainer by birth, who in his eleventh year saw his native province stolen by Germany. He chose to live in France and work for the day of restoration. His outlook was intensely nationalist. He was to the Right in domestic politics, and in character was stern and uncompromising. He had been Premier once before the War, and was President of France from 1913 to 1920, the very years of the French struggle to win the War and the peace that followed. Briand (1862–1932) began his political career as a socialist, but he soon moved over to the less extreme, but still Left Wing, radical groups. He had promoted the separation of

Church and State from 1905 onward, was twice Premier before the War and once during it. Temperamentally he was quicker, more adaptable, and more versatile than Poincaré, and although his French patriotism was undoubted, he possessed a wider international outlook than the Lorrainer.

Briand was Premier and in charge of foreign affairs from 1921 to 1922. In the latter year he was accused of leniency towards Germany over reparations, and forced to resign. Poincaré succeeded him, holding office from 1922 to 1924. The new Premier was intent upon exacting the full 'pound of flesh' from Germany, and in January 1923, following a technical default in German payments, Poincaré ordered the occupation of the Ruhr. The tragedy of this episode has been previously described. The cheers of his countrymen changed to murmurs of discontent as it became clear that the occupation was costing France far more than it was squeezing out of Germany. Poincaré had to impose new taxes upon France—and in 1924 he fell from office.

Early in 1925 Briand became Foreign Minister, later in the year succeeding to the Premiership as well, but the latter only for a short period. Briand remained in control of French foreign policy from 1925 to 1931, thus giving it a continuity that contrasted sharply with the changes of premiership that occurred during these years. This was the period of the Locarno Pact (1925), of Germany's admission to the League (1926), of the Briand-Kellogg Peace Pact (1928), and of Briand's vision of the United States of Europe. It is the domestic situation that must engage our attention just now, and here the worsening of the financial situation led to the recall of Poincaré to the premiership as the one man strong enough to give France the medicine she needed. In 1926 Poincaré formed a widely based coalition government, containing within it six former Premiers; it lasted till 1929—an unusually long span for a French government—when Poincaré resigned on account of ill-health. By then the government had achieved its task. By stringent methods the budget was balanced for the first time for many years. In the process the franc had been devalued to one-fifth of its pre-war value. All those with investments had lost four-fifths of the real value of their savings; from another angle, it meant that the French government's debt to its own people was reduced to one-fifth of its former value. The medicine was indeed strong, but it proved effective. On Poincaré's resignation in 1929 Briand had another short ministry which failed to see the year out. He continued as Foreign Minister till 1931, when he too retired from active politics.

THE NINETEEN-THIRTIES: WEAKNESS AND DIVISION

The story of the Third Republic in the years preceding the Second World War is not a happy one. The usual weaknesses continued to show themselves. Budgets were unbalanced, the value of the franc again fell, and in one period of thirteen months there were five different ministries. In 1934 corruption was uncovered in high places over the Stavisky affair. Stavisky was a Russian-born Jew, resident most of his life in France. He was a thoroughgoing scoundrel engaged in all sorts of financial swindles. When the police got on his track over his management of the Bayonne municipal pawnshop he committed suicide. Inquiries revealed that he had seven years earlier been caught in a swindle totalling 7,500,000 francs, but he had been released and the affair hushed up because too many big names, even in government circles, were involved. Many believed that his 'suicide' had been arranged by the authorities.

The Stavisky scandal was the signal for both fascist and communist riots in Paris in February 1934, when many lives were lost. People were losing faith in Parliamentary government. The ordeal passed off safely; but the fascist threat, both at home and abroad, led in 1936 to the formation of the Popular Front, a Left Wing alliance between the communists, socialists, and radical socialists. The Popular Front won the election, and the socialist leader, Léon Blum, a highly cultured and sincere man of Jewish origin, formed a government. The communists supported him by their votes, but refused to accept office. Blum dissolved the royalist and fascist societies, on the surface at any rate. He instituted a forty-hour working week with holidays with pay, nationalized the arms industry, and brought the Bank of France under government control. But it was hardly the time for 'bread and games' when the growing threat from Hitler, Mussolini, and maybe Franco demanded harder work and greater self-sacrifice. Production declined and prices rose. Blum's foreign policy, conditioned largely by that of Britain, was not sufficiently anti-fascist to please his friends on the Left, while his socialist policy had infuriated his enemies on the Right. In 1937 he resigned.

His successors repealed the forty-hour week and stepped up production and rearmament. But the political and economic weaknesses of France were too deep-seated to be got rid of overnight. France was in a poor position to withstand the German onslaught when it was launched with full fury in the spring of 1940.

Chapter 13

THE NEW EUROPE: OTHER COUNTRIES

THE SUCCESSION STATES

NEW STATES FOR OLD

THE Dual Monarchy of Austria-Hungary disappeared in 1918, and the last Hapsburg monarch, Charles I, went into exile. The old 'ramshackle empire' split into several parts, an arrangement which was confirmed by the Treaties of Saint-Germain (1919) and Trianon (1920) with Austria and Hungary respectively (see Chapter 10). The term 'succession states' is loosely given to those countries which either as a whole or in large part took the place of the old Dual Monarchy; they include, therefore, Austria, Hungary, Czechoslovakia, Yugoslavia, and possibly Roumania. This neat division of the Danube basin into its component racial groups satisfied national feelings, and was in accord with the Wilsonian doctrine of self-determination. But in so far as it solved old problems it created new ones. Minorities still existed, partly through necessity, partly through the vindictiveness of the victorious nations. Even more important, the succession states were (as is only to be expected) puffed up with pride in their newly acquired independence. They tried to make themselves as economically self-supporting as possible by stimulating new industries and by erecting tariff and other barriers against their neighbours. In this way they destroyed the former economic unity of the middle Danube basin, which had been one of the compensating advantages of the old Dual Monarchy to be set against its acknowledged disadvantages. In no case was this more illustrated than in the new republic of Austria.

AUSTRIA: A HEAD WITHOUT A BODY

The new Austria was simply the German part of the old empire left over when all the other parts had been taken away. It declared itself a republic, and established a Parliamentary system of government. Its chief difficulties were economic. The total population was six and a half millions, of which two millions lived in the capital, Vienna. The countryside was unable to support the capital, and very soon after the War Austria was faced with shortages and starvation. Far from exacting reparations from her, the Allies had to step in to assist her. From 1922 onward the League of Nations supervised the loans made by Britain, France, and others towards her recovery.

One solution of Austria's difficulties would have been to unite her with Germany. This union, or *Anschluss*, was desired by many Austrians (and, of course, by Germany itself), and agitation on its behalf continued for many years. But it was strongly opposed by France, Czechoslovakia, Poland, and others, which did not want an enlarged Germany as a result of the War. It was written into the peace-treaties that Austria could not unite with Germany without a unanimous vote of the League Council; this meant that France could always veto such a proposal. The Allied loans later made to Austria stipulated the continuance of her independence, and in 1931 when Austria and Germany proposed to join in a customs-union the scheme had to be abandoned.

It is somewhat surprising that the internal history of Austria during the 1920's was so peaceful. The chief clash was between the Social Democrats, who were strong in Vienna, and the more Right Wing Christian Socialists, who were strong in the countryside. As time went on the Right Wing parties, some of which were fascist, grew stronger. In 1932 the Christian Socialist, Dr Dollfuss, became Chancellor. In the following year, a few months after Hitler assumed office in Germany, Dollfuss made himself dictator. His policy was much like that of Mussolini's Fascism, and he strongly opposed the growing intrigues of the German Nazis to bring Austria under their control. The full story of Dollfuss and of Nazi designs upon Austria must await a later chapter.

HUNGARY: A KINGDOM WITHOUT A KING

The post-war years in Hungary, the other dominant partner in the Dual Monarchy, were even more tragic than in Austria. Hungary proclaimed herself a democratic republic, and chose as her ruler Count Karolyi, a pacifist-minded democratic nobleman who shared his own estates out among the poor. But as the Allied peace-terms became known they made Karolyi's position untenable. Hungary was to be reduced to a population of 8,000,000, practically all of Hun or Magyar descent. She had not expected to remain anywhere near her previous figure of 21,000,000; but what inflamed her was the loss of 3,000,000 Magyars to Roumania, Czechoslovakia, and Yugoslavia.

Following Karolyi's resignation (March 1919), power was seized by a young Jewish communist named Bela Kun, who had learned his creed from the fountain-head while a prisoner of war in Russia. From March to July 1919, Bela Kun imposed his Soviet Republic upon Hungary. It had the usual mixture of good and bad features; radical schemes of nationalization, land-reform, and social welfare were accompanied by a 'Red terror' in which political opponents were liquidated. The Allies in alarm authorized the Roumanian Army to suppress Bela Kun's régime. This it did, and for the next three months Budapest was subjected to a 'Roumanian Terror' accompanied by violence and wholesale looting.

When the Roumanians at length withdrew, the reactionary elements in Hungary seized power and exacted revenge upon Bela Kun's former associates, and all others of advanced leanings. This 'White Terror' was quite possibly the worst of all. The Jews were persecuted, the peasantry dispossessed, and the big landlords restored to their former vast estates. By various devices the franchise was restricted, and power concentrated in the hands of the wealthy. So Hungary remained in effect until the Second World War.

The White Terror saw the end of the Hungarian Republic proclaimed in November 1918. In March 1920 Hungary once more became a kingdom—but only in name, as the last Hapsburg, Charles, was in exile. So a regency was established with Admiral Horthy as Regent. This pretence was acceptable to the Allies so long as it remained a pretence. Charles did in fact make a few attempts to regain his throne, but the opposition of Czechoslovakia, Roumania, and Yugoslavia was too strong. When Charles died in 1922, never having legally abdicated, he left his claims to his ten-year-old-son, Otto.

Hungary continued as a kingdom without a king, dissatisfied with the peace-treaties and continually pressing for their revision.

CZECHOSLOVAKIA: A SUCCESSFUL DEMOCRACY

Czechoslovakia was formed out of Bohemia, Moravia, and other parts of the former Austro-Hungarian Empire. It contained about 14,000,000 inhabitants. The dominant groups were the Czechs and Slovaks, both Slavonic races, but with important differences between them. The Czechs numbered 7,000,000, and lived in the historic state of Bohemia. They had a long history behind them, with traditions of national aspirations against the Germans and Austrians, and among their remembered figures from past centuries were "good King Wenceslas" and their national hero, John Huss, who had forfeited his life in 1415 in defying the Catholic Church. Their University of Prague was one of the oldest in Europe. The Czechs were more advanced in all ways than their Slovak cousins, who consisted of 2,000,000 peasants, for the most part illiterate and downtrodden as a result of oppressive Hungarian rule. The most important minority was the 3,000,000 or more Sudeten Germans inhabiting the Sudeten and other mountains dividing Bohemia from Germany. In addition there were nearly 1,000,000 Magyars (who should have belonged to Hungary) and 500,000 Ruthenians, closely related to the Ukrainians of Russia.

The Czechoslovak Republic was proclaimed in October 1918, and its first president was Thomas Masaryk, the son of a Slovak coachman and a Czech servant-girl. Masaryk grew to be one of the most cultured and educated men of his country, and for a time held a professorship at Prague University. His marriage to an American heiress gave him useful social and political links with the U.S.A. The War provided him with the opportunity of realizing his life's ambition—namely, the independence of his country on the basis of Czech-Slovak unity. He was in the U.S.A. when the new republic was officially proclaimed in 1918, and was in his absence chosen to be its first president. He was re-elected several times, holding the office until his retirement in his eighty-fifth year in 1935; he died two years later. He was succeeded as president by his friend Dr Eduard Benes, who had been Foreign Minister through many changes of government over the whole period 1918 to 1935. Both Masaryk and Benes were men of wide vision and noble ideals. To them is largely due the fact that Czechoslovakia remained till her overthrow by Nazi Germany an island of enlightenment and democracy amid the invading seas of intolerance and dictatorship that beset her.

It must not be imagined that Czechoslovakia was free from all criticism or dissension. The minorities complained frequently of ill-treatment, although they were among the best treated in Europe. The new state incurred the hostility of Hungary when she joined with Roumania and Yugoslavia (her partners in the Little Entente) to prevent a Hapsburg restoration. The government's greatest achievement, in Masaryk's view, was the break-up of the large estates and the division of the land among the peasantry. Bohemia was also the centre of many industries, in which an eight-hour day with benefits during sickness, old age, and other contingencies was introduced. Hemmed in by other states, and with no seaboard, she found difficulties at times in marketing her products. In political matters she adopted in 1920 a democratic Constitution, in which women had the vote. Even more important, her people were for the most part imbued with a genuine democratic outlook, without which the best of Constitutions will not successfully work.

YUGOSLAVIA: A DIVIDED STATE

Yugoslavia, the country of the South, or *Yugo*, Slavs, was formed in 1918 by the union of Serbia, Montenegro, parts of the old Austro-Hungarian Empire, and a few small bits and pieces from Bulgaria. Its chief racial groups consisted of 6,000,000 Serbs, nearly 3,000,000 Croats, and 1,000,000 Slovenes, out of a total population of 13,000,000. Serbs, Croats, and Slovenes are all Slavonic, but with important differences. The Serbs are Orthodox in religion, and centuries of Turkish rule had left them backward. The Croats and Slovenes are Roman Catholic, and even under the Dual Monarchy had preserved certain rights which made them more advanced than their Serbian cousins.

The Croats and Slovenes wished the new state to be a federal one, in which the three main groups would enjoy a large measure of self-government. The Serbs, on the other hand, desired a unitary state in which they, as the majority group, would have the major control. The Serbs had their way, and their King, Alexander I, became the ruling monarch. This led to bitter strife, and in 1929 Alexander suspended the Constitution and established a royal dictatorship. In 1934 Alexander was assassinated at Marseilles by a Croatian-trained Macedonian terrorist. He was succeeded by his eleven-year-old son, Peter II, for whom a regency was proclaimed. Croatian agitation for greater independence continued down to the Second World War.

POLAND

PILSUDSKI AND THE PROBLEMS OF POLAND

The Poles are a Slavonic people, but their Roman Catholic religion has for centuries divided them from the Orthodox Slavs of Russia. Ever since the disappearance of Poland in the eighteenth century Polish patriots had dreamed of a revival of their country's independence. The outbreak of war in 1914 had, on the face of it, hardly increased the chances of this dream being realized. If Germany won it appeared likely that her hold over the Poles would be extended; similarly, if Russia won, the Russian frontier would be pushed further westward. By a curious turn of events both Germany and Russia lost, and the re-creation of Poland as promised in Wilson's thirteenth point was made possible.

The outstanding Polish patriot at this time was Marshal Pilsudski. Joseph Pilsudski was born of Lithuanian parents in Vilna, and grew up as a socialist with a burning hatred of Russian domination. He fought valiantly on the side of Germany—just as many other Poles, through the accident of their birthplace or dwelling, fought on the side of Russia. After Germany had occupied Warsaw Pilsudksi downed arms and awaited the German creation of a new Poland. The Germans had no intention of doing any such thing, and merely clapped Pilsudski into prison. The collapse of Germany in November 1918 gave Pilsudski his freedom and Poland her opportunity. A

Polish Republic was proclaimed, under Pilsudski as Chief of State and Minister of War (1918). Pilsudski chose the Polish pianist, Paderewski, as his Prime Minister, and sent him to Paris to plead Poland's cause.

We have already seen how the peace conference dealt with the many problems connected with Poland's frontiers; also how Poland pushed her frontier with Russia one hundred miles east of the Curzon Line, obtained Teschen from Czechoslovakia and Vilna (Pilsudski's birthplace) from Lithuania. The result was to increase Poland's already large minorities.

The political history of Poland in the inter-war years makes sorry reading. The Poles have never been noted for political wisdom, and for well over a century had suffered the disadvantages of partition and of subjection to three different systems of law and government. Paderewski failed to harmonize these differences, and resigned the Premiership at the end of 1919. Pilsudski resigned from the office of Chief of State in 1922. Numerous political parties and frequent changes of government brought unsettlement and divisions in a country whose crying need was for stability. At length in 1926 Pilsudski marched on Warsaw, overthrew the existing government, and made himself virtual dictator, a position he held till his death in 1935.

Poland had many other problems besides those of government. Her country was poor, and had been devastated during the War. Her people were for the most part illiterate and backward peasants, subjected to a wealthy feudal aristocracy. Efforts were made to break up estates and promote peasant ownership, but in general they achieved little. Her minorities proved a constant source of trouble. One-third of her population of about 30,000,000 were non-Polish. These included about 6,000,000 Ukrainians and White Russians, 3,000,000 Jews, and well over 1,000,000 Germans. The treatment of these minorities was unjust and in some cases cruel, and of course resulted in bad blood between Poland and her two powerful neighbours, Germany and Soviet Russia. The question of Danzig also raised difficulties, as Germany never ceased to regard this predominantly German port as rightfully hers. The Poles soon began to develop a rival port in Gdynia, and the Germans of Danzig complained of loss of trade. The appearance of Nazi Germany in the 1930's made the outlook for Poland very uncertain.

SPAIN

A BACKWARD COUNTRY

Spain had remained neutral during the First World War, and had made large profits. But in many respects she was still in the Middle Ages. Under her king, Alfonso XIII, were the three traditionally powerful elements in the State: the Church, the Army, and the Nobility. The Roman Catholic Church enjoyed considerable privileges; it was the biggest landowner in the country, and controlled the educational system. Despite its efforts, which in places were by no means inconsiderable, one half of the adult population could not read or write. The Army was officer-ridden, and in the position of a privileged caste. The nobles were large landowners who enjoyed their feudal rights while neglecting their obligations. The majority of the peasantry was landless, and lived in conditions of extreme poverty; many inhabited sunbaked holes or caves in the Spanish hillsides.

But even Spain could not escape the ferment of the modern world. The universities contained many advanced thinkers. Parts of Spain, especially Catalonia and the Basque country, were demanding rights of self-government. Above all, the industrial workers of the big towns were striving for a new order. All sorts of movements existed: socialists and trade unionists of more moderate aims; syndicalists who wished the workers to run the nation's industries; anarchists who opposed all authority and engaged in violence and murder; and communists who swore allegiance to the doctrines of Karl Marx.

THE DICTATORSHIP OF PRIMO DE RIVERA (1923–30)

Alfonso sought to divert attention from home affairs by planning a military expedition against Abd-el-Krim, leader of the tribesmen in the Rif Mountains who opposed Spanish rule in Morocco. His schemes were completely upset when the tribesmen slaughtered

10,000 Spaniards and captured 15,000 others with all their equipment (1921). Only one means existed of saving the Throne from popular indignation—to place a strong man at the top to act as dictator, and form a buffer between king and people. With Alfonso's backing, General Primo de Rivera, a popular soldier, proclaimed himself dictator in September 1923.

The new dictator was a big, bluff, hearty man, not too far removed in outlook from the people he now ruled. At first things went well. In alliance with France, which bore the brunt of the fighting, he avenged the Moroccan disaster by defeating Abd-el-Krim. He pleased the industrialists by erecting a high tariff wall to protect their manufactures. Spain was given new roads, railways, ports, schools, and hydro-electric undertakings which contrasted sharply with the medieval features that still remained. But the former elements of discontent soon began to raise their heads again. The Army lost confidence in de Rivera, and eventually only the Church remained. In 1930 Alfonso XIII dropped his strong man with as much readiness as six years earlier he had elevated him.

SPAIN A REPUBLIC (1931)

For just over a year Alfonso endeavoured to stem the tide of republicanism, but the tide proved too strong. Local elections in 1931 showed that the boroughs were solidly republican, although in the rural areas the monarchists still held their own. When the republican leader, Zamora, demanded the departure of the king, and the commander of the Civil Guard would not vouch for the loyalty of his troops, Alfonso deemed it prudent to leave the country (April 14, 1931). He never formally abdicated, but in effect the Bourbon dynasty dating from the War of the Spanish Succession was now ended. A Republic was proclaimed, with Zamora as its head. It had been a peaceful revolution for such a hot-blooded people—ominously so, as later events were to show, for within a few years the country was immersed in its blood-bath.

TURKEY

MUSTAPHA KEMAL'S REFORMS

We have seen in Chapter 10 how Mustapha Kemal, defying his own Sultan and the Western Allies, made himself master of Turkey and replaced the Treaty of Sèvres by the Treaty of Lausanne. In 1923 Turkey was formally declared a republic, with Kemal as its first president. To what ends would this vigorous and ruthless dictator use his powers? The answer was unmistakably given by Kemal's actions: he would hustle Turkey out of her backwardness, her Orientalism, and her Mohammedanism into the full glare of Westernization.

In 1924 he abolished the office of Caliph, and Islam was now without a head. He replaced Islamic laws, Islamic law-courts, and Islamic schools by counterparts based on western practice. The Koran lost its authority in the State, and school-children no longer learnt it by heart. Even the distinctive fez, with its convenience for religious prostration and prayer, was declared illegal; henceforth brimmed head-dress was compulsory. Caps were distributed to the Army. As for the ordinary Turks, they soon found that resistance even to this apparently small reform might incur the severest punishment, and their reaction is well described by H. C. Armstrong in his fascinating biography of Mustapha Kemal, *Grey Wolf*:[1]

> They wore old bowlers, ancient straw-hats, hats made out of a piece of cloth by their wives, with unskilled hands, caps imported in haste from Austria, anything with a brim that traders could get for them, anything that carried out the orders of the Gazi Mustapha Kemal, anything with a peak to save them from the prison, the bastinado, and the hangman's noose.

Efforts were made to bring women out of their Eastern seclusion. The veil was abolished, and European clothes encouraged. Schools for girls were opened, and professions no longer reserved for men. Ballroom dancing was introduced as a means of promoting the new freedom. The drive for women's emancipation created many

[1] Barker, 1932; Penguin, 1937.

problems, and even recoiled on Kemal's own head, for after encouraging women to take an active interest in politics, the dictator found his own wife interfering too much, and ended by divorcing her!

Kemal was keen upon education. To bring Turkey into line with Western Europe he replaced Arabic letters by Latin, and introduced European numerals, the Gregorian calendar, and the metric system. Place-names were changed from their Greek to Turkish equivalents; thus his capital Angora became Ankara, Constantinople became Istanbul, and Smyrna became Izmir. Technical education, together with schemes of public works, did much to modernize Turkey's economy.

In foreign affairs Kemal, unlike most dictators, pursued a policy of peace. His most notable achievement was the Convention of Montreux (1936) concluded with the main powers; this once more gave Turkey control over the Straits (subject to certain regulations), with the right to build fortifications.

Kemal died in 1938, and was succeeded by his right-hand man, Ismet. Under him and his successors the country has developed still further along the lines laid down by Kemal. Remarkable too is the fact that the one-party system has given way peacefully to methods of party government similar to those in the West.

Chapter 14

INTERNATIONAL RELATIONS (1920–32)

Contented and Discontented Nations

IN a broad way the settlement after the First World War left two sets of nations, the contented and the discontented, or, in other words, those who wished to maintain the *status quo* and those who wished to upset it. International affairs between the two world wars is largely the attempt to establish some working compromise between the two camps.

The discontented nations were naturally for the most part those that had lost the War, and suffered in consequence. Both Austria and Hungary regretted the loss of their former possessions. Bulgaria was resentful towards her neighbours, who had beaten her in the Second Balkan and the First World Wars. Italy had been on the side of the victors, it is true, but we have already seen her disappointment at her small gains, and the rise of Mussolini, determined, if possible, to right his country's wrongs. The two major discontented powers in Europe were obviously Germany and Soviet Russia. Germany's grievances were many. She had lost her overseas empire and valuable territory in Europe; she was held guilty of the War and saddled with enormous reparations; she was disarmed and in part occupied by Allied forces; the *Diktat* of Versailles and the post-Armistice Allied blockade rankled with her people; she was excluded like an outcast from the League of Nations. A still greater outcast was Soviet Russia, regarded by the ex-Allies as a deserter and a country imbued with dangerous revolutionary doctrines. The peace treaties had deprived her of territories to which perhaps she had no right, but territories, none the less, which she had ruled for a century or more: Finland, the Baltic states, Poland, Bessarabia. The wars of intervention by the ex-Allies had failed to unseat the Bolshevik leaders;

but they had enabled Poland to encroach on Russian territory, and had bequeathed a legacy of distrust between the two sides.

If we glance beyond Europe we find in Japan another discontented country. Japan had thought to despoil China of territory and rights while Europe was engaged in war; but the U.S.A. had stepped in, and by the Washington Conference (1921–22) forced Japan to disgorge her gains and agree to naval limitation and a settlement in the Pacific.

In their dealings with the dissatisfied nations the three major powers in the West were by no means united. The U.S.A. had refused to ratify the peace treaties or to join the League of Nations; at home she was to enjoy an economic boom in the 1920's, and European squabbles were not going to divert her from the pleasant task of growing rich. Her foreign policy was in general isolationist. France was obsessed by the danger of a German revival—and, with her memories of 1870 and of 1914, who could blame her? Her general policy was to keep Germany down, though under the leadership of Briand in the middle twenties a certain softening appeared in her attitude towards her defeated foe. Britain steered a course somewhere between. Though equally opposed to German militarism, Britain did not view the danger in the same light as France. She was inclined to be more sympathetic to German desires, and was at times isolationist in her small way towards Franco-German problems, as the U.S.A. was in a bigger way towards the whole European continent. It should be recalled that Britain and the U.S.A. had promised at the peace conference to guarantee France in return for the latter withdrawing her plan for a separate Rhineland state; but when the U.S.A. backed out Britain followed suit, and France was left without either plan.

The League of Nations in Action

The League of Nations was the new hope of the world in the 1920's. Despite many handicaps, it performed much valuable work. On the political side the Mandates Commission considered reports from the mandatory powers to decide whether the ex-enemy colonies were being justly administered. Likewise, complaints of minorities in many countries could be brought before the League. It arranged financial and economic assistance for Austria. The League governed the Saar territory successfully from 1920 to 1935, when it arranged for the plebiscite provided for in the peace treaties. At Danzig the League's High Commissioner acted as umpire between Polish and German interests. The Permanent Court of International Justice at The Hague gave judgment on a number of disputes between nations.

Valuable work was done in the social and humanitarian fields—work valuable in itself, and also as removing distress likely to lead to strife and war. Refugees were assisted, famine alleviated, and transfers of population—*e.g.*, between Greece and Turkey—smoothly made. International action was taken to combat the spread of disease or to send speedy assistance where needed; the traffic in dangerous drugs, such as opium or cocaine, was brought under closer control; the slave-trade, still existing in parts of Africa and Asia, was attacked. The International Labour Organization provided a means of regulating labour standards in many countries. It is interesting, and encouraging, to note that certain non-member countries like the U.S.A. and Soviet Russia co-operated in some of these humanitarian activities.

In the settlement of actual disputes between nations the League scored several successes. In 1920, when both Sweden and Finland claimed possession of the Aaland Islands, the matter was referred to the League; the decision was in favour of Finland, but with guarantees safeguarding the rights of the Swedish population. In 1924 the League was asked to decide upon the disputed ownership of Mosul, an area of very mixed population on the boundary between Turkey and the newly created state of Iraq, one of the British mandates. The decision went in favour of Iraq, and Turkey, after some initial reluctance, accepted it. In the middle of this dispute (1925) trouble flared up between Greece and Bulgaria, following the murder of two Greek soldiers by Macedonian bandits. A Greek force invaded Bulgaria, but as a result of League action the force withdrew, and Greece paid Bulgaria compensation for violating her territory. One further instance of successful League action occurred in 1927, when Lithuania brought forward the question of Vilna, whose seizure by Poland in 1920 (see page 134) still rankled in her mind. The League could in the circumstance do little about Vilna itself, which remained in

Polish hands, but it did persuade the two countries to end the animosities that had resulted from the dispute.

All this was very encouraging, as far as it went; but there was still a long way to go. The above disputes were mainly between smaller nations, and did not directly affect the rights of the great powers. The League had not dealt with the Corfu dispute between Italy and Greece in 1923 (see page 172) as firmly as the dispute between Bulgaria and Greece in 1925, and Greece might well wonder (as she did) whether different standards were applied when the aggressor was a fire-eating Mussolini instead of a small country like herself. The fact is that the League was only one instrument, and an imperfect one at that, in the quest for peace. France, for instance, sought security in the alliances we shall shortly describe, and when a major issue like the reparations question called for action she invaded the Ruhr rather than referring the matter to the League. During the 1920's the League endeavoured to promote the disarmament that had been looked forward to in the peace treaties: but, despite numerous commissions and conferences, nothing was really achieved, and as time went on Germany, which had been forcibly disarmed, grew impatient at the failure of other countries to follow suit.

Nor must these other countries, including France, be too readily blamed. The League suffered from too many imperfections. The U.S.A. was never a member, Germany was not admitted till 1926, Russia did not join till 1934—by which time both Germany and Japan had left! The League had no armed force at its disposal, and was dependent on the goodwill and co-operation of its members, among whom Italy and Japan were in many ways alien in spirit to its ideals. The League Covenant itself was not water-tight. There was the famous 'gap' in the Covenant which gave members the right to wage war three months after a decision with which they disagreed. Furthermore, arbitration over certain matters was not compulsory upon members. In 1924–25 the so-called Geneva Protocol attempted to remedy this. It suggested that all *legal* disputes should be submitted to the Hague Court; that other disputes should, if the League Council failed to reach a unanimous decision, go to a committee of arbitrators; and that even matters of domestic concern causing international friction should be submitted to a process of conciliation.

LENIN (1870–1924) AND STALIN (1879–1953)

Lenin ruled Russia from the 1917 Revolution until 1924, and was
succeeded by Stalin after the latter's overthrow of Trotsky.

Photo Sport and General

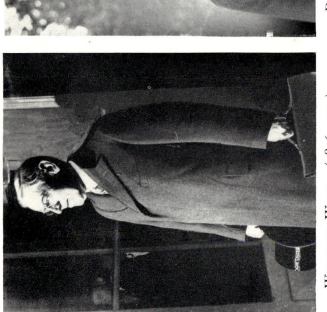

WOODROW WILSON (1856–1924)

President of the U.S.A., 1913–21; delegate to the Versailles Peace Conference, 1919.

Photo Sport and General

DWIGHT D. EISENHOWER (b. 1890)

American soldier and statesman; Supreme Commander for the Western invasion of Europe, 1944–45; President of the U.S.A. from 1953.

Photo Sport and General

All this, though complicated to the ordinary person, was praise-worthy in its intention of widening the field of the League's powers. But it met with much criticism, and eventually fell through.

In 1928 the Briand-Kellogg Peace Pact, described more fully later on, attempted to abolish war, but this was strictly not part of the League machinery. If, then, the League was but one of a number of threads during these years, we must now turn to some of the other threads to obtain a clearer view of the complete pattern.

Soviet Russia and the Outside World

For many reasons an attitude of mutual distrust and suspicion existed during these years between Soviet Russia and the rest of the world. For the time being Russia accepted the loss of her European territories; she was as yet too weak and too busy to do otherwise. But in 1919 Lenin had founded the Third International, usually known as the Comintern (short for Communist International). Its aim was the promotion of world revolution through the communist parties of other countries. This made it very difficult for foreign governments to establish normal relations with Russia. Throughout the whole of this period Russia was outside the League of Nations, which she denounced as a capitalist organization. Britain and France also maintained friendly relations with Russia's European neighbours in order to isolate Russia from the rest of Europe.

Slowly, however, a bridge was built to span the gap, but it remained a rickety affair always liable to collapse. In 1921 Britain opened up trade relations with Russia, and in the following year Russia attended an economic conference at Genoa. The conference achieved little, but following it the Russian and German delegates met at near-by Rapallo and signed a pact of friendship (1922) which was very unpalatable to the ex-Allies.

In 1924 the British Labour government recognized the Soviet government, and its example was followed by France, Italy, and other countries. But in the same year the newly built bridge almost collapsed again when, during the British general election, a letter from Zinoviev (president of the Comintern) was intercepted instructing the British communist party to overthrow the established system of government. Three years later the British government raided the

N

Russian trade centre in London, known as Arcos, on the grounds that it was the headquarters of revolutionary activity. It was not till the early 1930's that relations between Russia and the west improved—and then not because they loved one another any the more, but because they both feared the rise of common enemies in Nazi Germany and imperialist Japan.

Eastern Europe: The Little Entente

In Eastern Europe the division between the satisfied and the dissatisfied countries was clearly defined. The dissatisfied countries consisted of Austria, Hungary, and Bulgaria; the rest were non-revisionists, or supporters of the *status quo.*

In 1920–21 the Little Entente was formed, consisting of a series of alliances between Czechoslovakia, Roumania, and Yugoslavia. It was largely inspired by Dr Benes, Foreign Minister of Czechoslovakia, and was directed mainly against Hungary, on account of the latter's evident desire to regain the several million Magyars under foreign rule. The Little Entente also viewed with alarm the attempts of Hungary to restore the Hapsburgs, and it succeeded in forcing the Hungarian government to renounce all such attempts. France saw in these small countries, which desired the *status quo* in their own spheres, useful supporters of the *status quo* in the sphere in which she was interested—namely, Franco-German relations. From the outset there was close understanding; France supplied them with arms and technical assistance, and all their delegates worked in harmony at League meetings at Geneva. In the middle twenties France concluded definite alliances with the members of the Little Entente. Since 1921 France had also had a military alliance with Poland, whom she regarded as a useful counterpoise against German power in the east.

France and Germany: (1) Before Locarno

In many ways Franco-German rivalry still remained the central theme of European politics. Germany had recently been defeated, it is true, but France was acutely aware of the fact that it had been touch and go at the beginning, and that victory had been achieved only by the overwhelming resources in men and materials of the vast coalition that faced Germany at the end of the War. By herself

France possessed a population of about 40,000,000, as against Germany's 70,000,000; her industrial capacity, too, was much inferior to that of Germany. It is not surprising, therefore, that French foreign policy in the inter-war years was dominated by the search for security against a revived Germany, and that in the meantime France refused to countenance the general disarmament that had been provided for in the peace treaties. The important question, therefore, was how to achieve the necessary security.

Basically France thought that her only hope of security lay in keeping Germany weak—in repressing her, in isolating her, and in encircling her with French alliances. It was much the same policy as that adopted by Bismarck towards France herself after 1870. At the peace conference France had been foremost, though not alone, in pressing for German demilitarization, for heavy reparations, for the trial of war-criminals, and for the transfer of German territory to other nations. In some respects she succeeded, in others she failed. In particular she failed to create a separate Rhineland state, or to make the League of Nations an effective force by giving it an international army. Furthermore, first the U.S.A. and then Britain backed out of their promise to guarantee France against future German aggression, though it must always be remembered that Britain had her obligations to France as a fellow-member of the League of Nations.

With the peace conference over, French policy was to apply the terms of the Treaty of Versailles in their utmost harshness, as well as to use any other means that suggested themselves to keep Germany weak. She supplied her Polish ally with weapons and other sinews of war on cheap terms, and maintained a military mission in Warsaw. With the members of the Little Entente—Czechoslovakia, Roumania, and Yugoslavia—France was also on friendly terms, which ripened into alliances as time went on. But above all Germany must be kept weak, and in this connexion the chief weapon in the French armoury was reparations, a weapon regarded as a just one as well as an effective one, since it represented to the Frenchman compensation for damage actually done to his country. The successive attempts to extort reparations from Germany, and the French and Belgian occupation of the Ruhr (1923–24) have been described on page 165. The failure of the occupation pointed the way to different and more moderate methods. The Dawes plan was adopted in 1924 to solve the reparations problem. The French dismissed Poincaré in May 1924; early in 1925 Briand began his control of French foreign policy, which lasted till 1931. In Germany Stresemann had become Chancellor and Foreign Minister in the middle of the Ruhr occupation (August 1923). Although he soon resigned the Chancellorship he too controlled German foreign policy from 1923 till his death at the end of 1929. Stresemann defined his policy as one of 'fulfilment' —i.e., of fulfilling Germany's legitimate obligations under the Treaty of Versailles. Briand and Stresemann, together with Austen Chamberlain, the British Foreign Secretary, were the central figures in the events of the next few years, when, perhaps, more than at any other period in the inter-war years, it seemed as if old scars were healing, and the hands that had been for centuries clenched in anger were now to be clasped together in the spirit of friendship and peace.

France and Germany: (2) Locarno and After

It will be recalled that in 1924 an attempt had been made in the Geneva Protocol to widen the powers of the League of Nations in the field of arbitration. France had favoured this addition to the Covenant, but for various reasons Great Britain and other countries had rejected it in 1925. A new scheme immediately took its place; this was to take the form not of an addition to the Covenant, but of a treaty between various governments. Stresemann revived a suggestion that Germany had already made a few years earlier—namely, that the Franco-German frontier should be guaranteed against attack from *either* direction. Austen Chamberlain took up the suggestion, while the French insisted that in some form or other their allies in Eastern and Central Europe should also have their frontiers similarly guaranteed. The result was the Locarno Treaties of 1925, so called from the Swiss town on Lake Maggiore where the negotiations were concluded. It was agreed that Germany on the one hand, and France, Belgium, Czechoslovakia, and Poland on the other hand, should renounce war and accept arbitration in the settlement of future disputes. To make sure that this procedure would be adopted Britain and Italy guaranteed the frontier of Germany with France and Belgium from attack on *either* side. France likewise guaranteed the German boundary with Czechoslovakia and Poland. It was further understood that Germany would be admitted to the League of Nations.

Locarno was an ingenious arrangement appearing fair-minded to all sides, because not only were France and her allies guaranteed against German attack, but Germany was likewise guaranteed from attack. Hopes ran high following its conclusion, and Austen Chamberlain described it as "the real dividing-line between the years of war and the years of peace." But the arrangements were not altogether free from criticism. It appeared that Britain and Italy attached more importance to Germany's western frontier than to her eastern; might not this encourage Germany to think she had a freer hand in the east than in the west? Furthermore, the Covenant already covered the guarantees that had been given, which made it appear that the Covenant in itself was inadequate unless strengthened by extra treaties. This was hardly encouraging for the future of the League of Nations. Only time would show how far these criticisms were valid. Meanwhile, the next step was Germany's admission to the League.

A special session of the Assembly was summoned in March 1926 to admit Germany to the League, and to give her a permanent seat on the League Council alongside the other four permanent members, Britain, France, Italy, and Japan. Unfortunately, a hitch occurred when Poland, Spain, and Brazil also demanded permanent seats on the Council. The deadlock was so complete that the Assembly dispersed without having admitted Germany. Not till the following September was a compromise reached which secured Germany's admission with a permanent seat on the Council.

The Briand-Kellogg Peace Pact (1928)

On Germany's admission to the League the Allied Commission which had been supervising German disarmament was withdrawn, despite the fact that its latest report had alleged German evasion of her obligations. The League now set up a Preparatory Commission to pave the way for a full-scale Disarmament Conference. Year after year it laboured with no result. French distrust of Germany, even with Stresemann at the helm, was still dominant.

The most striking event of the next few years was the Briand-Kellogg Peace Pact, or Pact of Paris (1928), which, like Locarno, was outside the League Covenant. It arose from a proposal made by Briand to Frank Kellogg, American Secretary of State, that their two countries should agree never to wage war upon each other. Kellogg suggested that the undertaking should be thrown open to all nations. The result was that nearly every country in the world, including the U.S.A. and Soviet Russia (who, of course, were not members of the League), signed the pact renouncing war as "an instrument of national policy." This was encouraging as far as it went, but many doubted whether it went far enough. It was just a simple, if praiseworthy, declaration, and there was no machinery for enforcing it. Furthermore, the signatories made it clear that they still retained the right of self-defence—a right which might lead to all sorts of abuses in its interpretations. Thus in no sense was war renounced altogether, if a pretext could be found for justifying it. Still, the general intention was good, and efforts were made, without success, to incorporate the pact in the Covenant to give it greater validity.

The Close of an Era

During 1929–30 two further questions were tackled: the recurrent problem of reparations, and the evacuation of the Rhineland by Allied forces. France insisted that the reparations question should be settled first of all, and in 1929 the Young Plan replaced the Dawes Plan. For the first time the total of German indebtedness was fixed, and yearly payments were laid down lasting till 1988.

Satisfied on this score, France now agreed to discuss the evacuation of the Rhineland. Three zones had been fixed under the Treaty of Versailles, to be evacuated respectively in 1925, 1930, and 1935. The first had already been evacuated. Briand, Stresemann, and Henderson (who had replaced Austen Chamberlain) agreed that the Rhineland should be completely evacuated by June 30, 1930—i.e., five years before the time-limit for the third zone. This in fact came to pass, but before then Stresemann had died (October 1929). Austen Chamberlain had resigned in May 1929, on the fall of the Conservative Government. Briand continued till 1931, and in his closing years preached his vision of a United States of Europe.

These years witnessed the end of a definite era in the inter-war years, an era when men's hopes had been raised by Locarno, by Germany's admission to the League, by the Peace Pact, and by the apparent healing of old wounds under the skilful ministrations of Briand and Stresemann. A new and uglier period began when, in 1929, the worst economic crisis in history burst upon an unsuspecting world.

The World Economic Crisis (1929–33)

From 1929 to 1933 the world (outside Soviet Russia) experienced what economists call a 'slump' on an unprecedented scale. People and nations were unable or unwilling to buy goods from their neighbours, so that while every one was wanting to sell, no one was wanting to buy. Business-men were ruined, and the ordinary wage-earner dismissed. By 1932–33 the U.S.A. had 15,000,000 unemployed, Germany 6,000,000, and Britain nearly 3,000,000. The tragedy of it all was that, while human beings had insufficient food, clothing, and shelter, there was at the same time an abundance of foodstuffs and raw materials, and millions of idle hands only too anxious to be put to work; but as customers who could pay were lacking, there appeared no way of bringing labour and raw materials together.

The causes of the crisis were many and varied. The impoverishment and dislocation following the War was an obvious factor. Countries were saddled with huge national debts which demanded high taxation. The new countries of Central Europe erected tariff barriers against their neighbours, which obstructed the channels of international trade. The tangled question of reparations and war debts undoubtedly contributed to the final chaos. During the years 1924–29—i.e., from the Dawes to the Young plans—the U.S.A. had lent Germany vast sums; Germany paid her reparations out of these; Europe then paid her war-debts out of these reparations payments—which themselves had been paid out of American loans! It reads almost like the house that Jack built. But it was a house of cards, and it collapsed when in 1929 the American investor, realizing its instability, ceased to lend further sums, and demanded repayment of what he had already lent. It was this which precipitated the crisis.

A Turning-point in History

Britain soon found that her gold-supplies were going to the U.S.A., and were dwindling to a dangerously low level. So in August 1931 Ramsay MacDonald ended his Labour government and formed a National Government, which took Britain off the gold standard. Other countries soon took similar measures. In the same year President Hoover, of the U.S.A., arranged to postpone all war-debts and reparations for twelve months. Before the year was up Germany had announced that she would never again resume the payment of reparations; the ex-Allies had to accept this decision at a conference at Lausanne in 1932. Soon afterwards war debts followed the same course, despite American protests.

Politically, too, a new situation was emerging. New governments were appearing, destined to play a fateful part in the history of the next decade. We have seen the formation of the National government in Britain in 1931, first under Ramsay MacDonald, and later under Stanley Baldwin and Neville Chamberlain. In November 1932 Franklin D. Roosevelt was elected President of the U.S.A. The Republican Party, which had held power in the 1920's, was now discredited, and Americans turned to the Democrats, and their charming but forceful leader, to help them out of their mess. Roosevelt's New Deal policy of public works and governmental assistance put fresh confidence into the nation, and he was re-elected to the Presidency again in 1936, 1940, and 1944—an unprecedented tenure of office in a country where George Washington had established the tradition that two terms was the maximum period that any President should hold power.

Two further by-products of the economic crisis boded ill for the future. In 1931 Japan invaded Manchuria; in January 1933 the Nazi leader, Adolf Hitler, became Chancellor of Germany.

Japan and Manchuria

The Washington Conference of 1921–22 (see Chapter 10) had curbed Japanese activities in the Far East for the time being; but the general situation was still very unsettled. Sun Yat-sen, founder of the Kuomintang, or Chinese Nationalist Party, died in 1925. His successor, Chiang Kai-shek, set about suppressing the war-lords who continued to ravage much of China. As Chiang extended his authority over Northern China Japan became alarmed. Ever since the Russo-Japanese War of 1905 Japan had possessed special rights in Manchuria, which she regarded as a useful market, a source of foodstuffs and raw materials, and as a buffer-state between herself and Russia. There were also her rights in Port Arthur to be safeguarded. Japan saw the western world in the grip of a slump, and decided to strike.

In September 1931 the blow fell. An attempt by some Chinese to blow up the railway line near Mukden led to the movement of Japanese troops. In all probability the affair had been previously 'arranged' by the Japanese. The Chinese offered little resistance, and early in 1932 Japan was in complete control of Manchuria. She renamed it Manchukuo, and placed a puppet upon its throne—Pu Yi, the last Chinese emperor, who as a small boy had been deposed in 1912. Manchuria's iron and coal were harnessed to Japanese needs, and the level of Manchurian life lowered by the deliberate introduction of drugs and the destruction of university libraries.

By her aggressive action in Manchuria Japan had broken at least three international obligations: the League Covenant, the Washington Treaties of 1922, and the Briand-Kellogg Peace Pact. The U.S.A., it should be remembered, was a party to the last two. China, a member of the League, had appealed to Geneva in the very month of the invasion (September 1931). The League appointed a commission under Lord Lytton to investigate and report. It left Europe for China in February 1932, and reported in October 1932—fourteen months after the initial invasion. The Lytton Report condemned Japan's actions, and recommended the withdrawal of Japanese troops from the invaded areas. But what if Japan refused—as in fact she did? When the League Assembly adopted the report in February 1933 Japan left the League of Nations.

Nothing was done in fact to force Japan to mend her ways. For various reasons, some good and some bad, neither the U.S.A. nor the League was prepared to use force. Japan proceeded in the following years to nibble away at more parts of China, and by 1937 a full-scale conflict between the two countries was in progress.

The lesson of Manchuria was not lost on other would-be aggressors. Mussolini was biding his time. Most important, the Germany of Stresemann was during these very years giving way to the Germany of Hitler. To the events in Germany, which were to shape the world's destiny in the succeeding decade, we must now turn.

Chapter 15

NAZI GERMANY

Adolf Hitler: Early Life

WE saw in Chapter 12 some of the many difficulties which faced the Weimar Republic in the 1920's. The German people had no traditions of democratic government, and the influential classes of the old order (the military, the civil servants, the big industrialists, and the Junker landowners) were often hostile to the new republic. Moreover, the Weimar politicians were held responsible, quite unjustly, for accepting the humiliations of the Treaty of Versailles, with its armies of occupation, losses of territory, reparations, and so on. If Germany's new rulers co-operated with the Allies they were likely to earn the scorn of their own people; if they refused to co-operate they incurred the anger of the Allies. Add to all this the ruin of the middle classes in the inflation that accompanied the Ruhr occupation, and it will be appreciated that the Weimar Republic was sorely tried when the economic crisis of 1931 added to its woes. The German people were in the mood to try desperate remedies. In the event it was Adolf Hitler and his National Socialist Party which captured Germany.

Hitler was born in 1889 at Braunau, on the Austrian side of the river Inn. His father was a minor Customs official, who wished Adolf to follow in his footsteps. But the small boy fancied himself as an artist, and in any case he was too lazy at school to stand much chance of entering the Civil Service. When he was thirteen or so his father died, and five years later his mother died too. Hitler then betook himself to Vienna, where he spent five years during the impressionable age between eighteen and twenty-three. Here he became casual labourer, house-painter, and decorator, and lived in extreme poverty. Here, too, he picked up many of his later most characteristic ideas. In the bustling city of many nationalities he came to the conclusion that the German-Austrians were the superior race, and that all others, particularly the Jews, who formed the biggest minority, were inferior. Henceforth Hitler dreamed of a union of all Germans by once again reuniting Austria, expelled by Bismarck fifty years before, with the rest of Germany. The Hapsburg dynasty was an obstacle to such a reunion, and, together with its weak and party-ridden Parliaments, incurred Hitler's contempt. Likewise Hitler learnt to scorn the Social Democrats and their theories, and on one occasion was dismissed his job because he refused to join one of their trade unions.

In 1912 he moved to Munich, where he found German life and culture 'undefiled' by Jews, Czechs, and others. His emotions when war was declared in 1914 were later described in *Mein Kampf*:

"I am not ashamed to say to-day that overmastered by a storm of enthusiasm I sank down on my knees, and from an overflowing heart thanked Heaven for granting me the good fortune to be permitted to live at that time."

Hitler joined up as a volunteer and served throughout the War, winning an Iron Cross of the First Class for his bravery; but he never rose above the rank of corporal. He was in hospital in November 1918, recovering from the effects of mustard-gas, when the news of Germany's defeat reached him.

Hitler remained in the Army, being stationed in his beloved Munich. The German Army was taking its defeat and its restriction to 100,000 men badly, and Hitler's superiors employed him as a kind of spy to mix with people in cafés and clubs to discover what they were thinking. In July 1919 he was sent to report upon a small group known as the German Workers' Party. Its nationalist and racial ideas so appealed to him that he joined it, and soon became Number 7 on the committee, and the party's official propagandist. Other militarists followed Hitler's example, including Captain von Epp (commander of the Munich garrison) and Captain Ernst Röhm. The name of the party was changed to National Socialist German Workers' Party, abbreviated to Nazi from the German for its first two words, *National Sozialistische*. In February 1920 a programme of Twenty-five Points was adopted; this consisted of a mixture of extreme nationalism (to attract militarists and other opponents of Weimar) and socialism (to attract the workers and middle classes).

The Munich Putsch (1923) and "Mein Kampf"

The next few years were the formative period of the Nazi Party, when it acquired many of its distinct characteristics. It now recruited many of its later leaders, like Goering, Goebbels, and Hess. It obtained its own newspaper, adopted the swastika as its symbol, the outstretched arm as its salute, and the cry "Heil Hitler!" as its greeting. Captain Röhm organized its army in the Brownshirts, or *Sturmabteilung* (S.A.), a trained and uniformed body of men who acted as stewards at meetings and bodyguards in the streets. In fact they were often little more than thugs and gangsters, brutally silencing opponents, and engaging in fights with the rival armies of the Social Democrats and communists. Above all, Hitler consolidated his position as the undoubted Leader, or Führer, of the Party. Despite a somewhat unprepossessing appearance when off the platform, he became transformed when he mounted it, and with his magic oratory and compelling personality held his audiences spellbound often for hours on end. Every trick of pageantry was resorted to at his meetings, while Hitler himself roused his listeners to a frenzy by harping on a few simple themes—the wickedness of Jews, Marxists, and communists, the iniquities of Versailles, the treachery of the Weimar republicans, the superiority of the German race, and the betrayal of its Army in 1918 by money-grabbers behind the line.

In November 1923 the Nazis attempted a bid for power. It was the period of the Ruhr occupation, just after Stresemann had begun his policy of fulfilment. Hitler had secured the support of General Ludendorff, second in command to Hindenburg during the War. On the evening of November 8 Hitler and his Storm Troopers invaded a beer-house in Munich where members of the Bavarian government were meeting to hatch a plot of their own. Firing his revolver at the ceiling, Hitler announced the end of the Bavarian and the Weimar governments. But by the next day Hitler's *putsch*, or uprising, had collapsed, and both Ludendorff and Hitler were prisoners.

The Nazi leader was sentenced to five years' imprisonment. In fact, such were the influences at work on his behalf, he served only nine months. During his imprisonment he wrote the first volume of

Mein Kampf ("My Struggle"); the second volume was composed in the next two years. It did not at first have very large sales; but it was to become the Bible of the Nazi Party, and later of most of Germany, containing as it did an account of Hitler's life and struggle and a statement of his political views. Many of those views have already been given above, and need not be repeated; but one or two further points deserve mention. Hitler's contempt for the masses is plain and unconcealed. They are not capable or even desirous of reasoning, he says; all they want is to be told what to do. Hitler also elaborated his belief that the Aryan or Nordic race was superior to all others. It was in fact the master-race, or *Herrenvolk*. Among existing nations Germany was of the purest Aryan stock; but even she was tainted by Jewish blood inside her borders and by Slavonic blood along her eastern frontiers. To keep Germany pure the Jews must be exterminated, and Slavs such as Poles and Czechs be brought under subjection. Mankind would best be served if the Germans increased in numbers; in one place Hitler mentions an increase from 80,000,000 to 250,000,000. In this case Germany would require more living-space (or *Lebensraum*), to be found by an expansion eastward into Poland and Russia, particularly into the fertile region of the Ukraine. Anticipating his later foreign policy, Hitler also stated his belief that a policy of 'little by little' will gradually sap the morale of an enemy nation:

"A clever conqueror will always, if possible, impose his demands on the conquered by instalments."

Nazi-ism Marking Time

From 1924 to 1929–30 Nazi-ism made little headway. It was a period of relative prosperity for Germany, and of peaceful co-operation with the victors—the era of the Dawes Plan, of the American loans, of Stresemann and Locarno. Nazi representation in the Reichstag slumped. In May 1924 it was 32 seats; in December 1924 the Nazis won only 14 seats; in the 1928 elections they dropped to 12.

Nevertheless, the movement was still showing signs of activity. In 1925 the S.S. (*Schutzstaffel*), or Blackshirts, were formed; this was a select body which acted as a personal bodyguard to Hitler. It was regarded with jealousy by the S.A., or Brownshirts. Industrialists like Hugenberg and Thyssen were beginning to finance the party, whose nationalist aims now overshadowed the former socialist elements in its programme.

Hitler becomes Chancellor (January 1933)

The economic crisis played into Hitler's hands. American loans to Germany ceased, and world-trade dwindled. German exports dropped by about 35 per cent., and the unemployed numbered over 6,000,000. The German elector was bewildered, and ready to clutch at any straw. During these years the extreme parties on the Left and the Right gained ground at the expense of the moderate parties, but although the communists increased their seats in the Reichstag they were easily outdistanced by their enemies, the Nazis. The latter obtained seats as follows during these years:

YEAR OF ELECTION	1928	1930	1932 (July)	1932 (Nov.)
NAZI SEATS	12	107	230	196

The enemies of Nazi-ism were ever ready to point out two facts: (1) that at the height of their power, in July 1932, the Nazis, although the largest single party, never obtained a clear majority of seats or votes, but only about 37 per cent.; (2) that in the second election in 1932 the Nazi vote was on the wane, being about 2,000,000 fewer electoral votes than in July.

The Chancellor from March 1930 to May 1932 was a scholarly and enlightened man called Brüning, who did all he could to cope with the economic disaster. In doing so he overrode the Reichstag and ruled by emergency decrees under article 48 of the Constitution. He has for this reason been accused, perhaps unjustly, of killing democracy in Germany. President Hindenburg got rid of Brüning when the latter wanted to settle unemployed on the Junker estates in Prussia. In June 1932 von Papen, an ex-cavalry officer, became Chancellor. The domestic situation was growing uglier every day. The Reichstag had been suspended, and street-fights between S.A. and communists and others were common. In 1932 about 250 were killed and several thousands wounded as a result of these brawls. In

December Hindenburg replaced von Papen by von Schleicher, an Army general who had influence with the trade unions. It was no use; Hitler, as leader of the biggest single party, would not be denied. The old commander-in-chief of the First World War despised Hitler as a "Bohemian corporal," and at one stage in the negotiations offered him the Post Office to look after! But Hitler would accept nothing but the highest, and on January 30, 1933, he became German Chancellor.

Consolidation of Power (1933–34)

The new government was a coalition between the Nationalists of von Papen and Hugenberg and Hitler's Nazis. In less than two years Hitler's supremacy was absolute; the Nazis had crushed all rival parties in the State, and Hitler had crushed all rival leaders in the Party.

There were to be new elections to the Reichstag in March 1933. Hitler left nothing to chance. Goering, in charge of the Prussian Home Office, and thus of the police, ordered his men to kill all anti-Nazis, especially communists. On February 27 the Reichstag buildings went up in flames. Hitler proclaimed it a communist plot, arrested thousands of opponents, and muzzled the opposition Press and meetings. Many months later five men were accused at Leipzig of having started the fire. The Leipzig trial achieved world-wide publicity, and for once Nazi gangster methods had to proceed cautiously. Only one of the accused, a half-witted Dutchman named van der Lubbe, was found guilty. The rest, who were acquitted, included the Bulgarian communist Dimitroff, who at the trial had tied his Nazi accusers into knots, and confirmed the outside world's suspicion that the real 'Guy Fawkes' on this occasion had been Goering himself. In other words, the fire had been staged with a purpose.

The purpose was achieved when the elections were held at the beginning of March—after the fire, but well before the trial. Even so, the election results must have somewhat disappointed Hitler. The Nazis obtained 288 seats out of 646, representing 44 per cent. of the total electorate; with their allies, the Nationalists, they just had a majority. It was enough for Hitler. The 81 communists deputies were excluded, and the Reichstag was then persuaded into granting

HITLER (1889–1945) AND MUSSOLINI (1883–1945)

Adolf Hitler ruled Nazi Germany from 1933 to 1945;
Benito Mussolini ruled Fascist Italy from 1922 to 1945;
both were dictators who suppressed all opposition to their
rule.

Sir Winston Churchill (b. 1874)

British statesman; Prime Minister, 1940–45 and 1951–55;
ranks with William Pitt the Elder and David Lloyd George
as one of Britain's greatest war leaders.

Photo Associated Press

Hitler dictatorial powers. From now on the Reichstag was a mere sounding-board for Hitler's speeches, with no independent will of its own. Most of the Nationalists were soon ousted from office, leaving the Nazis in sole control.

There still remained party-rivals and old personal enemies to be dealt with. In particular Captain Röhm and his Brownshirt S.A.'s were proving a nuisance. Many of the S.A. leaders and men were anxious to develop the old socialist ideas of the pioneer days, which Hitler, drawing funds from Krupps and other big firms, was now just as anxious to forget. Further, Röhm wanted his S.A. incorporated in the regular German Army, with an important post reserved for himself. The Army resisted such a dilution, and Hitler, throwing all gratitude to the winds for services rendered, struck against Röhm and his Brownshirts. June 30, 1934, the so-called "Night of the Long Knives," witnessed one of the most extraordinary blood-baths ever perpetrated by a ruler in modern times. Röhm and many others, present colleagues or past enemies—all those, in fact, who had at any time incurred Hitler's enmity or aroused his suspicions—were brutally done to death. The S.A. was allowed to continue, but subordinate to the Army, and to the élite S.S., or Blackshirts.

Two months later, in August 1934, Hindenburg died. Hitler abolished the office of President, or rather amalgamated its powers with those he already possessed. A nation-wide plebiscite confirmed him by a huge majority in his now official title of Führer, or Leader. Hitler called his new Nazi Germany the Third Reich, or Empire, the First being the Holy Roman Empire of the Middle Ages, the Second being the Hohenzollern Empire established by Bismarck and ended in 1918. The Weimar Republic, dying since 1930, was now completely dead.

Nazi Totalitarianism

Ein Volk, ein Reich, ein Führer—"One Race, One Empire, One Leader"—this had been Hitler's rallying cry in the elections following Hindenburg's death. Logically this spelt totalitarianism—the dominance of one race, the Nordic or Aryan race, and its organization into a single state under one leader or dictator. Everything was henceforth subordinated to the Nazi Party, with its philosophy of

o

racial superiority, and inside the Nazi Party every one was subordinated to the Führer. All other political parties were dissolved, and
many of their leaders, especially the communists and Social Democrats, were sent to the concentration camps which Hitler soon established. Like Mussolini, Hitler claimed to have saved his country from
communism. The German trade unions were abolished, and their
funds taken over by the State. Strikes and lock-outs were forbidden,
for in theory the employers' organizations were also dissolved.
Freedom of speech, of association, of the Press, established by the
Weimar Republic, were now things of the past. Even the law was
tampered with, especially in the so-called People's Courts, where
political necessity overrode all other considerations, and was in fact
the supreme law itself.

Discontent, of course, occurred—witness the many thousands who
suffered the cruelties of the concentration camps—and there must
have been some opposition of a silent and inactive nature. But it was
all too little. A secret police, the Gestapo, was organized by Goering,
and later taken over and expanded by Himmler; it struck terror into
its victims. An intensive propaganda machine, conducted by all the
means at the disposal of the modern State, was directed by Dr Goebbels. Above all, the Nazis, like their totalitarian counterparts in Italy
and Soviet Russia, set out to win the minds of the next generation.
The schools, colleges, and universities were purged of unreliable
teachers; text-books were rewritten, and approved courses of study
drawn up. Pupils were encouraged to 'tell tales' about their teachers,
and even about their parents, so that the very privacy of family life
was assailed. Youth organizations, such as the Boy Scouts or the
Y.M.C.A., were replaced by the Hitler Youth Movement, in which,
alongside much praiseworthy physical training, there took place
instruction in the ideals of Nazi-ism, with, of course, insistence upon
the utmost devotion to the Führer.

Religion proved a problem, as with every Nero in history. Many
of the Nazis themselves were hardly Christian, and some tried to
revive rites and festivals associated with the gods of Norse and
Teutonic legends. But they found it impossible to persuade their
fellow-countrymen to follow suit. Although Hitler placed a puppet at
the head of the Lutheran Evangelical Church, he met with much

opposition in this quarter from the fearless Pastor Niemöller, who was at one time confined to a concentration camp. Likewise the Roman Catholic Church, strong in Southern Germany, proved a source of opposition, and the Pope eventually condemned many Nazi doctrines as being in conflict with Christianity.

When, however, Hitler vented his spleen upon the Jews he had things entirely his own way. The 600,000 or so Jews in Germany were regarded by the Nazis as an inferior—nay, a defiled—race. They were alleged to dominate many of the professions to a degree out of all proportion to their numbers. Their international contacts conflicted with the Germanic nationalism of the Nazi philosophy. They were held to be on the one hand responsible for the worst abuses of capitalism, and on the other hand the brains behind Marxist communism. They had played a large part, it was said, in the treacherous 'stab in the back' which it was now fondly believed had caused the collapse of the German armies in 1918. They also provided a convenient scapegoat for governmental mistakes—a target upon whom the people could vent their discontent whenever things went wrong. They were therefore excluded from the universities and from the professions; their property was attacked, their synagogues despoiled: their persons were subject to all kinds of indignities, or, in times of extreme wrath, to indescribable brutalities. The Nuremberg Laws of 1935 robbed them of their citizenship, systematized the hardships under which they suffered, and inflicted severe penalties upon anyone with the faintest drop of Jewish blood in his veins. Despite the obstacles placed in their way by their very tormentors, many managed to escape to other countries. It may be added here that the German conquest of most of Europe during the Second World War extended her power over millions of Jews in countries like Poland and Roumania. Nazi barbarism was unleashed upon them, and, although exact figures will never be known, something like 5,000,000 are known to have been massacred.

Nazi Economics

When Hitler took office the unemployed in Germany numbered 6,000,000; by 1936 the figure had been reduced to 1,000,000; by 1938 there was a shortage of labour. This was the result of many factors.

Young people had to engage in six months' compulsory labour service upon tasks such as forestry, land-reclamation, or road-building. When Hitler introduced military conscription this too absorbed many of the young men. Schemes of public works were set in hand. In particular, the vast motor-roads, or *Autobahnen*, were built with a dual carriage-way, each one capable of taking four streams of traffic. These had a strategic as well as an economic significance, since many of them were built to point like daggers at Czechoslovakia, Poland, or Austria. Vast schemes of rearmament were also set on foot, which again served both a military and an economic purpose.

There was nothing magical, therefore, in Hitler's conquest of unemployment. The really important question was how Germany could be made to pay for such measures, for the more there was of concrete or metal the less there was to eat and drink. This was the basis of the famous dilemma of "Guns or Butter" which faced the German people, and the answer they gave (or their leaders gave for them) was "Guns." Germany had little surplus for export wherewith to purchase necessary imports, such as rubber, cotton, or fats. She did all she could to bring the Balkans and the adjacent countries under her economic control, obliging them to send her their food and raw materials in exchange for whatever surplus articles Germany herself had. Even so, the German was short of many things, and German ingenuity was directed towards salvage campaigns and the production of substitute, or *ersatz*, materials. By these means it was intended to make Germany as self-supporting as possible, ready for the eventual war to which Nazi policy was surely tending. Years before 1939 German life in most of its aspects was organized upon a war footing.

Chapter 16

THE ROAD TO WAR (1933–39)

Germany leaves the League (1933)

On February 2, 1932, the full-scale Disarmament Conference of the League opened at Geneva. It was attended by about sixty nations, including some not members of the League, like the U.S.A. and the U.S.S.R. This was a good omen, counterbalanced, unfortunately, by the continued aggression of Japan, which *was* a member of the League, in the Far East.

The Conference soon ran into difficulties. There were many problems of detail—of how best to achieve disarmament—but overshadowing these were important matters of principle. In a much-quoted phrase the Russian delegate, Litvinov, insisted that "peace was indivisible." So long, that is to say, as peace was anywhere in jeopardy, as in the Far East, it was everywhere in jeopardy. Russia, therefore, would not disarm so long as Japan was armed. This immediately led Germany to retort that, so long as Russia was armed, *she* ought not to be disarmed. This was but one aspect of what soon became the most important obstacle of all—the German demand for equality.

It became clear that if equality through disarmament were not achieved, then Germany would seek equality through rearmament. This immediately provoked France to emphasize the need for her own security. Very soon, therefore, the Conference was bogged down in the problem of how to reconcile the German demand for equality with the French demand for security. No solution to this dilemma being found, the German delegates withdrew from the Conference in September 1932.

During the next few months a formula was sought to bring Germany back, and in February 1933 Germany returned to the conference-table. Hitler was now German Chancellor, and the international atmosphere more electric. France was understandably more reluctant than ever to budge from her position, and after a summer's protracted negotiations Germany withdrew from the Conference and, a few days later, from the League itself (October 1933). Japan had likewise resigned from the League earlier in the year.

The League of Nations was patently failing in its quest for peace. Instead of disarming, the nations of the world were soon rearming.

Nazi Germany: Europe's First Reactions

Although the danger of a revived Germany had never been completely absent since 1918, the establishment of Nazi rule brought it much nearer, and within a few years made it into a reality. Hitler had never made any secret of his scorn for the Versailles system, and of his determination to upset it, and thus restore German self-respect. His views on race, his creed of the *Herrenvolk,* or master-race, his insistence on the German need for *Lebensraum*—all these were bound to alarm his neighbours, especially such as had German minorities, or occupied lands taken from Germany in 1918–19. His gangster methods at home revealed an unscrupulousness which he would inevitably be tempted to repeat abroad. It was well known in official quarters (though no action had been taken) that Germany had for long been rearming contrary to the Versailles Treaty. With the failure of the Disarmament Conference and Germany's resignation from the League of Nations, German rearmament gathered pace. Small wonder, therefore, that Europe took alarm!

Among the smaller powers the Little Entente (Czechoslovakia, Roumania, and Yugoslavia) feared that Germany as a country wishing to revise the Treaty of Versailles would encourage Austria, Hungary, and Bulgaria in their revisionist desires also. Czechoslovakia was aware too of the fact that she had over 3,000,000 Sudeten Germans inside her borders. The position of Poland was also fraught with dangerous possibilities. She was painfully aware that both Germany and Russia had grievances against her: Germany because of the German minorities, the Polish Corridor, and Danzig, and Russia because of the strip of territory seized by Poland in the wars of intervention (1918–21). In January 1934 she concluded a Ten-year Peace Pact with Germany. Time alone would show the value of such an assurance.

Among the great powers the reactions of Soviet Russia, France, and Italy call for special comment. Soviet Russia was already apprehensive of the growing aggressiveness of Japan, her old rival in the Far East. Now on her other flank was the threatened revival of Germany. Hitler was the avowed enemy of communism, whose disciples he was busy suppressing or herding into concentration camps. In *Mein Kampf* he had clearly stated that German *Lebensraum* was to be sought eastward, in the Ukraine and elsewhere:

"When we speak of new territory in Europe to-day we must principally think of Russia and the border states subject to her."

Russia accordingly sought ways and means of strengthening her position. Early in 1934 France championed Russia's admission to the League of Nations, and in September she was admitted to membership with a permanent seat on the council. Russia also concluded numerous non-aggression pacts about this time. Among these may be noted a Pact of Mutual Assistance with France in 1935, and a similar pact with Czechoslovakia a fortnight later.

France was naturally very alarmed at the turn of events in Germany. The whole edifice she had been creating since Versailles was now tumbling about her ears. "France is and will remain by far the most dangerous enemy," Hitler had written in *Mein Kampf*. In population and industrial capacity France was far below Germany, and once Hitler succeeded in harnessing the Ruhr industries to German rearmament French striking-power would soon be outstripped by that of her sworn enemy. As far back as 1929 André Maginot, French Minister of War, had begun the construction of his famous line of fortifications along France's eastern frontier. The Maginot Line was not completed when its originator died in 1932; but in the succeeding years France hastened to finish the construction of what many hoped would for ever preserve her territory from yet another German invasion. The Maginot Line and the false sense of security it produced were not without their critics; chief among them was a staff colonel, Charles de Gaulle, who foresaw the swift, mechanized warfare of the future, against which such fortifications would prove useless. Politically too France was going through a period of exceptional difficulty even for her (see Chapter 12). The German danger stimulated France to action, and she weathered her internal storms for the time being. In the realm of foreign policy she redoubled her efforts to encircle Germany with a ring of steel. Poland was at the moment cooling off, preferring to test the genuineness of Germany's peaceful professions rather than relying solely upon the assistance of such a distant ally as France. Britain also was disinclined to do anything about the new menace. Many in Britain felt that perhaps after all the Treaty of Versailles had been too harsh, and that Germany's reaction was justified; many were inclined to regard Hitler as a ridiculous lunatic; almost all were still influenced by the traditional sense of security created by the English Channel. With her other traditional friends France was more successful. We have seen how she backed Russia's application for membership of the League, and how in 1935 the two countries concluded a definite Pact of Mutual Assistance. She strengthened her ties with the Little Entente, and welcomed their conclusion of a security pact with Turkey.

What finally of Fascist Italy? At first Mussolini patronized Hitler, with whose ideas he had much in common, but very soon he too began to share in the general alarm. For the explanation of this we must turn to the situation in Austria.

Hitler, Mussolini, and Austria

For ten years Mussolini had cultivated the friendship of Austria and Hungary, the two revisionist powers of the Danube basin. The appearance of a strong and aggressive Germany upon the scene threatened to undo the patient work of the past ten years. Despite League loans and other assistance, Austria was still in a condition of weakness. If only the *Anschluss*, or union with Germany, were effected, she would be immeasurably strengthened. In 1931, during the economic crisis, Austria and Germany had proposed a customs union between themselves, but France and others had vetoed it. Now, two years later, Hitler was in control of the destinies of Germany. Austrian-born himself, and with an avowed policy of uniting all Germans into a Greater Germany, he made no secret of his intention of carrying through the *Anschluss* at the first favourable opportunity. This would not only destroy Italian influence in Central Europe, but would bring German might to the Brenner Pass and the Italian frontier. Determined to prevent this, Mussolini quickly developed a new fellow-feeling for France and other countries that were likewise opposed to the new Germany.

In Austria itself the situation was somewhat confused. There were two main parties: the Christian Social Party, which was strongly Catholic, totalitarian, and fascist, and which was supported by Mussolini, and the Social Democrats, who were Marxists, drawing their support chiefly from the townsfolk of Vienna. Since May 1932 the Christian Social Party had been in power, with Dr Dollfuss as Chancellor. The struggle between these two groups was already bitter enough, both parties possessing their own armies, when in 1933 there appeared a third party, the Austrian Nazis. The object of these latter was clear enough—namely, union with Germany—and in pursuance of their aims they received all kinds of assistance from the Third Reich.

During the whole of 1933 the Austrian Nazis, backed up by their German masters, were making themselves a nuisance. Dollfuss fought them with determination, but the struggle threw him more than ever into the arms of Mussolini. At length the Italian dictator, in return for his subsidies to the Austrian government, demanded that Dollfuss should suppress the Viennese Socialists. Dollfuss was not unwilling, for, anti-Nazi that he was, he was none the less reactionary and totalitarian in his own way. In February 1934 a battle raged for four days in Vienna between the Austrian government and the Socialists, the latter using as fortresses the model tenements they had once built. Many hundreds of lives were lost. Dollfuss scotched one enemy; but in so doing he had destroyed the only party that might eventually have saved Austria from his other enemy, the Nazis.

In the following month a Danubian Agreement between Italy, Austria, and Hungary sought to bind these countries more closely together. But Hitler and his Austrian disciples were not yet ready to give up the struggle. In July 1934 the Austrian Nazis attempted a *coup d'état*. They occupied the Chancellery, shot Dollfuss in cold blood, and refused him medical attendance while for three hours he bled to death. But the government forces were too strong, and

Mussolini moved three divisions to the Austrian frontier ready to move in if Germany stirred. The *coup* was suppressed, and for the next three years Hitler soft-pedalled over the Austrian problem. Dollfuss's successor, Dr Schuschnigg, ruled his country with Mussolini in the background pulling the strings. The situation seemed to have stabilized itself. In January 1935 Mussolini secured additional support for his policy when he concluded an agreement with the French Foreign Minister, Laval. The independence of Austria was asserted, and France accorded greater rights to Italians living in Tunis, as well as transferring to Italy a few strips of French African territory.

1935: The Last Year of Peace

1935 has been called the 'last year of peace.' It began peacefully enough with a settlement of the Saar question, but it ended with Italy engaged in a full-scale war with Abyssinia.

It will be recalled that the Treaty of Versailles had placed the Saar under the control of the League of Nations for fifteen years, while at the same time awarding France the coal-mines as compensation for damage done to her own mines during the War. By 1935 the period of League rule was due to end, and arrangements were made for a plebiscite among the Saarlanders to determine their future status. On January 13, 1935, the plebiscite was held, with troops from Britain, Italy, Holland, and Sweden present to see fair play. Three choices were open to the voters: one, continuance of League rule; two, union with France; three, union with Germany. Intensive propaganda preceded the elections, especially on the part of the Nazis, against whom charges of unfairness were made. None the less, the elections proceeded quietly, and the result was so overwhelming that none could doubt the real wishes of the Saarlanders. Over 90 per cent. voted for Germany, 9 per cent. for the League, and less than 1 per cent. for France. On March 1 the Saar was formally restored to Germany. Hitler visited the territory in person, declaring that this was the last territorial claim Germany had against France, and assuring the world of "our deep desire to preserve the peace." In return for regaining the coal-mines Germany paid France 900,000,000 francs compensation.

A few weeks later came the first of Germany's 'surprise' actions which kept an anxious world on tenterhooks for the next four years. Just now France was about to enter upon the results of the low birth-rate during the war years as far as her numbers of conscripts were concerned. There was a sudden drop from 230,000 to 118,000. To counteract this the French government proposed an extension of service. It was announced on March 15 that for conscripts called up in 1935 the period of enlistment would be extended from one year to eighteen months; those called up in the following four years would serve for two years. On the following day the German government introduced conscription and declared its intention of building up a standing army of 550,000 men. This was Germany's first *avowed* and unilateral breach of the Versailles system, though it was well known that for years she had in fact been breaking the disarmament clauses. France, Britain, and Italy issued a strong protest, and in April their representatives met at Stresa, in North Italy, and jointly condemned Germany's action.

The "Stresa front," as it was called, did not last long. The first blow came from Britain, which, without consulting its other partners, concluded a Naval Pact with Germany on June 18, 1935. Germany was to be allowed warships in excess of the disarmament clauses of Versailles, and France was understandably angry with Britain. The British defence was that Germany was already building warships, including submarines, and it was desirable that the scope of her building should be defined and restricted. But if Britain was guilty of an indiscretion, France's other partner in the Stresa front— namely, Italy—was soon to be guilty of far worse, for throughout the spring and summer of 1935 she was preparing for war against Abyssinia.

The Italo-Abyssinian War

On October 3, 1935, Italian forces crossed the frontier and began the invasion of Abyssinia. Nearly a year previously, on December 5, 1934, a frontier clash had occurred between Italian and Abyssinian troops at Wal Wal; very probably the incident had been 'arranged' by Italy as an excuse for war. Even as early as 1932 the idea of a war against Abyssinia had been in Mussolini's mind, as in that year he had sent a military mission to Eritrea to investigate the problems that such a war would produce.

Mussolini had many motives in launching this long-prepared attack. Abyssinia (or Ethiopia) was the only remaining part of Africa still open to European conquest. Its population of 6,000,000 was largely Christian, but very backward. The ruling Emperor, Haile Selassie, had done something to modernize his country, but he was faced with problems of poverty and ignorance and the opposition of many of his tribal chiefs, or Rases. Strategically the country was a tempting prize to Italy. It would link her two East African colonies of Eritrea and Italian Somaliland; it might eventually prove a springboard for an attack upon the Anglo-Egyptian Sudan, and in any case might enable its possessor to browbeat the Sudan and Egypt by threatening to interfere with the Nile waters.

We have already seen (page 47) how in 1896 Italy had suffered defeat at Adowa in a previous attempt to conquer Abyssinia; this humiliation had rankled ever since, and it was Mussolini's desire to avenge it. It is true that since then Italy had signed various agreements promising to respect Abyssinian integrity, the last being a Treaty of Friendship in 1928. Both Italy and Abyssinia were also members of the League of Nations and signatories of the Briand-Kellogg Peace Pact. But Mussolini recked little of such undertakings. He had never concealed his fascist belief in the virtues of war as the supreme test of a nation's strength, and he thought it altogether wrong that the 'Have' nations like France and Britain should impose barriers to the ambitions of the 'Have-not' nations like Italy. The Manchurian affair had demonstrated the impotence of the League to restrain an aggressor, while the rise of Nazi Germany was likely to engage the full attention of France. Add to all these factors the increasing population of Italy, her poverty, and her continually unbalanced budgets, and it can be seen that a successful war would serve also as a distraction from economic difficulties. For propaganda purposes much was said of Abyssinia's backwardness, even savagery, and of the slavery that still persisted in many parts. While this was true, it did not excuse Italy's actions; in any case, her own colonies were not altogether innocent of slavery and slave-trading.

The Italian invasion, beginning on October 3, 1935, was on two fronts; the main thrust was in the north from Eritrea, with a subsidiary thrust from Italian Somaliland in the south. The objective of both forces was the capital, Addis Ababa. Apart from geographical factors—the mountainous nature of the country, lack of roads, and heavy rains—the advantages lay entirely with the Italians, and the large numbers of African troops assisting them. The Italian forces outnumbered their opponents, and had the advantage of a unified command. Haile Selassie's only regular forces, entirely under his control, were his Imperial Guard; his other troops consisted of levies serving for irregular periods under the leadership of the Abyssinian chieftains, or Rases. Mussolini endeavoured by lavish gifts and promises to win the Rases to his side, but he had little success in this connexion. Above all, the Italians fought with modern weapons and equipment, while their opponents had no tanks, aeroplanes, heavy artillery, or anti-aircraft guns, and were short even in light arms and ammunition. Both sides fought ruthlessly, and there were many charges and counter-charges of atrocities. The Italians, however, possessed greater facilities for barbarism, and they used them to the full. Helpless villagers were bombed from the air, mustard gas sprayed on civilians and soldiers, and Red Cross depots and vehicles attacked.

Mussolini, in fact, was all out for a quick decision, and he achieved his object. After several months of heroic resistance the Abyssinians, commanded by their Emperor, made a last stand at Lake Ashangi. They were defeated, and the road to the capital lay open. Haile Selassie escaped to Jibuti, in French Somaliland, where a British cruiser took him off to Palestine (May 2, 1936). On May 5 the Italians occupied Addis Ababa, and five days later Mussolini formally announced the annexation of Abyssinia and the bestowal of the title of Emperor upon the King of Italy. The war was virtually over, though guerrilla resistance continued till December.

The Abyssinian War and the League

The Italo-Abyssinian War was an important milestone on the road towards the second Armageddon of the twentieth century. It marked the death of the League. It gave Germany greater freedom of action in breaking the Versailles system. It completely shattered the Stresa front by detaching Italy from Britain and France and throwing her into the arms of Germany. The Abyssinian War had been no sudden breach of the peace launched upon an unsuspecting world. Mussolini had long been making open preparations for the conflict, and in January 1935 Haile Selassie made the first of many appeals to the League to take action to prevent the war. Nothing in effect was done, and when the war did break out only entirely ineffective measures were taken against the aggressor. It will be helpful to review the factors at work during this crisis.

First, it must be remembered, as always, that the League could only do what its member-states were prepared to do, and that among those member-states it was the great powers alone which could take effective action; this placed the responsibility upon Britain and France. Secondly, the situation was complicated by the growing threat from Nazi Germany. We have seen that in March 1935 (during the period, that is, of Italian war preparations) Germany introduced military conscription. We shall see that in March 1936 (during the actual war) German forces reoccupied the Rhineland. Consequently Britain to some extent and France above all were unwilling to tie up their forces in opposing Italy, and thus bare themselves against the next German moves. Indeed, they (especially France) were desirous of Italian support rather than Italian hostility. Action against Italy might easily provoke a large-scale European war, and no one could foretell where it would stop. Finally, there were many factors connected with the special case of Abyssinia itself. Some felt with Mussolini, even if they did not always confess it openly, that a colonial war against an uncivilized non-European nation was more excusable than a war between two 'civilized' states —though this was to ignore the warning that the Russian Litvinov had given years before that 'peace is indivisible.'

Repeated appeals by Abyssinia from January 1935 onward were turned down by the League on one pretext or another. Not till September did the matter come before the League Council. There the British Foreign Secretary, Sir Samuel Hoare, raised expectations high once more when he declared that the British government "will be second to none in their intention to fulfil, within the measure of their capacity, the obligations which the Covenant lays upon them."

This did not deter Mussolini from commencing war three weeks later on October 3. Four days later the League Council declared that Italy had broken the Covenant, and in November sanctions were imposed under article 16. Loans and credits to Italy were forbidden, imports from Italy were stopped, and a ban was imposed on the export to Italy of arms and materials necessary for war. Italy was injured by these measures, but not enough. In fact, they served to rally the Italian people round Mussolini without seriously impairing his ability to wage war. In particular, the sanctions did not include the export of oil, which was indispensable to Mussolini's war-machine. There might, it is true, have been difficulties in getting the U.S.A. to share in such an embargo, though she might very well have joined in had the League members appeared more in earnest. But the real reason why oil was not banned was simply and solely not to offend Mussolini!

The ordinary person in Britain and France was still further startled when, on December 9, 1935, a peace plan arranged between Hoare and Laval was made public. Under this Italy was to obtain about half of Abyssinia (more than she had by then conquered), while the Emperor was to receive small compensations elsewhere. The Hoare-Laval Plan roused public opinion to a high pitch of indignation, and Sir Samuel Hoare had to resign the Foreign Secretaryship. His successor, Anthony Eden, declared some months later that Britain would impose an oil embargo if other League members would join in it. But by now it was too late, and when a few days later Germany marched into the Rhineland European statesmen had other matters to think about.

As we have already seen, the Italians occupied Addis Ababa on May 5, 1936. Thereafter the continuance of sanctions was, in the British government's view, the "very midsummer of madness." They were officially ended by the League Council on July 15. For the first and only time the League had taken measures (or rather half-measures) to restrain aggression on the part of a great power. Its failure to achieve its purpose marked the virtual death of the League, though its ghost continued to haunt the world for another few years. No single person, no single country, no single action, killed it. Responsibility for its death must be shared in varying degrees by the whole world.

The European Scene (1936): The Rhineland and the Axis

The preoccupation of Britain and France with the problem of sanctions, and the necessarily strained relations between these two countries and Italy, gave Hitler greater freedom of action. On March 7, 1936, German troops marched into the Rhineland. This meant military occupation of the zone which had been demilitarized by the Versailles Treaty and confirmed by Locarno, which latter Hitler had promised to observe. Hitler's justification was that the Franco-Soviet Treaty had already destroyed the Locarno Treaty. It has since been revealed that the German military commanders carried sealed orders to retreat at the first sign of any French counter-moves. But none came—that is to say, none that meant actual physical resistance, though the air was soon thick with paper protests. The average Englishman was inclined to regard Germany as well within her rights in occupying what was after all her own territory, and France was afraid to act alone. Hitler sought to allay fears by offering a new peace pact and the possibility of Germany's re-entry to the League, but this came to nothing. During the remainder of the year further pages from Versailles were torn up. German conscription was extended from one to two years; Germany assumed complete control over her waterways, including the Kiel Canal; in January 1937 Hitler repudiated the war-guilt clauses and declared the Versailles system at an end.

The Abyssinian war dealt also the final blows to the Stresa front of Britain, France, and Italy. However much France attempted to appease Italy by softening the sanctions against her, the fact remained that France *was* in the opposite camp. Britain was even more clearly pro-League and anti-Italian, and had at times only been restrained by France. Hitler, of course, had no League commitments and had studiously done nothing to embarrass Mussolini. In July 1936 Hitler concluded a pact with Austria, recognizing her independence. Whether Mussolini believed Hitler's word or not, the two dictators now drew closer together, and in October 1936 an agreement was made on the common lines of policy to be adopted by the two countries over such questions as Spain (where civil war had broken out), the League, the Rhineland, and so on. In other words, the so-called Rome-Berlin Axis was now formed. The grouping went a stage further when in the next month Germany and Japan signed an Anti-Comintern Pact against the U.S.S.R. and communism, a pact to which Italy subscribed a year later.

Between Italy on the one hand and France and Britain on the other relations were henceforth very strained. Mussolini denounced his previous pact with Laval. One way and another France's position was growing weaker; Poland and the Little Entente powers were less ready than ten years before to put their faith in France. Between Britain and Italy relations continued bad long after the Abyssinian war was over. Italy resented British power in the Mediterranean, and did all she could in Palestine and elsewhere to stir up anti-British feeling. At length in 1938 agreement was reached between the two countries over the British recognition of Italian rule in Abyssinia and other matters. Differences were thus patched up, but no one could describe the new relationship as friendly.

Spain: (1) An Unsettled Republic

As the fires of war died down in Abyssinia, so they were being kindled in a new trouble-spot, Spain. On July 15, 1936, the League sanctions against Italy were ended; on July 17 military revolt in Spain ushered in a civil war that was to last till 1939.

With the establishment of the Spanish Republic in 1931 power passed into the hands of Left Wing moderates—of men like the liberal Catholic, Zamora, who became president, and the moderate socialist, Azaña, who became Prime Minister. Azaña's ministry (1931-33) tried to curb Spain's traditional reactionary forces, the Church, the Army, and the landed and industrial upper classes. But the government proceeded with caution, partly through choice and partly through the force of circumstance. Laws were passed attacking the wealth of the Church, the religious orders, and their control over education; but in practice many concessions had to be made. Thus the Jesuits were allowed to continue their educational work because otherwise there would not be enough teachers for the educational schemes the government had in hand. The power of the Army was reduced by pensioning off half the excessively large number of officers; but this did not prevent them from plotting in private to

P

regain their old powers. In economic affairs the government nation-alized the railways, brought the Bank of Spain under its control, and introduced better working conditions and old-age pensions. Attempts were made to settle peasants on the large estates; but these achieved much less success than was intended because of opposition from the landowners, and the difficulty of providing an independent peasantry with implements, seed, stock, etc., at such short notice.

Azaña's government fell between two stools. On the Left were the anarchists, syndicalists, and other extremists who were dissatisfied with the slow pace of reform. On the Right were the traditional forces of reaction, whose wealth and privilege had been so far only threatened, and whose powers for mischief remained intact. The Right Wing parties quickly formed a united front under the leader-ship of an ardent Catholic, Gil Robles, and in the 1933 elections defeated the socialists. A Right Wing government under Lerroux assumed power, and proceeded to undo the work of its predecessor. The Church regained its privileges; the grandees retained their estates. Gil Robles and others were more to the Right than the government itself, and began to preach fascist doctrines threatening democracy and the very republic. The workers in alarm combined, and in October 1934 strikes and insurrections occurred throughout the country. In the Asturias the rebels held out for several weeks, and were only put down with cruel barbarism by Moorish troops. Some thousands of lives were lost, and the prisons were filled with 30,000 rebels following the October risings.

For another year Spain continued on the verge of civil war. In February 1936 fresh elections were held for the Cortes, or Parlia-ment. This time the Left had united to form a Popular Front, and they reaped the reward of their tactics. It is impossible to say exactly how the voting went, with so many parties of all shades from one extreme to the other. It is quite clear, however, that the Left gained a majority of seats—about 260 to 270, out of a total of 473. But these figures did not reflect accurately the actual electoral votes cast; here the verdict was fairly even between Right and Left. However, the Right Wing government resigned, and a moderate Left Wing government (at first under Azaña again) took over.

The next few months were merely the prelude to civil war. The government embarked on a see-saw policy of reverting to its measures of 1931–33. This failed to satisfy its extreme supporters, who seized lands, destroyed churches, and attacked opponents. The Right engaged similarly in violence and acts of sabotage against authority; furthermore, it had for some time been negotiating with Fascist Italy and Nazi Germany for outside assistance. On the night of July 17–18 Right Wing Army leaders seized key points in Spanish Morocco. The next day troops landed in Spain itself, where military insurrections immediately occurred in every big garrison town. The civil war was on.

Spain: (2) Civil War and 'Non-Intervention'

Leadership of the insurgents soon passed into the hands of General Francisco Franco. He had seen long service in the Spanish Army, both at home and in Spanish Morocco, where he had helped to form the Spanish Foreign Legion. He had taken part in the brutal crushing of the Asturian rising in 1934, and after the 1936 elections had been exiled by the new Left Wing government to the Canary Islands. At the beginning of the revolt Franco arrived in Morocco by air. It was soon apparent that Franco's rebel forces controlled South and North-west Spain, while the government controlled much of the centre, the north, and the east, with the important towns of Madrid, Bilbao (in the Basque country), and Barcelona (in separatist Catalonia). The rebel headquarters were at Burgos, and the rebels possessed most of the regular Army, with corresponding superiority in weapons. The government forces possessed the country's gold reserves, and controlled most of the seaports; but they had very few arms.

In the first few weeks of the war Britain and France began to press for non-intervention on the part of outside powers, and early in September a Non-Intervention Committee, representing most European states, met in London. Mr D. C. Somervell, in his *Between the Wars*, aptly remarks: "Few committees have ever listened to as many lies as the London non-intervention committee." While paying lip-service to the theory of non-intervention, certain powers (especially Italy and Germany) used every device of evasion, falsehood, and delay to prevent its application. Italian planes were in

Morocco a few days before the rebellion started; German planes appeared in Spain a few weeks afterwards. Thereafter military equipment of all sorts, together with numerous troops (often referred to as 'volunteers'), were sent to Franco's assistance. The Fascist powers claimed to be fighting communism, but they were also thinking of the rôle of Spain in any future European war. For Hitler a Fascist Spain would be a useful 'backdoor' threat to France. For Mussolini a Fascist Spain would also be a useful partner in his moves against British sea-power, and in his efforts to turn the Mediterranean once more into a Roman lake. At one period during the war, in 1937, Italian submarines and planes were actually attacking British merchant and naval ships on various pretexts connected with the patrolling of the Spanish coast and its approaches. The non-Fascist powers could hardly take all this completely lying down; but they rarely rose much from their recumbent position. Britain painfully asserted minimum rights on the seas. France (afraid of becoming too involved in Spain in view of the German menace) sent a little assistance to the Spanish republicans, as likewise did Soviet Russia, which was hampered by geographical reasons. An International Brigade of genuine 'volunteers' was also formed to assist in the struggle against Franco. A few figures will illustrate approximately the proportionate amounts of assistance given on both sides. Two years after the outbreak of the war there were on the one side 80,000 Italian and 20,000 German troops, on the other side 10,000 international volunteers and several hundred technicians from Russia; the details of equipment sent would present an even more lop-sided picture.

The war was fought with ferocity, and both sides were guilty of atrocities. Those on the part of Franco's troops and his Fascist assistants were on a larger scale, and were systematically inflicted in order to terrorize their opponents, civilian as well as combatant. The insurgents began the war with the advantages of surprise and preparation. By November 1936 they were besieging Madrid, but the timely appearance (for the first occasion) of Russian aeroplanes and tanks helped to save the capital. In 1937 Franco's forces concentrated on an offensive in the North to subjugate the Asturias and the Basque country. In the course of this campaign the small town of Guernica was completely destroyed from the air, mainly by German aeroplanes—one of the most horrible of many atrocities. By the end of the year the North had been conquered, and in 1938 the insurgents turned to the eastern districts, to Aragon and Catalonia. By reaching

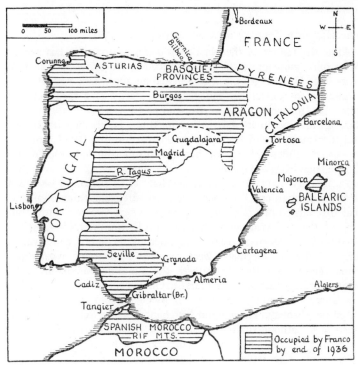

THE SPANISH CIVIL WAR, 1936–39

the sea near Tortosa they drove a wedge between the republican forces in the north and those in the south. Early in 1939 Barcelona surrendered, and in April the war ended with the fall of Madrid.

After three years of war Spain was prostrate. Franco was henceforth Spanish dictator—El Caudillo (Leader, or Chief of State), as he called himself. His Falangist party embodies many fascist and totalitarian features: suppression of opposition groups, of individual rights, of trade unions, and other workers' organizations. But during the Second World War he kept his exhausted country neutral, and Italy and Germany failed to reap full benefits from the amount of 'non-intervention' they had given to their fascist brother.

The German Seizure of Austria (March 1938)

After the failure of the Nazi *coup d'état* of 1934 Austria settled down once more under its new Chancellor, Dr Schuschnigg. Two years later (July 1936) Germany signed an agreement with Austria promising to respect her independence. Partly as a result of this guarantee (for what it was worth), and partly as a result of sanctions during the Abyssinian war, Mussolini threw in his lot with Hitler, and the Rome–Berlin Axis (October 1936) resulted. Italy's interest in Austria's independence was henceforth subordinated to her desire for the friendship of Germany.

In January 1937 Hitler declared that "The period of so-called surprises is at an end." Perhaps the most surprising thing of all was that this turned out to be true during the next twelve months, but early in the new year events moved with lightning rapidity. At the beginning of February 1938 a number of the more conservative Army leaders in Germany were replaced by extreme Nazis, and Hitler announced that henceforth the supreme command of all armed forces was vested in himself. On February 12 Schuschnigg was summoned to Germany to interview Hitler—a summons he dared not disobey. Throughout his chancellorship Schuschnigg had ruled as a Catholic right-wing politician, opposed to Social Democrats and to Nazis alike, and with leanings towards a Hapsburg restoration. The latter would have killed Hitler's hopes of the *Anschluss*, or Austro-German union, on which his heart was set. With the threat of invasion if he failed to comply, Schuschnigg returned to Vienna to carry out Hitler's demands. A prominent Nazi, Dr Seyss-Inquart, was made Austrian Minister of the Interior (with control of the police), and Austrian Nazis were given greater freedom, and imprisoned members released. Austria's impending fate was clear enough. The British Prime Minister, Neville Chamberlain, chose this moment to try to come to terms with Mussolini on outstanding differences concerning intervention in the Spanish war; he probably hoped that Italy would be offended with Germany over the turn of events in Austria. The British Foreign Secretary, Anthony Eden, regarding appeasement of the dictators as short-sighted, disagreed with the Prime Minister, and resigned. The general result was to weaken British policy at this juncture and to create bewildered dismay in France.

Schuschnigg tried one more card. On March 9 he announced that the people of Austria would be given a chance of voting on the following Sunday (March 13) on their own political future. This was more than Hitler was prepared to risk. It was reckoned that between 60 per cent. and 80 per cent. would have voted for the continuance of Austrian independence; but no one can know with certainty, because the plebiscite was never held. Hitler massed troops on the frontier, and demanded Schuschnigg's resignation. Rather than see his country immersed in a blood-bath, the Austrian Chancellor complied. Seyss-Inquart succeeded him, and invited German troops in to restore order in a country where there were no disorders except those manufactured by the Nazis themselves. On March 11 Germany invaded Austria, and on the following day Hitler himself revisited the land of his birth. Short of launching a European war, the democracies could do little but protest. Mussolini too had to accept the *fait accompli*, and derive whatever consolation he could from a telegram sent by Hitler which read: "Mussolini, I shall never forget you for this."

Austria was now a province of Greater Germany. The usual results of Nazi-Fascist rule quickly followed, in the shape of executions, murder, suicide, or the concentration camp for socialists, communists, royalists, Catholics, Jews, and others. Schuschnigg himself was imprisoned under conditions of extreme cruelty. The two dead assassins of Dollfuss four years earlier were now honoured as heroes. When all opposition had been thus silenced Hitler held his own 'free and secret' plebiscite to confirm his action.

The international consequences were far-reaching. Despite the fact that the Germans of the Third Reich were now reunited with their 7,000,000 kinsmen in Austria (a blood-reunion which soothed the consciences of many in Britain), it could not be overlooked that this was the first *territorial* infringement of the Versailles Treaty. It gave Hitler new sources of timber, iron, and other products. Strategically, it gave him control of the upper Danube, and linked the Italian–German frontiers. Above all, it extended the German frontier with Czechoslovakia, and added to that country's encirclement.

Czechoslovakia: First Bite (September 1938)

The German occupation of Austria was accompanied by assurances that Germany had no hostile intentions towards Czechoslovakia; but by now such assurances meant little. Rather they might be interpreted as an indication as to who was the next victim on Hitler's list.

The racial composition of Czechoslovakia has already been given in Chapter XIII. Of obvious significance at this stage was the existence of just over 3,000,000 Sudeten Germans on the mountain-fringe bordering Germany. These Germans had never been under the rule of Germany, but had formed part of the Austro-Hungarian Empire. They lived on the Czech side of the mountain-frontier, and for obvious geographical reasons could not have been incorporated in the new Austria. To have given them to defeated Germany in 1919 would have been unthinkable, as well as an offence to geographical and strategical considerations. The Germans, like the other racial minorities of Czechoslovakia, had grievances, it is true, but in general they were treated much better than minorities in most other countries. They formed their own party, and were represented in the Czech Parliament and government. In 1933, with Hitler's accession to power in Germany, many of them joined the new Sudeten German Party, which was Nazi in outlook, and led by Conrad Henlein. The latter was a native of Bohemia, a bank-clerk and teacher of gymnastics by profession, and in character mild and persuasive. For some years after 1933 he continued to profess loyalty to the Czechoslovak Republic.

The German conquest of Austria completely altered the situation. Henlein soon became little more than the mouthpiece of Germany, and his demands were stepped up. In April 1938 he delivered a speech embodying the Carlsbad Programme, which the Czech government agreed to discuss. Briefly, Henlein demanded complete self-government for the Sudeten Germans inside the general framework of the state; but these demands were merely a smoke-screen behind which Germany developed her plans. A campaign of abuse, full of the most blatant lies, was launched against the Czechs and their President, Dr Benes, who in 1935 had succeeded Thomas Masaryk. German troops were massed on the frontier, and it looked in May as if Germany were about to strike. The crisis passed, and Britain used the breathing-space to send out Lord Runciman to attempt a settlement between Henlein and the Czech government. The attempt failed, because Germany (the real power behind Henlein) refused to let it succeed. By September Henlein was demanding complete secession; the Czech government was refusing a demand which would dismember their country; Germany was again massing troops, and war seemed inevitable.

It was at this stage that the British Prime Minister, Neville Chamberlain, now in his seventieth year, made his first aeroplane flight to visit Hitler at Berchtesgaden (September 15). Here he was informed that, failing self-determination on the part of the Sudeten Germans, Hitler would go to war. Within a week Britain and France had obliged the Czech government to agree to a plan for handing over to Germany all districts where more than 50 per cent. of the inhabitants were German. Exactly a week after his first flight, Chamberlain again flew to meet Hitler, this time at Godesberg, in the Rhineland, to present the Anglo-French plan. Hitler now raised his terms, demanding, for instance, plebiscites in districts where the Germans were in a minority. In the meantime also Germany had encouraged Hungary and Poland to put forward claims against Czechoslovakia. Agreement proving impossible, Europe began to mobilize as if for war. Then, at the eleventh hour, Chamberlain appealed to Mussolini to use his good offices with the German dictator. Hitler yielded, and on September 30 Britain, France, Germany, and Italy met in conference at Munich to work out a settlement.

By the terms of the Munich agreement Germany obtained the Sudetenland, which the Czechs were to evacuate, without the destruction of any fixed capital, within the next ten days (October 1 to 10). Final frontiers were to be fixed by an international commission, and plebiscites were to be held in debatable districts. Alongside the dismemberment of Czechoslovakia went also an undertaking signed by Chamberlain and Hitler "never to go to war with one another again." The four powers also guaranteed the new frontiers, the two dictator countries only after Poland and Hungary had also satisfied their claims by seizing minority areas—which they did in November. All told, Czechoslovakia lost one-third of her territory, one-third of her population, and more than one-half of her industries.

'Munich' is the outstanding example of many acts of appeasement made by Britain and France in an attempt to satisfy the dictators. As such it has naturally excited controversy ever since. When Chamberlain returned to London he claimed (following Disraeli in 1878) to have brought back "peace with honour," and the London crowds cheered him wildly. Faced with the terrible alternatives of agreeing to Hitler's demands or almost certain war, Chamberlain deserves every sympathetic consideration. He chose peace—even though it lasted less than a year. He realized that Germany, as over the Austrian crisis, had a superficial case, since she was demanding territories predominantly German. A war against her over the Sudetenland question would not have evoked support from many in the West who were prepared, like Chamberlain himself, to test the genuineness of Hitler's professions that he was interested only in Germans, and not in Czechs. Nor would such a war have saved Czechoslovakia from immediate invasion. Britain was grossly un-prepared for war in September 1938 (for which the government must take much blame); Chamberlain immediately launched a large re-armament campaign, which was an ironical commentary on his stated belief that he had brought back "peace for our time."

In general the country backed Chamberlain in plucking peace from the threatening fires of war, though most people had few illusions as to its endurance. But he had to face critics of outstanding quality like Winston Churchill and Anthony Eden. The former spoke bluntly of the "total, unmitigated defeat" suffered by the democracies, which had, when all was said and done, yielded to the threats of a bully. The exact set-up of the Munich conference can also be criticized. Czechoslovakia herself was not represented, and during the crisis her government resigned and gave way to one more amenable to German demands. The exclusion of Soviet Russia was also of doubtful wis-dom, though with Hitler and Mussolini strongly objecting to her presence any other course would have been difficult in the circumstances. Soviet Russia had a pact of mutual assistance with Czechoslovakia, operative only if France honoured her pact also; this France had chosen not to do, so that Soviet Russia cannot be blamed for her inactivity. None the less, she was an interested party, and when she was excluded from the conference she naturally concluded

THE DISMEMBERMENT OF CZECHOSLOVAKIA, 1938-39

that the Western democracies were quite ready to do a deal with the dictators at anybody's expense but their own—including Russia's.

'Munich,' in brief, symbolized an ever-recurring dilemma facing those who cherish peace in their dealings with those who reck nothing of plunging the world into war: how far can the former go in seeking to appease the latter without being guilty of sacrificing other principles of conduct? There is no clear answer.

Czechoslovakia: Second Bite (March 1939)

For some months following Munich the international situation was relatively quiet, though in Spain Franco was gradually crushing republican resistance, and in the other half of the world Japan was at war with China. But Hitler's pressure on his chosen victim remained unceasing. Henlein was appointed ruler of the Sudetenland, and 300,000 Germans still under Czech rule clamoured for special privileges, while at the same time Hitler encouraged Slovaks and Ruthenians to demand independence. The country was fast disintegrating. Then on March 14, 1939, the aged and ailing President Hácha (who had succeeded Benes) was summoned to Berlin, and under threat of the immediate aerial bombardment of Prague, forced to sign away his country's independence. German troops had already crossed the frontier, and on March 15 Czechoslovakia ceased to exist. Most of it, including the Skoda armaments works, was incorporated in Hitler's Third Reich, though Hungary was allowed to occupy Ruthenia.

At the same time Hitler forced Lithuania to return the port of Memel to Germany.

The Last Months of Peace

March 15 made war inevitable, unless the miraculous happened and Hitler mended his ways. Hitler had seized his first non-German colony in Europe—an action which betokened pure conquest and domination. Two questions were now uppermost. Could the anti-Axis powers at this late stage combine sufficiently to frighten Hitler into a reformation of his ways? If not, when and in what circumstances would war burst upon Europe, and maybe the rest of the world?

It was obvious that Poland was cast for the rôle of Hitler's next victim. For some years her position had been becoming more and more unenviable. Her friend and ally, France, was declining in power and influence, and Poland felt herself increasingly at the mercy of her two powerful neighbours, Germany and Soviet Russia. The latter still remembered Poland's seizure after 1918 of a strip of territory a hundred miles east of the ethnic Curzon line. German grievances concerned Danzig and the Polish Corridor dividing Germany proper from East Prussia. The port of Danzig was indisputably German in population, but it was Poland's natural outlet to the sea along the river Vistula. It had been made into a Free City, with Polish commercial rights safeguarded, and with a League of Nations High Commissioner appointed to see fair play between the rival interests. The Polish Corridor was of mixed population, but predominantly Polish. German complaints can be easily imagined. About 1,500,000 Germans were under Polish rule—an insult to the master-race. Germany was cut off from East Prussia. Danzig was mainly German, and its trade was injured by the new Polish port of Gdynia.

In 1934 Poland had been glad to conclude with Germany a Pact of Mutual Non-Aggression. It had been worth trying, but it was proving a broken reed. The Nazis in Danzig grew stronger and bolder with every increase in the power of their German masters. Eventually they controlled the City Council, and Hitler's representative, Herr Forster, who was not even a citizen of Danzig, acted at times as the city's ruler. The authority of the League dwindled almost to nothing. From the end of 1938 onward Hitler formulated his demands: the return of Danzig to Germany, and the control, with complete sovereign rights, of road and rail communications across the Corridor. Poland resisted, not only on the merits of the demands themselves, but also because they would obviously be the first steps to further demands. During the spring and summer of 1939 mounting German agitation followed the familiar pattern: manufacture of incidents, stories of oppression and brutalities, massing of troops, and so on.

Hitler's seizure of Czechoslovakia had at long last stimulated Britain and France to action—the latter, weakened by political divisions, following Britain's lead at this juncture. In a speech at Birmingham on March 17 Chamberlain announced the end of appeasement. On March 31 Britain gave Poland a guarantee of assistance in case of attack; geographical reasons would obviously exclude any effective *direct* assistance, though many in Britain failed to realize this at the time.

A week later, on April 7 (Good Friday), Italian forces invaded Albania and drove out its royal family. For many years Albania had been under the 'protection' of Italy; it now became an Italian possession. This added to the threat to Yugoslav and Greek independence, and disturbed the balance of power in the Mediterranean. As a consequence Britain, on April 13, guaranteed assistance to Greece and Roumania in case of attack; France did likewise. Towards the end of April Britain introduced a moderate form of compulsory military service—the first time in history that she had applied conscription in times of peace. At the same time Hitler denounced the 1934 Non-Aggression Pact with Poland, and the 1935 Anglo-German Naval Treaty. On May 12 Britain and Turkey signed an agreement pledging mutual assistance in the event of war in the Mediterranean. Germany and Italy replied by concluding a definite ten-year military alliance. The powers were thus lining up once more for a second Armageddon. There remained one enigma—Soviet Russia.

Soon after the extinction of Czechoslovakia in March Britain and France had begun negotiations with Russia in an attempt to include her in the Peace Front they were now building up. These negotiations continued throughout the anxious summer months of 1939 without producing any definite result. In May Litvinov, who had always shown certain leanings towards the Western democracies, was replaced at the Russian Foreign Office by Molotov, who proved a much less sympathetic negotiator. All sorts of difficulties arose. The West, for instance, desired Russian guarantees to be limited to Poland and Roumania only; Russia wished to include the Baltic states (Latvia, Esthonia, and Lithuania) under her umbrella. The Baltic states made it clear that they preferred the risks of neutrality to the assistance of their powerful neighbour, whose ultimate designs they strongly suspected. Poland also intimated that she would oppose the entry of Russian troops into her territory. These and other difficulties were still unsolved when on August 21 the 'bombshell' burst upon an unsuspecting world—Russia and Germany announced a Pact of Non-Aggression! Two days later the German Foreign Minister, Ribbentrop, signed the pact in Moscow.

The Russo-German Pact startled even a world which for the past six years had experienced its fill of surprises. Nazi Germany, the persecutor of communism, was now linked in friendship with communist Russia, the sworn enemy of fascism. Germany, of course, was only too glad to neutralize Russia, and thus avoid the war on two fronts (for she could soon settle Poland's account). As for Russia, the pact gave her peace in the event of a German attack on Poland, whereas the western democracies were offering her war in that contingency. If it was objected that Russia's policy was short-sighted, and that her turn at the hands of the German invader would come next, Russia had her own answers ready. Stalin probably looked forward to a war of annihilation between Germany and the West, leaving Russia a free hand in European affairs. After Munich and other acts of appeasement by Britain and France he regarded the Western democracies as quite capable of turning Hitler's fury away from themselves to Russia; if he could beat them at their own game, why not? Secret clauses of the pact also gave Russia definite advantages, which the events of the next few months made apparent to all. Russia was to regain her strip of Poland, and her 'interests' in the Baltic states and in Bessarabia (all of which she had lost in 1918) were to be restored.

Whatever the validity of Stalin's reasoning, or the wisdom of his policy, it was quite clear that the pact of August 23 brought war immeasurably nearer.

The Outbreak of War

Appeals for peace were made by the Pope, President Roosevelt, the King of the Belgians, and others; even Mussolini proposed at the eleventh hour another conference reminiscent of Munich. It all fell on deaf ears. Hitler was determined on his chosen course—an appeal to the God of Battles.

At 5.30 A.M. on September 1, 1939, German troops invaded Poland. At 11 A.M. on September 3 Britain was at war with Germany; at 5 P.M. France had followed suit.

Chapter 17

EPILOGUE: THE SECOND WORLD WAR
AND AFTER

THE SECOND WORLD WAR

THE FIRST WINTER

THE first period of the war may be aptly described as *blitzkrieg* (lightning-war) in the east and *sitzkrieg* (sitting-war) in the west.

The German invasion of Poland was a text-book demonstration of the speed and effectiveness of the most modern weapons of war, particularly aeroplanes and mechanized armour, which penetrated deep into the enemy territory, and made the establishment of any line of battle an impossibility. Literally within a few weeks Poland had collapsed. On September 17 Soviet troops invaded Poland without warning, and the secret terms of the Russo-German Pact were put into operation. Russia obtained Polish territory roughly up to the Curzon Line of 1919, and took over the Baltic states.

In the west it was otherwise. There the opposing forces ensconced themselves in the Maginot and Siegfried Lines and spent the winter in relative inactivity. Even the much-dreaded air raids on the civilian population of either side failed to materialize. Only at sea was there much activity, the British fleet rounding up enemy raiders as in the first months of 1914. American correspondents referred to the 'phoney war,' and people began to doubt whether the contesting powers were in earnest.

During this first winter, from November to March, Soviet Russia engaged in a war with Finland in an attempt to push the Finnish frontier away from its dangerous proximity to Leningrad. The Finns resisted valiantly, and Britain and France began seriously to make plans for sending them assistance. Before this happened Finland had surrendered, and Russia annexed small parts of Finland, including the Karelian isthmus west of Leningrad.

THE FALL OF FRANCE (JUNE 1940)

On April 9, 1940, the *sitzkrieg* in the west was transformed over-night into *blitzkrieg*, when Germany suddenly attacked Denmark and Norway. The former was soon occupied; the latter took slightly longer, and the Allies sent the Norwegians assistance. But Germany had the advantage of proximity for her air and naval arms, and was aided by the Norwegian Nazi leader, Major Quisling, whose name has since become synonymous with 'traitor.' By May effective Nor-wegian resistance had ended.

Then on May 10 a full-scale attack upon France was launched, taking in the neutrals, Holland, Belgium, and Luxembourg. The events of the next month stupefied the world. German armour swiftly swept aside all resistance and drove deep into France. At the end of May occurred the 'miracle of Dunkirk,' when over 300,000 British and French troops were evacuated to Britain with the help of the Navy and a host of hurriedly collected small ships. As France reeled under the German onslaught Mussolini's courage mounted, and on June 10 Italy (which had hitherto remained neutral) declared war on Britain and France to join in the final kill. The French Premier, Reynaud, resigned, and was succeeded by the aged Marshal Pétain, veteran commander of the First World War. On June 22 France surrendered. Germany occupied two-thirds of France; the remainder was under Pétain's puppet government at Vichy. General de Gaulle, who had escaped to Britain, raised the flag of Free France, and became the rallying-point for those Frenchmen who refused to accept German domination.

THE BATTLE OF BRITAIN (AUGUST TO SEPTEMBER 1940)

The British Empire was now virtually alone, though many Allied leaders and fighting-men had escaped to continue the struggle under British direction. Only twenty miles of water saved Britain from the fate of France, and to prevent French warships from falling into Hitler's hands the British Navy had to attack and destroy certain naval units of their ex-ally. While Italy attacked British bases in Africa Germany concentrated on the Battle of the Atlantic, and made preparations for Operation Sea-lion, Hitler's code-name for the invasion of Britain. Leadership of the British people had passed on May 10 to Winston Churchill, who, in a memorable phrase, offered them nothing but "blood, toil, tears, and sweat." Under Churchill's inspiring leadership the British worked hard in their factories to repair the losses of Dunkirk, and after the long day's toil manned Home Guard and Air Raid Precaution services. The U.S.A., neutral in deed if not in thought since the outbreak of war, sent Britain small arms, and transferred fifty 'over-age' destroyers in return for a lease of naval bases in the British West Indies.

Daylight control of the air over Britain was essential before Germany could safely launch Operation Sea-lion. Early in August Field-Marshal Goering ordered the Luftwaffe to attack Britain. Beginning with the South Coast harbours, it soon turned its attention to the R.A.F. fighter stations, and when it failed to put these out of action it subjected London to a month's bombardment. The numerically smaller Royal Air Force inflicted heavy losses on the enemy, whom, with the aid of the newly invented radar, it was often able to intercept at a distance. The "Battle of Britain" saved Britain, and maybe the world, from Nazi domination. In the words of Churchill, "Never in the field of human conflict was so much owed by so many to so few."

During the winter of 1940–41 the Luftwaffe engaged in indiscriminate night-bombing of Britain, but when this failed as a war-winning weapon Germany turned her attention elsewhere, and by the end of 1941 the whole world was at war.

1941: THE WORLD AT WAR

German influence in the Balkans had been spreading with her victories against her Continental enemies. This had alarmed Russia, and already in 1940 there were signs of strain between the two countries. In Yugoslavia there was a strong anti-Axis party, while Greece was already at war with Hitler's ally, Mussolini, and was receiving British assistance. In early April 1941 Germany attacked Yugoslavia and Greece. They were soon subjugated, though the British attempt to hold on to Crete proved an important interruption in Hitler's timetable. Germany's interest in the eastern theatres of war was also shown by the dispatch of troops under General Rommel to North

Africa, where Italian forces were not doing too well against the British. In May the German battleship *Bismarck* escaped to the Atlantic to prey upon convoys; she sank H.M.S. *Hood*, but was herself soon afterwards sunk.

On June 22, 1941, Germany invaded Russia without notice—an event long expected by many observers. The Russo-German Pact of 1939 was shown up for what it really was, a mere marriage of convenience to be dissolved at will whenever it suited either party. Winston Churchill immediately promised Russia every assistance, and supplies were got through despite many hazards; but naturally Russia had to rely mainly upon her own resources. The Russian armies took the utmost advantage of their country's vast distances. They held on to no 'line' long enough to risk annihilation, and with every mile they retreated they stretched German communications. They were determined, however, to save Moscow and Leningrad, and before winter set in they had even launched limited counter-offensives against an enemy in sight of their historic cities. In 1942 an Anglo-Russian Treaty (unfortunately usually forgotten in the post-war years) bound the two countries together in friendship and alliance for the next twenty years.

After the U.S.S.R. came the turn of the U.S.A. During the 1930's the U.S.A. had endeavoured by various neutrality devices to cushion herself against the ever-increasing shocks and ensure her isolation in the event of war. This was indeed only possible in 'Never-Never Land,' and quite unattainable in the grim realities of the twentieth-century world. Very soon after the outbreak of war the U.S.A. became the acknowledged arsenal of democracy, and when the democracies could no longer purchase supplies she instituted Lend-Lease (March 1941) which postponed the sordid details of finance until the end of the War. In August 1941 Churchill and Roosevelt met at sea, and issued a statement of war aims known as the Atlantic Charter. Its lofty idealism is reminiscent of Wilson's Fourteen Points, and it makes strange reading in the post-war years. Perhaps the most remarkable fact about it is its association with the U.S.A., a country not yet at war. The U.S.A. was also, as usual, deeply concerned with the Far East, whence in fact the first blows against her came. Here Japan had since 1937 been waging full-scale war against China. The

U.S.A. was alarmed at the spread of Japanese power. At first American business-men had supplied Japan with oil, steel, scrap-metal, and other necessities of war; but as time went on the American government had imposed restrictions which threatened to interfere considerably with the Japanese war-machine. Negotiations between the two countries were still proceeding when, without warning, Japan struck. On December 7, 1941, she attacked the American Hawaiian base at Pearl Harbour, inflicting enormous damage. Attacks on British bases in the Far East occurred at the same time.

The U.S.A. and Britain were now alongside China in being at war with Japan. A few days later Germany and Italy declared war on the U.S.A. The god of war had indeed put a girdle round the world. Russia and Japan continued nominally at peace with each other; they were both too busy slaughtering the other's allies.

1942–43: DEFEAT AVERTED

The overall picture during the next two years may be simply stated. For nearly a year the enemy pressed his advantage to the utmost, but the second year saw a definite turning of the tide. Defeat had been averted, but there was still a long road to travel to final victory.

In the Far East Japan scored notable successes. On December 10, 1941, she sank H.M.S. *Repulse* and H.M.S. *Prince of Wales*, and by February 15, 1942, she had taken Singapore. In May she conquered the Philippines, after a prolonged resistance by General MacArthur. With Japanese forces occupying Burma and the East Indies, both India and Australia intensified their efforts to keep out the invader. As early as August 1942 the Pacific counter-attack began with American landings in the Solomon Islands.

On the European front the Germans succeeded in capturing Sebastopol in July 1942, but Leningrad and Moscow were still outside their grasp. The stubborn and heroic Russian defence of Stalingrad gave the Western Allies time to prepare their forces, though it was to be another two years before they felt able to open the much-desired second front on the Continent. Already in May 1942 the thousand-plane British attack on Cologne had foreshadowed the later massive air-attacks on Germany, carried out in the following years largely by British planes at night and American planes by day.

It was in North Africa that the most spectacular land-fighting occurred on the part of American and British Commonwealth troops. Rommel had launched an offensive which by the summer of 1942 had taken him to within fifty miles of Alexandria. Here he was halted, and on October 23, 1942, the Eighth Army under Montgomery counter-attacked at El Alamein. This, Churchill later remarked, "was the turning-point in British military fortunes during the world war. Up to Alamein we survived. After Alamein we conquered." Two weeks later, on November 8, American forces landed in Morocco and Algeria, at the other end of the Mediterranean. The enemy was caught in a pincer-movement, and retreated with heavy losses. By May 1943 North Africa was cleared, and on July 10 the Allies landed in Sicily. Little more than a month later they had crossed to the mainland. Mussolini's empire had disappeared, and the very home-land was threatened. On July 25, 1943, he was deposed from office, and when, at the beginning of September, Allied landings on the mainland began in earnest, the new Italian government surrendered unconditionally. Italy was officially out of the War, but her territory still very much in it. The Germans rescued Mussolini, made him puppet-head of a new Italian state, and themselves occupied as much of the peninsula as they could. A bitter struggle ensued till near the end of the War, with the fires of battle raking Italy's length from south to north.

THE FINAL PHASE (1944–45)

In the summer of 1944 London and other parts of South-east England were subjected to new forms of attack by Hitler's boasted 'secret weapons,' the V 1 flying-bombs, or 'doodle-bugs,' followed later by the V 2 rockets. Aerial bombardment attacked their launch-ing-bases, but full deliverance could come only from conquest. The second front was opened up on June 6, 1944 (D-Day), when British and American forces landed in Normandy under the supreme com-mand of General Eisenhower. While British and Canadian forces held on grimly to the pivot at Caen the Americans engaged in a great wheeling movement deep into the French interior. Germany was also distracted by French and American landings on the Mediterranean coast. By August 25 the Allies had captured Paris, and by September they were lined up along the German frontier. This rapid advance was facilitated by events in Eastern Europe, where for the past three years millions of men had been locked in conflict. At terrible cost to themselves and the enemy, the Russians had by now reached Poland, Bulgaria, Roumania, and other German bastions. Germany was now at bay.

Early in 1945 attacks from east, west, and south soon led to Germany's downfall. In April the Germans in Italy surrendered, and on April 28 Mussolini was killed by his own countrymen while attempting to escape into Switzerland. A few days later the Russians had reached Berlin. With fighting only a few streets away, Hitler and his devoted companion, Eva Braun, committed suicide in their concrete dug-out in the Chancellery garden (April 30); their bodies were burned to remove all traces. VE Day came on May 8 with the unconditional surrender of Germany.

There remained the Far East. There the Japanese hold on Southeast Asia was being seriously undermined; but above all the Americans at great cost were capturing Pacific islands whence they could launch air-attacks on the Japanese homeland. The capture of Okinawa in April 1945 brought them only 350 miles from the nearest point on the Japanese mainland. Aerial bombardment culminated in the most deadly weapon hitherto devised by man—the atom bomb, dropped on August 6 on Hiroshima, and three days later on Nagasaki. The resulting casualties and material destruction defy exact reckoning. One official estimate based on all available data puts the deaths alone at well over 100,000 in the two cities combined. Between the two bombs, on August 8, Russia declared war on Japan, and proceeded to occupy Manchuria. On August 15 (VJ Day) the Japanese Emperor announced his readiness to accept unconditional surrender.

For six years "blood, toil, tears, and sweat" had been the common lot of mankind—not only of the fighting-man, but of countless others whose story can find no place in a brief outline such as this: the Merchant Navy, men and women workers in factories and fields, air-raid officials, refugees and displaced persons, slave-workers in the

Nazi war-machine, prisoners of war and inmates of concentration camps, harassed housewives, members of resistance movements in occupied countries. With the fighting over, blood and tears passed into human memory; toil and sweat were still man's lot to make good the destruction of war.

EUROPE IN THE POST-WAR WORLD

THE UNITED NATIONS ORGANIZATION

No full-scale peace conference followed the Second World War comparable with the Paris Conference of 1919. Instead, the post-war arrangements depended in the first instance upon a number of special meetings or declarations dealing with specific topics. In February 1945, with the European war in its closing stages, the Big Three (Roosevelt, Stalin, and Churchill) met at Yalta, in the Crimea, and laid down an agreed policy upon a large variety of topics concerning the post-war world. Many of these will be considered later. Here we are concerned with their decision to promote international co-operation through a new United Nations Organization. In consequence delegates from fifty nations assembled at San Francisco on April 25 to draw up a Charter for the new organization. After two months their labours were finished, and the Charter was signed on June 26.

The new body resembled its predecessor, the League of Nations, in many respects. Its aims included security from war, the promotion of international justice and welfare, and the establishment of human rights irrespective of race, sex, language, and religion. Six major organs were created to achieve these aims: a General Assembly meeting once a year, in which every member-state had one vote; a Security Council consisting of five great powers (the U.S.A., the U.S.S.R., Britain, France, and China) and six others elected by the Assembly, whose special function it was to maintain international peace and security; an Economic and Social Council; a Trusteeship Council, whose work was to be roughly similar to that of the Mandates Commission of the League; an International Court of Justice, which, like the old court, was to meet at The Hague; and a Secretariat directed by a Secretary-General.

Differences from the old League existed, and were fastened upon as signs of hope by a war-weary world. Although ex-enemy countries like Germany, Italy, and Japan were excluded, the membership was much more impressive than that of the League; with the U.S.A., the U.S.S.R., and the members of the British Commonwealth, it included the major strength of the world. The Security Council, through ambassadors or other representatives, was to be in permanent session at the new headquarters at Lake Success, New York. There were even provisions (which have so far remained a dead letter) for a Combined Staff for directing any military sanctions found necessary to keep the peace. Finally, the Economic and Social Council was much more important than any counterpart in the League, and it was soon co-ordinating the work of numerous 'specialized agencies,' such as the Food and Agriculture Organization (F.A.O.) or the United Nations Educational, Scientific, and Cultural Organization (U.N.E.S.C.O.).

But over the supremely important question of national sovereignty the new organization marked no advance upon the old. In the final resort every nation was still its own judge and executioner, if it were strong enough to get its way. The Charter itself gave the great powers the right of veto on certain matters coming before the Security Council. The United Nations has done, and is still doing, invaluable work in many matters concerning food, health, refugees, drugs, education, and so on; but in the supreme task of world peace it can, like the League, do no more than its powerful members will individually permit it to do. There is no easy way out.

EUROPE AFTER THE WAR

A host of problems confronted Europe at the end of the War. In the social and economic sphere there were devastated areas to repair, and run-down capital to replace. Millions of soldiers, refugees, and displaced persons needed resettlement; relatives and homes had in many cases disappeared in the turmoil. Plans had been made well before the end of the War for tackling these problems, and these were immediately put into operation. Two important bodies concerned were the International Refugee Organization (I.R.O.) and the United Nations Relief and Rehabilitation Administration

CENTRAL AND EASTERN EUROPE AFTER THE
SECOND WORLD WAR

(U.N.R.R.A.). Drawing financial and material support from many nations, the latter did a tremendous job of work for two years after the end of the War. Immediately after the War, with the cessation of Lend-Lease, the U.S.A. and Canada made loans to Britain to help in her recovery. It soon became apparent that these loans were insufficient, and that in effect the rest of Europe needed assistance from the New World to put it on its feet again. In June 1947 the American

Secretary of State, Mr George Marshall, in a speech at Harvard University, offered Europe the assistance that very soon materialized in the Marshall Plan, or European Recovery Programme.

Political problems were no less manifold and urgent. Most European countries were without settled forms of government; usually there was a government in exile representing pre-war influences and a government on the spot formed out of the various resistance movements. Areas of occupation on the part of the great powers were inevitable, for military reasons in the closing stages of the War, and for purposes of law and order immediately following. Germany presented a major problem, not only in itself, but because its collapse would create a vacuum in Central Europe which would revolutionize the pre-war balance of power. Quite obviously Soviet Russia was unrivalled on the Continent, as a military giant amid so many dwarfs.

The Big Three Yalta conference of February 1945 had reached agreement on many immediate post-war problems; the application of its terms to Germany received additional attention at the Potsdam conference in July and August 1945. Under Yalta spheres of occupation and influence were sketched out as between the Western and the Soviet armies. France, the Low Countries, and Italy obviously came within the Western sphere; eastern and Balkan countries like Poland, Czechoslovakia, Hungary, Roumania, and Bulgaria were allotted to the Russian sphere. Yugoslavia had liberated itself under Marshal Tito, who was subsequently confirmed as ruler by his countrymen; as a communist he entered the Russian camp—for the time being. Greece, although a Balkan country, was regarded as a British sphere (partly for reasons of Mediterranean sea-power), and in the closing stages of the War Britain sent forces to prevent Greek communists from seizing power. These arrangements were intended to be temporary, the occupying powers pledging themselves "to the earliest possible establishment through free elections of governments responsive to the will of the people."

The Yalta and Potsdam arrangements on Germany were naturally more complex. By way of compensation for the territory she had lost to Russia, Poland was to receive new areas in the north and west; she did this by extending her frontier to include Danzig and most of East Prussia, and also a substantial strip of Germany up to the Oder-

Neisse line. The rest of Germany was divided into four zones, to be administered by Russia, the U.S.A., Britain, and France. Berlin, situated wholly within the Russian zone, was similarly to be shared by the four occupying powers. Despite those divisions, the whole country was to be treated as a single economic unit. There were included also in the German arrangements the so-called 'five *d*'s' of Allied policy: (1) demilitarization; (2) denazification—witness the later Nuremberg and other trials of war-criminals; (3) de-industrialization, or the limitation of Germany's level of industry—*e.g.*, in steel; (4) decentralization, or the promotion of local and provincial councils; (5) democratization, through whatever means—*e.g.*, education—were thought applicable.

Austria, with Vienna, was divided among the four powers much like Germany and Berlin. One important difference was that Austria was allowed to elect a government with limited powers over the whole country, while Germany was not.

A conference at Paris in 1946—on no such impressive scale as that of 1919—drew up certain peace treaties, which were signed early in the following year. These applied to Italy (which lost its African empire, and certain districts along the north-east Adriatic coast), Roumania, Bulgaria, Hungary, and Finland. In all cases their armed forces were limited. Agreement on Germany and Austria proved more difficult. It was not till May 1955 that an Austrian treaty was concluded, and at the time of writing, all efforts to draw up a treaty for a united Germany have proved unsuccessful. The explanation lies in the so-called cold war which developed between the Western democracies and the Soviet bloc shortly after the War.

THE COLD WAR: BEGINNINGS

The cold war can be regarded from many different angles. Some observers view it primarily as a clash of power between the two 'giants' of the present day, the U.S.A. and the U.S.S.R., each striving for world domination. Others view it as a struggle between conflicting ideologies. In the West the emphasis is upon the individual's rights and freedom; in the communist countries the emphasis is upon the power of the State, and upon planned economies, in which the individual, though often well provided for, is left with little choice. While both sides boast of being democratic, their inter-pretations of the word are poles apart; the one-party system of the communists is repugnant to the Western outlook. The extreme com-munist view of the West is that the capitalist countries are reaction-ary, outdated, and bound to collapse sooner or later; the extreme capitalist view of the communist countries is that they are little better than huge slave-camps held down under the iron heel of tyranny. Average opinion on both sides is probably not far removed from these extremes. From this angle there is much truth in the view that the cold war began, in fact if not in name, in 1917. Certainly since 1917 relations between Soviet Russia and the outside world have been almost continuously strained. It needed Hitler's invasion in June 1941 to bundle Russia and the democracies into the same camp. At the end of the War there was in western countries a tremendous fund of goodwill and admiration towards Russia for her invaluable contribution to victory. Within a few years most of this had gone. Clashes occurred everywhere, and over every possible topic.

Germany naturally witnessed many of these clashes. The different zones soon reflected the creeds of their respective rulers. In the Russian zone were State control of industry, regimentation of the individual, a one-party system, and other totalitarian features which caused millions of German refugees to flock to the West. In the western zones greater political and economic freedom was allowed; the Russians seized upon any shortcomings in the way of high prices or the emergence of near-Nazi parties to vilify their ex-Allies. All efforts to work out agreed policies on reparations, free German elec-tions, the level of industry, and many other issues having failed, the two sides drifted apart, though in Berlin and along the so-called Iron Curtain they were obliged to live in sight of one another.

The rest of Europe likewise was soon split in two. In the countries liberated by the West there was in general a return to pre-war forms of government and society. Norway, Denmark, Holland, and Bel-gium received back their royal families. In Italy and Greece plebis-cites were held over the monarchies. In Italy King Victor Emmanuel III had retired from public life in 1944; he had not strictly 'abdi-cated,' and the Crown Prince Umberto ruled as Lieutenant-General. The voting in 1946 gave a narrow majority for a republic, which

Italy then became. In Greece the voting, supervised by over a thousand foreign observers, gave a big majority the other way, and King George of the Hellenes returned; the communists had boycotted the elections, which they then claimed to be unrepresentative. In France the discredited Third Republic was not resurrected. The Vichy government, which had collaborated with the Germans, was of course dissolved, and many of its members were tried and punished. In 1946 a new Constitution, the Fourth Republic, was painfully born; in practice it is proving little different from its predecessor.

If in the West it was mainly a return to 'as you were,' in Russian-occupied Europe it was far otherwise. There without exception communist governments soon held sway. The general 'pattern' of events was for an immediate post-war government to be formed from the various parties on the spot and in exile, with a communist as Minister of the Interior, and thus in charge of the police. Within a year or so the other parties were outmanœuvred (maybe their leaders were accused of treason and executed), the communists were left in charge, and single-party elections were then held to confirm them in power. In this way 'People's Democracies' were established in Poland, in Roumania (where the king abdicated), in Bulgaria (again where the king abdicated), and in Hungary (where the fiction of Admiral Horthy's regency came to an end). Yugoslavia, which had been liberated by Marshal Tito's communists without Russian assistance, pursued a somewhat different path; but here the end was much the same, as King Peter, in exile in London, was dethroned. When the communists supplanted their rivals in Czechoslovakia in February 1948 the tale was complete.

The West was by now thoroughly alarmed at this extension of Russian power—for such, in fact, it was. Certain benefits may be said to have followed in the wake of communism in the parcelling-out of large estates among the peasantry; but these were accompanied by communist persecution and subordination to Moscow. The Russian satellites were forbidden to accept Marshall Aid from the U.S.A., and a campaign of abuse against it was forthwith commenced. During the War, as an ally of the West, Russia had dissolved the Communist International; now, at the end of 1947, she established a successor in the Cominform to bind the satellites to her side, and to foment trouble in countries like France and Italy. Only Tito of Yugoslavia was strong enough to shake off Russian domination. Well might the West accuse Russia of breaking her Yalta pledge to establish "through free elections governments responsive to the will of the people."

At the other end of the world were further occasions for mutual suspicion and hostility. As a result of her week's war against Japan, Russia controlled key-points in Manchuria, as well as Port Arthur and North Korea. The Americans were in control of Japan and many of her former possessions, including South Korea. Efforts to unify Korea proved as unsuccessful as similar efforts in Germany, and across the dividing-line of the 38th Parallel there was a barrage of wireless propaganda. Russia regarded with suspicion the American establishment of fresh Pacific bases, especially in view of events in China. There the collapse of Japanese power was followed by civil war between the Chinese communists and Chiang Kai-shek's Nationalist Party, which latter had departed from the ideals of its early days, and was now corrupt and reactionary. Not wishing China to become communist, the U.S.A. supplied the Nationalists with vast supplies of money and materials. In Indo-China, Malaya, and to a less extent in Indonesia (which had wrested its independence from Holland) the communist threat was also apparent.

THE COLD WAR: (I) DEVELOPMENTS IN EUROPE

As their respective areas of control became more clearly defined, the two sides pressed more heavily against each other. The communist bloc exerted pressure at various points in an effort to break out. The western bloc, pursuing a policy of 'containment,' applied counter-pressure to stop up any threatened gaps. Thus the communists conducted guerrilla warfare against Greece, and a 'war of nerves' against Turkey. President Truman, who had succeeded Roosevelt on the latter's death in April 1945, sent material aid to these two countries. In the early summer of 1948 the Russians began their blockade of Berlin by closing road and rail communications from the West German zones to the German capital. Their object was clearly to drive the western nations from Berlin, but they were foiled by the air-lift which the U.S.A. and Britain developed to supply the West Berliners with essential goods and maintain a foothold in the capital. By the summer of 1949 the Russians admitted defeat and lifted the blockade. Before the year was out both sides had established completely separate governments in their German zones; in the west a new German capital was created at Bonn, and Dr Adenauer became first Chancellor of the West German Federal Republic.

For some time the western nations had been contemplating a more permanent military alliance to further their policy of containment. Already in 1947 Britain and France had signed the fifty-year Dunkirk Treaty of mutual assistance; in the following year the Benelux countries (Belgium, Netherlands, and Luxembourg) were added under the Brussels Treaty. These agreements were obviously somewhat limited in scope, and furthermore had been made chiefly with the danger of a German revival in mind. Something larger was now needed, and in April 1949 the twenty-year North Atlantic Treaty was signed in Washington by the U.S.A. and Canada plus ten European nations: Britain, France, Benelux, Norway, Denmark, Italy, Portugal, and Iceland. Three years later Greece and Turkey were added. The signatories declared in the preamble to the treaty their determination "to safeguard the freedom, common heritage and civilization of their peoples founded on the principles of democracy, individual liberty, and the rule of law." Professing adherence to United Nations principles, they claimed to be uniting for self-defence as permitted under the Charter, and agreed that "an armed attack against one or more of them in Europe or North America shall be considered an attack against them all." It was made clear that this included occupation forces in Europe. Since its formation various commands have been created, many combined exercises have been held, and a permanent North Atlantic Treaty Organization (N.A.T.O.) has been set up in Paris.

The question of the limited rearmament of Western Germany to enable her to contribute to N.A.T.O. forces has raised many difficulties, especially in view of Germany's military record and the French fear of a German revival. A scheme was proposed whereby German forces would be integrated with those of France, Italy, and Benelux in a European Defence Community (E.D.C.) inside the general framework of N.A.T.O., but this was finally rejected by France in August 1954. Further attempts were immediately begun to find another solution to this difficult problem. Such a solution was found at a conference in London in October, when it was agreed to enrol West Germany and Italy in the Brussels organization, and Britain promised to keep certain forces on the Continent to allay French fears. This new organization of seven nations was given the name of Western European Union.

Despite such setbacks the North Atlantic Treaty has succeeded in stabilizing frontiers in the west. Other factors have also contributed, notably the superiority (less now than formerly) of the U.S.A. in atomic power. Nor must it be overlooked that stabilization has resulted from Russian policy as well as from Western, and the motives influencing Russia, whether they be fear or desire for peace, cannot be stated with certainty. But if containment has hitherto succeeded in Europe, the same cannot be said with equal truth of the Far East.

THE COLD WAR: (2) DEVELOPMENTS IN THE FAR EAST

The U.S.A. has always had a special interest in the Pacific, with a 'soft spot' towards China. Her efforts to help Chiang Kai-shek in his struggle against the Chinese communists proved unavailing, and by the middle of 1949 China was in communist hands. While Britain recognized the new government soon afterwards, the U.S.A. refused to follow suit. Communist China is still excluded from the United Nations, and the U.S.A. supports the remnants of Chiang Kai-shek's forces which sought refuge in Formosa. With a complete turn-about in her traditional Far Eastern policy, the U.S.A. has taken Japan under her wing, democratized her (on the surface), and seeks to rearm her as a counterpoise to the communist threat from the mainland. Soviet Russia naturally welcomed the addition of 600,000,000 Chinese to the communist camp, and in February 1950 the two countries signed a treaty of friendship. Shortly afterwards—possibly as a result, though this cannot be proven—the Korean War broke out.

At the end of the war Korea was divided along the 38th Parallel between Russian and American occupying forces. When the two sides failed to agree upon the steps necessary to give Korea its free-dom and independence the U.S.A. turned the matter over to the United Nations, and in 1949 both sides withdrew their occupying forces. North Korea refused to allow a United Nations commission to enter its territory, and in June 1950 war broke out between the North and South. The Security Council of the United Nations declared the North to have been the aggressor, and called on member-states to repel the attack. There followed a bitter war lasting three years, in which the U.S.A. played the major part, alongside about fifteen other countries, on the United Nations side, and in which Russia and China gave assistance to the North Koreans.

During the post-war years Indo-China and Malaya were also the scenes of communist and anti-colonial activities. The war in Indo-China proved a heavy drain on French resources, and prevented her from playing a full part on the European stage. In an effort to raise living-standards in South-east Asia the British Commonwealth embarked in 1950 on the Colombo Plan.

PEACEFUL CO-EXISTENCE?

With agreement proving impossible over the many issues dividing the two camps, the utmost that it seems possible to hope for is some form of 'peaceful co-existence.' If we cannot be one big family, we can at least try to live peacefully as two separate families, respecting each other's ideas and interests.

The death of Stalin in March 1953 brought new rulers to the fore in Soviet Russia, chief among them being Malenkov. First signs were that the new régime might prove more co-operative than the old. In July 1953 the fighting in Korea ended with a truce that really settled nothing. But a conference at Berlin early in 1954 again failed to produce agreement over the German and Austrian questions. In the Far East the Indo-Chinese war was ended by a conference at Geneva, which gave the communists control of the northern part of Viet Nam.

The year 1955 witnessed important developments which can only be barely recorded here. In February Malenkov was replaced as Soviet leader by Marshal Bulganin, assisted by Krushchev and others. In May the Federal (West) German Republic received its sovereignty

R

and was admitted to N.A.T.O. Her government immediately took steps to raise the military forces agreed upon. In the same month an Austrian peace treaty was at long last signed, and a Soviet delegation including the highest leaders visited Yugoslavia to heal the breach which had existed since 1948. Most important of all, in July the four heads of governments (President Eisenhower for the U.S.A., Marshal Bulganin for the U.S.S.R., Sir Anthony Eden for Great Britain, and M. Faure for France) met at Geneva to discuss differences, and to seek methods of peaceful solution. This conference 'at the summit' succeeded in establishing a framework for future discussions between the Foreign Ministers of the four countries. Such discussions, it was urged, should concentrate upon three topics: (1) the security of Europe, including the unity of Germany, (2) the improvement of relations between the two rival camps, and (3) disarmament.

The end of the year, however, witnessed a falling off in the new "Geneva spirit" of trust and goodwill. In November a Foreign Ministers' conference at Geneva failed once more to solve the problem of German unity. At the same time the Russian bloc began to supply arms to Egypt, while Marshal Bulganin and Krushchev toured India and adjoining countries, delivering speeches calculated to sow bad blood between Asia and the West. It is to be hoped that the future will see a change for the better.

Appendix I

TIME-CHART OF CHIEF EVENTS

Date	Event
1815	Treaty of Vienna.
1830.	Belgian Independence (confirmed by Treaty of London, 1839).
1848.	Year of Revolutions; Louis Napoleon ruler of France.
1852.	Cavour Prime Minister of Piedmont.
1861.	Kingdom of Italy; death of Cavour; emancipation of Russian serfs.
1862.	Bismarck Chancellor of Prussia.
1864.	International Red Cross formed.
1866.	Austro-Prussian War.
1867.	Austro-Hungarian Dual Monarchy; *Das Kapital*.
1869.	Suez Canal opened.

1870	Franco-German War; Papal Infallibility; Italy obtains Rome.
1871	Treaty of Frankfort; German Empire; Paris Commune
1872	*Dreikaiserbund*.
1873	First May Laws (*Kulturkampf*).
1875	Third French Republic; Disraeli and Suez Canal shares; International Postal Convention.
1876	Bulgarian atrocities; Dual Control in Egypt.
1877	MacMahon crisis in France.
1878	Treaty of Berlin.
1879	May Laws suspended; Bismarck's tariff policy; Austro-German Alliance.

| 1881 | Alexander II of Russia assassinated; France annexes Tunis. |
| 1882 | Britain suppresses revolt in Egypt; Triple Alliance (Germany, Austria, Italy). |

Date	*Event*
1883	Bismarck's Social Insurance.
1884	German colonies in Africa.
1885	Berlin Act (Africa); Penjdeh incident (Afghanistan).
1886	Boulanger crisis begins.
1888	Accession of William II in Germany.
1889	Panama scandal begins.
1890	Dismissal of Bismarck; Anglo-German African agreement.
1892	Beginning of Witte's reforms in Russia.
1894	Dreyfus affair begins; Sino-Japanese War (1894–95).
1895	Franco-Russian Alliance; Kiel Canal.
1896	Battle of Adowa, in Abyssinia.
1898	Spanish-American War; Battle of Omdurman; Fashoda.
1899	Boer War (1899–1902); first Hague Conference.
1900	Boxer Rebellion (China)
1902	Trans-Siberian Railway completed; Anglo-Japanese Alliance.
1903	Bolshevik Party formed.
1904	Russo-Japanese War (1904–5); Anglo-French Entente.
1905	Church disestablished in France; revolution in Russia; separation of Norway and Sweden.
1906	Dreyfus declared innocent; Russian *Dumas*; Algeciras Conference.
1907	Anglo-Russian Entente; second Hague Conference.
1908	Young Turk revolt; Austria annexes Bosnia-Herzegovina.
1910	Portugal a Republic.
1911	Turco-Italian War (1911–12); Agadir; China a Republic.
1912	First Balkan War (1912–13).
1913	Second Balkan War.
1914	Panama Canal completed; First World War (1914–18).
1915	Italy joins Allies.
1917	U.S.A. enters the War; revolutions in Russia (March and November).

Date	*Event*
1918	Treaty of Brest-Litovsk; end of War; abdication of Kaiser William II.
1919	Treaty of Versailles, etc.; League of Nations; Weimar Republic.
1920	Little Entente formed (1920–21).
1921	Treaty of Riga (Poland and Russia); Lenin's New Economic Policy.
1922	Mustapha Kemal at Chanak; Washington Treaties; Mussolini's March on Rome.
1923	Treaty of Lausanne; occupation of Ruhr (1923–24); Primo de Rivera Spanish dictator.
1924	Death of Lenin; Dawes Reparations Plan; Geneva Protocol.
1925	Locarno Treaty (Stresemann, Briand, Austen Chamberlain).
1926	Germany joins League.
1928	Briand-Kellogg Peace Pact.
1929	Lateran Treaty; Stalin's first Five-Year Plan.
1930	Allies evacuate Rhineland.
1931	Spain a Republic; economic crisis; Japanese invasion of Manchuria.
1932	Disarmament Conference opens; end of Reparations.
1933	Hitler Chancellor; Japan and Germany leave League.
1934	Murder of Dollfuss; U.S.S.R. joins League.
1935	Saar plebiscite; German conscription; Stresa front; Abyssinian War opens.
1936	Germany reoccupies Rhineland; Spanish Civil War (to 1939); Rome-Berlin Axis.
1937	Sino-Japanese War (1937–45).
1938	Germany annexes Austria; Munich Conference on Czechoslovakia.
1939	End of Czechoslovakia; Second World War begins.
1940	Fall of France; Battle of Britain.
1941	German invasion of U.S.S.R.; Atlantic Charter; Pearl Harbour.
1942	Stalingrad; El Alamein.

Date	*Event*
1943	Allied invasion of Italy; Mussolini deposed.
1944	Second Front in Europe.
1945	Yalta Conference; VE and VJ Days; United Nations Charter.
1946	Fourth Republic in France.
1947	Dunkirk Treaty; Marshall Plan; Cominform; Italian Republic.
1948	Brussels Treaty; Czechoslovakia communist; Berlin Blockade.
1949	North Atlantic Treaty; Bonn and East German governments; Communist China.
1950	Korean War opens; Colombo Plan.
1952	Greece and Turkey join North Atlantic Treaty.
1953	Death of Stalin; Truce in Korea.
1954	Indo-Chinese War ends; France rejects E.D.C.
1955	Geneva Conference of Heads of Governments.

Appendix II

TIME-CHART OF RULERS AND FORMS OF GOVERNMENT

	France	Germany, etc.	Russia	Italy	Other Countries
1840	1848. Second Republic (Louis Napoleon)	1848–1916. Francis Joseph (Austria)		1849. Victor Emmanuel II (Piedmont)	
1850	1852. Second Empire (Napoleon III)		1855. Alexander II		
1860		1861. William I (Prussia) 1866. Austria expelled from Germany 1867. Dual Monarchy		1861. Kingdom of Italy	

Year	France	Germany	Russia	Italy	Other
1870	1870. End of Second Empire 1875. Third Republic	1871. German Empire (Kaiser William I)		1878. Humbert I	1876–1909. Abdul Hamid II (Turkey)
1880		1888. Frederick III 1888. William II	1881. Alexander III		1886–1931. Alfonso XIII (Spain)
1890			1894. Nicholas II		
1900				1900. Victor Emmanuel III	1905. Haakon VII (Norway) 1909. Mohammed V (Turkey)

1910. Portuguese Republic 1911. Chinese Republic	1918. Poland, Czechoslovakia, Hungary Republics	1920. Regency in Hungary	1923. Turkish Republic (Mustapha Kemal, died 1938)
		1922–43. Mussolini	
1917. Bolshevik Revolution (Lenin)		1923. U.S.S.R.	1924–29. Stalin v. Trotsky 1929. Stalin
1916. Charles I (Austria) 1918. German and Austrian Republics 1919. Weimar Constitution			

1910

1920

	Spain	Italy	Russia	Germany	France
1930	1931. Spanish Republic 1939. Franco régime in Spain		1936. Stalin Constitution	1933. Hitler's Third Reich	
1940		1944. Victor Emmanuel III retires; Crown Prince ruler		1945. Allied Zones	1940. Vichy Govt (Pétain) 1944. De Gaulle
	1946–47. Republics in S.E. Europe 1949. Communist China	1946–47. Republic established		1949. Bonn and East German Republics	1946. Fourth Republic
1950			1953. Malenkov 1955. Bulganin		

INDEX

Treaties, pacts, and similar international agreements will be found listed under Treaties. Similarly, all battles are listed under Battles.